T0119846

Let the Law Catch Up

Also edited and introduced by Cathy Cambron

The Way Women Are: Transformative Opinions and Dissents of Justice Ruth Bader Ginsburg

Let the Law Catch Up
THURGOOD MARSHALL IN HIS OWN WORDS

Edited with an Introduction by
CATHY CAMBRON

Welcome Rain Publishers
NEW YORK

Let the Law Catch Up

Original content copyright © 2022 Welcome Rain Publishers LLC

All rights reserved. The arguments, opinions, and dissents presented in federal courts in the United States are in the public domain to the best of the publisher's knowledge. However, the editing, organization, cover design, foreword, introductions, summaries, commentary, and so on that are included in this book are original and copyrighted and may not be used without the prior written permission of the publisher.

Cover photo used by permission of the photographer, Cecil Williams

Designed by Laura Smyth, Smythtype Design

Library of Congress Cataloging in Publication Data is available from the publisher.

Direct any inquiries to Welcome Rain LLC.

Printed in the USA

10 9 8 7 6 5 4 3 2 1

ISBN: 978-1-56649-413-7

Contents

Introduction

Many words have been written by and about Thurgood Marshall, who led a life packed with dramatic events and epic undertakings. Among many other accomplishments, Marshall, as an attorney with the National Association for the Advancement of Colored People (NAACP), argued the appeal that outlawed segregation in public schools, *Brown v. Board of Education of Topeka*, in 1954; he then became the first Black solicitor general of the United States (the nation's top lawyer) in 1965 and served as the first Black U.S. Supreme Court justice from 1967 to 1991. This book contains only a few of his words, but they serve to illuminate the long, awe-inspiring career of a truly remarkable man.

With its post–Civil War amendments designed to eradicate the stigma of slavery and create equality between the races, the U.S. Constitution promised much to Black citizens, but delivered little justice. Marshall spent his career as an attorney—the "greatest attorney of the twentieth century," according to Supreme Court Justice Elena Kagan, who clerked for him—determined to make the Constitution live up to its promises. He once described his philosophy: "You do what you think is right and let the law catch up."[1]

Marshall persisted in doing what he thought was right in the face of grave danger, wresting from the Supreme Court a series of stunning victories in the 1940s and 1950s that demolished the legal edifice of racial segregation in the United States. He summed up his indomitable attitude in 1969: "It takes courage to stand up on your own two feet and look anyone straight in the eye and say, 'I will not be beaten.'"[2] And for the most part, he was indeed not beaten: his record of successful appearances before the Supreme Court, in which he won twenty-nine of the thirty-two cases he argued before the Court, is still unbroken.[3]

The United States of Jim Crow

Thurgood Marshall was born in Baltimore, Maryland, on July 2, 1908, in an America that held many hardships and terrors for its Black citizens. The early decades of the twentieth century, when Marshall was growing up, were some of the worst for Black Americans since the end of Reconstruction in the 1870s. Most Black citizens were prevented from voting—by poll taxes, literacy tests, and arbitrary actions of racist election officials. Party primaries routinely excluded Black voters. Threats and violence were directed at those who tried to vote anyway. Without any means of obtaining representation, Black Americans were powerless to prevent the election of racist officials.

Across the nation, Jim Crow laws enforcing racial segregation were passed as Woodrow Wilson, a Virginian elected president in 1912, imposed segregation on the previously unsegregated federal government. Following World War I, things became even worse for Black Americans in a surge of violence that occurred at the same time as many Confederate memorials were constructed in the South.[4]

During the years 1890–1940, nearly five thousand Black Americans—accused, often groundlessly, of various offenses against whites—were lynched and tortured by white mobs. Frequently, the lynchings were social occasions, and attendees included white children. Black criminal defendants, if they avoided lynching, were tried by all-white juries who often had wide latitude in imposing the death penalty. And Black communities were constantly vulnerable to punishing "race riots"—more accurately, destruction, violence, and murder inflicted on Black communities by local whites in reaction to incidents as minor as a fistfight or as flimsy as a false accusation.[5]

It is worth retelling even a few of these stories, which are not generally taught in U.S. schools. In July 1917, three thousand white rioters gathered in downtown East Saint Louis and burned Black homes and businesses; the National Guard, called in to restore order, in some cases participated in the violence. More than a hundred Black residents lost their lives, and six thousand were left homeless. In the summer of 1919, white Americans directed so much violence against Black veterans and Black communities that poet James Weldon Johnson dubbed the season the "Red Summer." And in spring 1921, a young Black man who worked as a shoeshine boy was accused of assaulting a white, female elevator operator, setting off a chain of events that led white rioters, again with the assistance of National Guard, to ransack and burn "Black Wall Street," a prosperous thirty-five-block area in North Tulsa, Oklahoma, and to attack and murder Black residents. Three hundred people were killed, and ten thousand lost their homes.[6]

Baltimore offered something of a safe harbor for young Thurgood. Officials considered the city the only place in Maryland to securely keep Black criminal defendants accused of crimes against whites and in danger of being lynched while they awaited trial. Old West Baltimore, where the Marshall family lived, was fairly integrated when Thurgood was born. Beginning in 1911, however, first laws were passed and then racially restrictive covenants were used in real estate deeds to keep Black people out of majority-white neighborhoods, and Baltimore became more segregated by race.[7]

Early Life

Thoroughgood, as his name was originally spelled, was the second son of William Marshall and the former Norma Williams, who were both from hard-working families of grocers. William worked as a waiter; Norma was a schoolteacher who was ever active on behalf of her children. William Marshall was an assertive man who taught Thurgood not to tolerate racist mistreatment. Thurgood grew up to be tall, handsome, and "disputatious," like his father, with a gregarious personality.[8]

Thurgood was known as a prankster at school but graduated near the top of his high school class and went on to earn his undergraduate degree in 1930 at Pennsylvania's Lincoln University, a college many considered the "Black Princeton." During college, he met Vivien "Buster" Burey at a Baptist church in Philadelphia, and they married in his senior year. After graduation, ineligible for admission to the University of Maryland School of Law purely because he was Black, Marshall applied and was admitted to Howard University's law school in Washington, D.C. [9]

Howard University, a Mentor, and a Mission

At Howard, Marshall fatefully encountered Charles Hamilton Houston. Houston, a Black Harvard Law School graduate and the head of the law school, was, in Marshall's words, "one of the greatest lawyers I've ever been privileged to know."[10] Houston attracted famous speakers to the school, such as Clarence Darrow and Harvard Law School dean Roscoe Pound, and held students to high standards while exposing them to the workings of the legal system in the District of Columbia. Marshall took the opportunity while in Washington to hear lawyers presenting oral arguments in the U.S. Supreme Court, including South Carolinian John W. Davis, who would be opposing counsel one day in the cases consolidated as *Brown v. Board of Education*. Marshall applied himself to his schoolwork as he never had before, and by his third year he was a favorite student, on whom Houston called for assistance with a criminal case referred by the National Association for the Advancement of Colored People.[11]

A fervent opponent of racial segregation, Charlie Houston helped set Marshall on a path that would lead to the overturning of the U.S. Supreme Court ruling in *Plessy v. Ferguson*, 163 U.S. 537 (1896). This ruling allowed the government to require segregated ("separate but equal") facilities for Black Americans despite the guarantee of the Fourteenth Amendment to the U.S. Constitution that all citizens of the United States are entitled to equal protection of the laws. "Charlie saw the big picture," Marshall said later. "He taught us all to be social engineers."[12]

Marshall became intimately familiar with the legal edifice created after the Civil War promising equal treatment of the races, which he summarized in a 1944 speech at the NAACP's Wartime Conference:

> The Thirteenth Amendment to the Constitution, abolishing slavery, the Fourteenth Amendment, prohibiting any action of state officials denying due process or the equal protection of its laws, and the Fifteenth Amendment, prohibiting discrimination by the states in voting, are well-known to all of us. In addition to these provisions of the Constitution, there are the so-called Federal "Civil Rights Statutes" which include several Acts of Congress such as the Civil Rights Act [of 1870] and other statutes which have been amended from time to time and are now grouped together in several sections

of the United States Code…The United States Supreme Court…in one case stated that "the plain objects of these statutes, as of the Constitution which authorized them, was to place the colored race, in respect to civil rights, upon a level with the whites. They made the rights and responsibilities, civil and criminal, of the two races exactly the same."[13]

The realities of life for Black Americans belied the spirit and indeed the letter of these laws. It became Thurgood Marshall's mission to hold the United States to these promises of equality.

Thurgood Marshall, Attorney at Law

The summer that he graduated law school, in June 1933, Marshall took his first trip through the Deep South, accompanying Charlie Houston on a tour to document the state of Black schools. The miserable conditions made a lasting impression on Marshall, as did the gruesome lynching of George Armwood on Maryland's Eastern Shore a few months afterward. In response to that event, the neophyte lawyer went to the governor's office to press for an investigation of the state police, in an early demonstration of the insistent advocacy that would alter U.S. history.[14]

For her part, Marshall's wife, Buster, became a leader in the "Buy Where You Can Work" movement in downtown Baltimore to pressure businesses to hire Black employees. Picket lines at stores that turned away Black applicants caused a dramatic decrease in the stores' sales during the holiday shopping season of 1933 before a court order put a stop to the demonstrations.[15]

Marshall had been so eager to embark on a legal career after graduating that he had turned down a doctoral fellowship from Harvard University so that he could open his own practice right away. But the United States was in the throes of the Great Depression when he became a lawyer in 1933. Marshall barely covered his expenses with the fees he collected. Anyway, he was interested in more than representing Baltimore's prominent Black businesses and processing uncontested divorces. Increasingly, he worked on cases referred by the NAACP.[16]

1. Mr. Civil Rights: 1934–1950

Marshall worked with the NAACP as counsel for the Baltimore Regional Office until 1936, when he became assistant special counsel for the NAACP in New York. In 1940, he became the first director and counsel for the NAACP Legal Defense and Education Fund, where he worked until he was appointed to the United States Court of Appeals for the Second Circuit in 1961.[1]

In Baltimore in 1935–1936, Marshall won acquittals or obtained sentences less than the death penalty for Black defendants in five capital cases. He succeeded in insisting on the indictment of a police officer for fatally shooting a Black motorist in the back while processing the driver's arrest following a minor traffic accident, although a jury then found the officer not guilty. And working with Charlie Houston, Marshall, no longer a powerless student, took on the Maryland law school that had refused to admit him back in 1930.

In what is now recognized as a first step toward school desegregation, Marshall and Houston represented rejected Black applicant Donald Murray in a successful lawsuit against President Raymond A. Pearson of the University of Maryland School of Law in 1935. Marshall intended to begin a campaign of showing that "separate but equal" educational facilities for Black students were in fact not at all equal. At trial in state court, Marshall demonstrated the falsity of the university's claim that Princess Anne Academy, a state school for Black students, provided an equal education in the law. The trial judge, in a move that stunned observers, ordered Murray to be admitted to the law school. The university's appeal of the state court ruling was unsuccessful.[2]

Beginning in 1936, Marshall launched lawsuits attacking the statutes that permitted Black public school teachers in Maryland to be paid little more than half what their white counterparts earned. Marshall's efforts ultimately had the effect of doubling the pay of the largest professional group in the Black community at the time. Litigation challenging teacher pay discrimination spread throughout the South, with Marshall's assistance, and helped spawn the development of hundreds of NAACP branches nationally.[3]

During these years, Marshall traveled and toiled relentlessly, identifying cases that would enable him and his colleagues to fight back against racial discrimination and segregation, and assisting Black criminal defendants in perilous circumstances throughout the South. Posters advertising Marshall's appearances in local communities labeled him "Mr. Civil Rights." Traveling through the South by train, Marshall would stay in the homes of local Black residents, because hotels usually would not accept Black travelers. He accommodated insults and endured threats from local whites so he could get his legal work done.[4]

Marshall was revered by the Black residents of the communities he visited. His secretary at the NAACP, Alice Stovall, recalled what happened when Marshall appeared at courthouses in small Southern towns: "They came in their jalopy cars and their overalls. All they wanted to do—if they could—was just touch him, just touch him. *Lawyer Marshall,* as if he were a god. These poor people who had come miles to be there."[5]

The NAACP was among the few recourses for Black Americans who were paying the price of racism in those years, and Marshall seemed to be personally involved in every case that came to the organization's attention. Traveling to towns with "sundown laws," where any Black person in town after dark was in mortal danger, and intervening in episodes of terrible racial tension, Marshall put himself in grave peril again and again.

In 1946, Marshall barely escaped a lynching in Columbia, Tennessee. When a white mob gathered following a fight between a white radio repairman and his Black customer's son, armed Black veterans prepared to prevent a lynching and defend their community. Shots were fired, and police responded with a raid on the Black community, ransacking and looting Black businesses and arresting more than a hundred Black residents. Marshall and his colleagues defended twenty-five Black men charged with assault with intent to commit murder. After twenty-three were freed, Marshall returned to defend the last two accused, winning an acquittal for one and a limited sentence for the other.[6]

Infuriated, police followed Marshall as he was leaving town with a colleague, stopping Marshall's car to take him out in a place where he could see the lynch mob waiting for him down by Duck River. Police told Marshall's colleague, Nashville lawyer Z. Alexander Looby, to drive away and not look back, but Looby followed the group to try to keep Marshall safe. Looby's presence as witness dissuaded the police from giving Marshall over to the mob. Instead, the police brought him before a magistrate on charges of drunken driving; sniffing Marshall's breath, the magistrate proclaimed, "You're crazy. This man hasn't even had a drink." On his way out of town, Marshall traded cars with another colleague to avoid being followed. Marshall said that colleague was then stopped and beaten "bad enough that he had to stay in the hospital for a month. I mean, they didn't play around."[7]

The unrelenting stress of Marshall's work took its toll. He had little time to spend with his wife, Buster, and a series of miscarriages was heartbreaking for the childless couple. A chain smoker and a drinker, Marshall was flattened by pneumonia in 1946; the head of the NAACP, Walter White, said, "Mr. Marshall's condition is due solely to the fact that he has worked himself almost to death without any thought of self." Marshall recuperated with Buster in the Virgin Islands before throwing himself back into his work.[8]

Marshall's record before the U.S. Supreme Court during his years with the NAACP Legal Defense and Education Fund remains unparalleled. He won twenty-nine of the thirty-two cases that he argued in the Court, beginning with *Chambers v. Florida*, 309 U.S. 227 (1940). In this case, after an elderly white man in the small town of Pompano, Florida, was robbed and murdered, dozens of Black residents were arrested, jailed, and interrogated relentlessly for a week, including overnight without respite. Marshall persuaded the Court that the confessions thus obtained, which ultimately led to death sentences for several men, were coerced and that convictions based on the confessions violated the due process clause of the Fourteenth Amendment.

Marshall racked up a number of landmark rulings years before the *Brown v. Board of Education of Topeka* school desegregation case. He successfully challenged Texas's all-white Democratic primary in *Smith v. Allwright*, 321 U.S. 649 (1944). In *Shelley v. Kraemer*, 334 U.S. 1 (1948), he persuaded the Supreme Court that racially restrictive real estate covenants, which sustained residential segregation, were unenforceable under the Fourteenth Amendment.

Other Supreme Court wins during this time included *Morgan v. Virginia*, 328 U.S. 373 (1946), striking down a Virginia law requiring racial segregation on commercial interstate buses as a violation of the commerce clause of the Constitution; *Patton v. State of Mississippi*, 332 U.S. 463 (1947), holding that systematic racial discrimination in juror selection violates the equal protection clause of the

Fourteenth Amendment; *Sipuel v. Board of Regents of the University of Oklahoma*, 332 U.S. 631 (1948), requiring a qualified applicant, whose application had been rejected because she was Black, to be admitted to the University of Oklahoma's law school; and *Watts v. Indiana*, 338 U.S. 49 (1949), holding that it violated the due process clause of the Fourteenth Amendment to allow into evidence at trial a confession obtained by holding the defendant—who had not been charged with a crime and had been permitted neither access to counsel nor contact with anyone besides police—in solitary confinement in a bare cell where he was interrogated by relays of police officers for nearly a week.

Any lawyer could be justifiably proud of having successfully argued even one of these important cases before the Court. And yet these victories, accomplished in less than a decade, represent only part of what Marshall would accomplish as an attorney.

The NAACP continued to push for civil rights legislation. In 1948, President Harry S. Truman gave a historic address to Congress requesting legislation to better protect voting rights, deter lynchings, and prohibit discrimination in interstate commerce, as well as the establishment of a permanent civil rights commission and civil rights division within the Justice Department. Marshall communicated with the Truman administration and offered testimony to Congress in support of this effort. On meeting resistance, however, Truman's effort fizzled; it would be another decade before Congress enacted a civil rights bill.[9]

In 1949, Marshall met with Black residents of Clarendon County, South Carolina, with the goal of testing the constitutionality of segregation in public schools. This case became *Briggs et al. v. Elliott et al.*, one of the cases consolidated by the Supreme Court into the ruling for which Marshall may be most well known, *Brown v. Board of Education* (discussed in the next chapter).

Marshall was not deterred by exhaustion or threats of violence. Around this time he told *Collier's Magazine*, "I intend to wear life like a very loose garment, and never worry about nothin'."[10] His equanimity, humor, and gregarious nature may help explain how he summoned such remarkable moral and physical bravery and persistence in the face of the cruelty and brutality of American race relations. Marshall himself, however, scoffed when congratulated on his courage, insisting that the Black people he represented were the brave ones: "There isn't a threat known to men that they do not receive. They're never out from under pressure. I don't think I could take it for a week. The possibility of violent death for them and their families is something they've learned to live with like a man learns to sleep with a sore arm."[11]

Smith v. Allwright, 321 U.S. 649 (1944)

When this suit was filed, the Texas Democratic Party held all-white primary elections. At the time, Texas was essentially a one-party state: the only primaries held in the state were for the Democratic Party, and only Democratic nominees for Congress, the state senate, and the governor's office had been elected in Texas since 1859, with just two exceptions. Barring Black voters from participating in the party primary thus effectively denied them any role in choosing their representatives in government. Lonnie Smith, a Black member of the Texas Democratic Party who had been barred from voting in the state's all-white Democratic primary, challenged the party's policy as violating his rights under the Fourteenth, Fifteenth, and Seventeenth Amendments to the Constitution.

The lower courts decided in favor of the Texas Democratic Party, on the ground that voting in the Democratic primary was a private "political party affair," which did not involve the state (i.e., governmental) action required for discrimination to be considered a violation of a person's constitutional rights. On appeal to the Supreme Court, Thurgood Marshall argued in the brief included here that state action was involved in the Texas Democratic Party's exclusion of Black Democratic voters from primary elections.

The Supreme Court decided that states must make voting in their primary elections equally accessible to voters of all races, even if the state itself does not manage the political parties' election process, because the primaries are an integral part of the machinery for choosing federal and state officials.

In a speech at the 1944 NAACP Wartime Conference, Marshall said:

> The civil rights statutes...can be used to enforce the right to register and vote throughout the country. The threats of many of the bigots in the South to disregard the ruling of the Supreme Court of the United States in the recent Texas Primary decision have not intimidated a single person. The United States Supreme Court remains the highest court in this land.[12]

PETITION FOR WRIT OF CERTIORARI AND BRIEF IN SUPPORT THEREOF

[*Some citations and footnotes have been omitted for ease of reading. Other omissions are noted in the text with ellipses or an ornament for longer omissions.*]

In the Supreme Court of the United States

October Term, 1943

Lonnie E. Smith, Petitioner, vs. S. E. Allwright, Election Judge, and James J. Luizza, Associate Election Judge, 48th Precinct of Harris County, Texas, Respondent.

—

To the Honorable, the Chief Justice of the United States and the Associate Justices of the Supreme Court of the United States:

—

PART ONE. Summary Statement of Matter Involved.

I. Statement of the Case.

The amended complaint alleged that on July 27, 1940, and on August 24, 1940, the respondents, acting as election judges of the 48th Precinct of Harris County, Texas, denied the petitioner and other qualified electors the right to vote in the primaries for selection of candidates of the Democratic party for the offices of U.S. Senator and Representatives in Congress. Petitioner sought damages for himself and a declaratory judgment on behalf of himself and others similarly situated that the actions of the respondents in refusing to permit qualified Negro electors to vote in these primaries violated Sections 31 and 43 of Title 8 of the United States Code in that they had subjected him to a deprivation of rights secured by Sections 2 and 4 of Article I, and the 14th, 15th, and 17th Amendments of the United States Constitution. The amended answer admitted that respondents refused to permit petitioner to vote, but denied that their actions violated the United States Constitution or laws, because the Democratic primary in Texas was "a political party affair" not subject to federal control. Both parties agreed to stipulations as to certain material facts.

The case was heard upon the stipulations, depositions, and oral testimony. On May 11, 1942, District Judge T. M. Kennerly filed Findings of Fact and Conclusions of Law, and on May 30, 1942, entered a final judgment that: (1) the petitioner "take nothing against" respondents, and (2) issued a declaratory judgment "that the practice of the defendants (respondents here) in enforcing and maintaining the policy, custom, and usage of which plaintiff (petitioner here) and other Negro citizens similarly situated who are qualified electors are denied the right to cast ballots at the Democratic Primary Elections in Texas, solely on account of their race or color, is constitutional, and does not deny or abridge their rights to vote within the meaning of the Fourteenth, Fifteenth, or Seventeenth Amendments to the United States Constitution, or Sections 2 and 4 of Article I of the United States Constitution."*

Notice of appeal to the United States Circuit Court of Appeals for the Fifth Circuit was filed by petitioner on June 6, 1942. On November 30, 1942, the United States Circuit Court of Appeals for the Fifth Circuit affirmed the judgment of the lower court.† Petition for rehearing was promptly filed and denied on January 21, 1943, without opinion.

II. Salient Facts.

All parties to this action, both petitioner and respondents, are citizens of the United States and of the State of Texas, and are residents and domiciled in said State.

Petitioner is a Negro, native born citizen of the United States residing in Houston, Harris County, Texas, and has been a duly and legally qualified elector under the laws of the United States and the State of Texas, and is subject to no disqualification.

Petitioner is a believer in the tenets of the Democratic party and, as found by the district judge, is a Democrat.

On July 27, 1940, a primary, and on August 24, 1940, a "run off" primary were held in Harris County, Texas, for nomination of candidates upon the Democratic ticket for the offices of U.S. Senator, U.S. Congressman, Governor and other State and local officers. Prior to this time the respondents were appointed and qualified as Presiding Judge and Associate Judge of Primaries in Precinct 48, Harris County, Texas.

On July 27, 1940, petitioner presented himself to vote in the said Democratic primary, at the regular polling place for the 48th Precinct with his poll tax receipt and requested to be permitted to vote. Respondents refused him a

---

*The District Court reached the conclusion: "I, therefore, follow *Grovey v. Townsend*, and render judgment for defendants."

† The *per curiam* opinion of the Circuit Court of Appeals concluded: "The opinion in that case (*U.S. v. Classic*) did not overrule or even mention *Grovey v. Townsend*. We may not overrule it. On its authority the judgment is affirmed."

ballot because of his race and color, in accordance with alleged instructions of the Democratic party of Texas.

The State of Texas has prescribed the qualifications for electors in Article 6 of the Texas Constitution and Article 2955 of the Revised Civil Statutes of Texas, which statute sets forth identical qualifications for voting in both "primary" and "general" elections. Primaries in Texas are created, required and controlled in minute detail by an intricate statutory scheme.*

According to the stipulations of facts made a part of the Findings of Facts of District Court: "At all times material herein the only State-Wide Primaries held in Texas have been for nominees of the Democratic Party."

While there is a statutory provision requiring the payment of certain primary election expenses by the candidates, all other expenses are borne by the State of Texas. The County Clerk, the Tax Assessor and Collector, and the County Judge of Harris County all performed duties required of them under Articles 3100–3153, Revised Civil Statutes of Texas, in connection with holding of the primaries on July 27, 1940 and August 24, 1940, without cost to the candidates, or the Democratic party, or any official thereof.

After such primary the names of the candidates receiving the nomination are certified by the County Executive Committee to the State Executive Committee; the State Executive Committee, in turn, certifies said nominees to the Secretary of State who places the names of these candidates on the General Election Ballot to be voted on in the General Election. Such services are rendered by the Secretary of State as a part of his governmental function and are paid for by the State of Texas. Said Secretary of State also certifies other Party candidates as well as Independent candidates for places upon the General Election Ballot; such services as rendered by the Secretary of State are paid by the State of Texas.

Although some of the expenses of the primary elections are paid by the Harris County Democratic Executive Committee, it is admitted: "that it received the funds therefor by levying an assessment against each person whose

---

* The present election laws of Texas originated with the so-called "Terrell Law," being "An Act to regulate elections and to prescribe penalties for its violation" (General Laws of Texas, 1903, Chapter 51, p. 133). Sections 82 to 107 of this statute set out the requirements for the holding of primary elections. In 1905 that Statute was repealed and in place thereof Chapter 11 of the General Laws of Texas, 1905, was enacted. These statutes established almost identical requirements for both the "primary" and "general" elections as integral parts of the election machinery for the State of Texas....

name was placed upon the Primary Ballot for the two Primaries named, and that the funds unused therefor, and which remained in the possession of the Harris County Democratic Executive Committee, were returned pro rata to each candidate for Democratic nominee who had made a contribution to the Harris County Democratic Executive Committee, following the assessment so levied."

The stipulation of facts agreed upon by petitioner and respondents provides that: "Since 1859 all Democratic nominees, for Congress, Senate and Governor, have been elected in Texas with two exceptions."

PART TWO. Question Presented.

Does the Constitution of the United States prohibit the exclusion of qualified Negro electors from voting in primary elections which are an integral part of the election machinery of the State and which are determinative of the choice of federal officers?

PART THREE. Reasons Relied on for Allowance of the Writ.

I. The decision of the Circuit Court of Appeals in this case is inconsistent with the decision of this court in *United States v. Classic* [313 U.S. 299 (1941)].

II. Ratio decidendi [*the reason for a judicial decision*] of *Grovey v. Townsend* [295 U.S. 45 (1935)] should be re-examined in the light of new facts disclosed by the present record.

III. Inconsistency between the decisions of this court in *Grovey v. Townsend* and *United States v. Classic* apparent in their application to the instant case should be resolved.

A. *Grovey v. Townsend* and *United States v. Classic* present inconsistent theories as to federal authority over primaries which decide elections.

B. *Grovey v. Townsend* and *United States v. Classic* present inconsistent theories of what constitutes "state action" in the conduct of primaries.

Argument
I. The decision of the Circuit Court of Appeals in this case is inconsistent with the decision of this Court in *United States v. Classic.*

In his complaint petitioner charged that respondents had violated Sections 31 and 43 of Title 8, United States Code, in that they had subjected him to a deprivation of rights secured by Sections 2 and 4 of Article I and the 14th,

15th, and 17th Amendments of the Constitution of the United States. The courts below held that the petitioner, a qualified elector of the State of Texas, could not maintain an action for damages against the respondents, Democratic primary election judges, who refused to permit petitioner and other qualified electors to vote in the Democratic primary election held July 27, 1940, and August 24, 1940, in voting precinct 48, Harris County, Texas. Those rulings were inconsistent with the decision of this Court in *United States v. Classic*, 313 U.S. 299 (1941).

Petitioner seeks to maintain this action to obtain redress for deprivation of a constitutional right specifically recognized and described by this Court in the *Classic* case. There, relying on Section 2 of Article I this Court said: "The right of the people to choose (Congressmen)...is a right established and guaranteed by the Constitution and hence is one secured by it to those citizens and inhabitants of the state entitled to exercise the right" (313 U.S. 299, 314).

In the *Classic* case, as in the instant case, the acts complained of had been committed in connection with primary elections. Nevertheless, this Court concluded that those acts were an interference with a right "secured by the Constitution," saying:

"Where the state law has made the primary an integral part of the procedure of choice, or where in fact the primary effectively controls the choice, the right of the elector to have his ballot counted in the primary, is rightfully included in the right in Article I, Section 2. This right of participation is protected just as is the right to vote at the election, where the primary is by law made an integral part of the election machinery, whether the voter exercises his right at a party primary which invariably, sometimes or never determines the ultimate choice of the representative" (313 U.S. 299, 318).

In the instant case the record demonstrates that the laws of the State of Texas have made the primary "an integral part of the procedure of choice." No valid distinction can be drawn between the Texas and Louisiana statutes in this connection. Moreover, the history of Texas elections shows that the Democratic primary "effectively controls the choice" of the elected representatives in the State, and respondents in this case have so stipulated.*

While *United States v. Classic* was a criminal case, the statutory prohibition (18 *U.S.C.* sec. 51, 52), involved there closely parallels Section 43 of Title 8 of the United States Code upon which petitioner here relies. These sections of

* Both parties agreed to the following stipulation: "Since 1859 all Democratic nominees, for Congress, Senate and Governor, have been elected in Texas, with two exceptions."

the United States Code are parts of the same Acts of Congress, the legislative history of which demonstrates that they were intended to provide both civil and criminal redress for the same wrongs.* Both the criminal sanction of Section 52 of Title 18 and the civil sanction of Section 43 of Title 8 are aimed at any deprivation of constitutional right "under color of any statute, ordinance, regulation, custom, or usage of any state or territory." Election judges in Texas, just as in Louisiana, have authority to act in primary elections only by virtue of the State laws. The decision of the Court below is inconsistent with the determination made by this Court in the *Classic* case that the "alleged acts of appellees were committed in the course of their performance of duties under Louisiana statutes requiring them to count the ballots, to record the result of the count, and to certify the result of the elections. Misuse of power, possessed by virtue of state law and made possible only because the wrongdoer is clothed with the authority of state law, is action taken 'under color of' state law" (313 U.S. 299, 325–326).†

---

*After the adoption of the 13th Amendment, a bill, which became the first Civil Rights Act (14 Stat. 27), was introduced, the major purpose of which was to secure to the recently freed Negroes all the civil rights secured to white men including language similar to that in Section 43 of title 8 and section 52 of title 18. The 2nd Civil Rights Act (16 Stat. 140-16 Stat. 433) was passed for the express purpose of enforcing the provisions of the 14th Amendment. The third civil rights act, adopted April 20, 1871 (17 Stat. 13), re-enacted the same provisions.

Section 43 of Title 8 and Section 52 of the United States Civil Code were both parts of the same original bill and although one provides for civil redress and the other for criminal redress, the language of the two sections is closely similar:

Section 43 of Title 8
"Every person who, under color of any statute, ordinance, regulation, custom, or usage, of any State or Territory, subjects, or causes to be subjected, any citizen of the United States or other person within the jurisdiction thereof to the deprivation of any rights, privileges, or immunities secured by the Constitution and laws, shall be liable to the party injured in an action at law, suit in equity, or other proper proceeding for redress. R. S. Sec. 1979."

Section 52 of Criminal Code
"Whoever, under color of any law, statute, ordinance, regulation, or custom, willfully subjects, or causes to be subjected, any inhabitant of any State, Territory, or District to the deprivation of any rights, privileges, or immunities secured or protected by the Constitution and laws of the United States, or to different punishments, pains, or penalties, on account of such inhabitant being an alien, or by reason of his color, or race, than are prescribed for the punishment of citizens, shall be fined not more than $1,000, or imprisoned not more than one year, or both."

† Section 43 of Title 8 has been used repeatedly to enforce the right of citizens to vote without discrimination because of race or color. See: *Myers* v. *Anderson,* 238 U.S. 368 (1914); *Lane* v. *Wilson, 307* U.S. 268 (1939).

Moreover, this Court having found that the misconduct of primary election officials in the *Classic* case constitutes action taken "under color of state law" within the meaning of Section 52 of Title 18, United States Code, it necessarily follows that similar misconduct here involves "state action" within the meaning of the 14th Amendment. Where such misconduct is discrimination on account of the race or color of the complaining voter, there is, likewise, a violation of the 15th Amendment and section 31 of Title 8 of the United States Code which is a part of an original act entitled, "A Bill to Enforce the Right of Citizens of the United States to Vote in the Several States of this Union and for other purposes" (17 Stat. 13).

It is, therefore, submitted that the decision of the Circuit Court of Appeals affirming the action of the District Court in this case is inconsistent with the decision of this Court in *United States v. Classic*.

II. Ratio decidendi of *Grovey v. Townsend* should be reexamined in the light of new facts disclosed by the present record.

The record formerly before this Court in *Grovey v. Townsend*, 295 U.S. 45 (1935), failed to reveal or present facts essential to an adequate legal appraisal of the so-called "white primary." That decision had no proper basis in the actualities of the Texas system, and should be re-examined in the light of facts now revealed for the first time in the present record. In the words of Mr. Justice Brandeis:

"Not only may the decision of the fact have been rendered upon an inadequate presentation of then existing conditions, but the conditions may have changed meanwhile." *Burnett v. Coronado Oil and Gas Co.*, 285 U.S. 393, 412 (1932).

In *Grovey v. Townsend*, this Court decided that the present method of excluding Negroes from voting in the Texas Democratic primary elections did not involve such state action as is comprehended by the 14th and 15th Amendments. Because the exclusionary practice was predicated upon a resolution of the State Democratic Convention, and in the light of the record then at hand, this Court failed to find any decisive interposition of state force in the primary election.

Grovey v. Townsend was decided upon demurrer to a petition for damages filed in Justice Court, Precinct No. 1, Position No. 2, Harris County, Texas. That record provided no factual picture of the organization and operation of the so-called Democratic party of Texas and permitted the assumption that the "party" had the basic structure and defined membership which are characteristic of an organized voluntary association. Moreover, on that record, this Court assumed that the privilege of voting in the Democratic primary election was an incident of "party membership" and restricted to members of an organized voluntary association called the "Democratic party."* The present record and the following analysis will show that these supposed facts, vital to the decision in *Grovey v. Townsend,* did not exist.

The problem in *Grovey v. Townsend,* as in the present case, was the determination and evaluation of the participation of government on the one hand, and the so-called "Democratic party" on the other hand, in Texas primary elections with a view to deciding whether the conduct of these elections was, in legal contemplation, a governmental function subject to the restraints of the 14th and 15th Amendments or a private enterprise not so restricted. The complaint described in detail the state statutes creating, requiring, regulating, and controlling the conduct of primary elections in Texas. These circumstances were summarized in the opinion of this Court (295 U.S. 45, 49–50).

In contrast, the nature, organization and functioning of the "Democratic party" were nowhere adequately described. Instead, the Court found it necessary to rely upon a general conclusion of the Supreme Court of Texas in *Bell v. Hill,* 123 Tex. 531, 74 S. W. (2d) 113 (1938), that the "Democratic party" of Texas is a voluntary association for political purposes, functioning as such in determining its membership and in controlling the privilege of voting in its primaries.†

Now, for the first time, this Court has significant facts before it which permit an independent examination of the "party" and its functioning and a meaningful comparison of the roles of state and "party" in Texas primary elections. The present record shows that in Texas the Democratic primary is not, as was assumed in *Grovey v. Townsend,* an election at which the members of an organized voluntary political association choose their candidates for public office.

* "While it is true that Texas has by its laws elaborately provided for the expression of party preferences as to nominees, has required that preference to be expressed in a certain form of voting, and has attempted in minute detail to protect the suffrage of the members of the organization against fraud, it is equally true that the primary is a party primary..." (296 U.S. 45, 50).

† *Bell v. Hill* was decided by the Supreme Court of Texas on an original motion for leave to file a petition for mandamus. As in the *Grovey* case there were no facts presented or evidence of either the "Democratic Party" or the actual functioning of the election machinery.

First, any white elector, whether he considers himself Democrat, Republican, Communist, Socialist, or non-partisan, may vote in the "Democratic" primary. The testimony of the respondent Allwright is positive and stands unchallenged on this point.

"Q. Mr. Allwright, when a white person comes into the polling place during the primary election of 1940 and asks for a ballot to vote do you ever ask them what party they belong to?

A. No, we never ask them.

Q. As a matter of fact, if a white elector comes into the polling place to vote in the Democratic primary election, he is given a ballot to vote; is that correct?

A. Right.

Q. And Negroes are not permitted to vote in the primary election?

A. They don't vote in the primary.

Q. But any white person that is qualified; regardless of what party they belong to, they can vote?

A. That is right.

Q. And you do let them vote?

A. Yes."

Second, the "Democratic party" of Texas has no identified membership and no structure which would make its membership determinable. Under these circumstances, it is impossible to restrict voting in the primary election to "party members." The testimony of E. B. Germany, Chairman of the Democratic State Executive Committee, illustrates this point.

Third, the "Democratic party" in Texas is not organized. Officials claiming to represent the "party" testified positively that the "party" has no constitution nor by-laws, and is a "loose jointed organization." No minutes or records of the periodic "party" conventions are preserved. The "party" has no officers between conventions. Beyond the lack of organic party law, there is no formulated body of party doctrine. No resolutions of the state conventions are preserved. Even the resolution upon which the exclusion of Negroes from the primaries is predicated is not a matter of record and has no existence as a document. At the trial, the alleged contents of the resolution were proved, over the objection of the petitioner, by the recollection of a witness who testified that he had introduced such a resolution, and was present when it was adopted.

The only rules and regulations governing the "Democratic party" and the "Democratic primary" elections are the election laws of the State of Texas. This startling state of affairs is perhaps the most striking evidence of a one-party political system where for all practical purposes the "Democratic party" is co-extensive with the body politic and, hence, needs no private organization to distinguish it from other parties.

In such circumstances the legal character of the primary elections, and the status of those who conduct them, can be derived only from the one organized agency, which creates, requires, regulates and controls these elections, namely, the State of Texas. The factual material supplied in this record, but not available in the record of *Grovey v. Townsend*, compels this conclusion.

Inadequately informed, this Court sanctioned the practical disenfranchisement of 540,565 adult Negro citizens, 11.86% of the total adult population (citizens) of Texas.* It is for the correction of this error and the resultant deprivation of constitutional right that the present petition is submitted.

III. Inconsistency between the decisions of this Court in *Grovey v. Townsend* and *United States v. Classic* apparent in their application to the instant case should be resolved.

The District Court and the Circuit Court of Appeals refused to follow the decision in *United States v. Classic*, because of their belief that the instant case was controlled by the earlier decision in *Grovey v. Townsend*. The District Court concluded: "I, therefore, follow *Grovey v. Townsend*, and render judgment for Defendants." The Circuit Court of Appeals likewise followed the *Grovey* case in affirming the lower court. In a per curiam opinion it was stated:

> "The Texas statutes regulating party primaries which were considered in *Grovey v. Townsend* are still in force. They were held not to render the primary an election in the constitutional sense. There is no substantial difference between that case and this. It is argued that different principles were announced by the Supreme Court in *United States v. Classic*, 313 U.S. 301. The latter was a criminal case from Louisiana, and did not involve the Texas statutes. It differs in many points from this case. The opinion of the court in that case

* United States Census (1940)....

did not overrule or even mention *Grovey v. Townsend*. We may not overrule it. On its authority the judgment is affirmed."

In thus following the *Grovey* case rather than the *Classic* case, the District Court and the Circuit Court of Appeals made a choice between apparently inconsistent legal theories of this Court as to federal control over primaries.

A. *Grovey v. Townsend* **and** *United States v. Classic* **present inconsistent theories as to federal authority over primaries which decide elections.**

The decision in the *Grovey* case was based on the theory that the right to participate in the Democratic Primary is one of the privileges incidental to membership in the Democratic Party of Texas and should not be confused with "the right to vote." Thus, the opinion stated:

"The complaint states that...in Texas nomination by the Democratic party is equivalent to election. These facts (the truth of which the demurrer assumes) the petitioner insists, without more, make out a forbidden discrimination.... The argument is that as a Negro may not be denied a ballot at a general election on account of his race or color, if exclusion from the primary renders his vote at the general election insignificant and useless, the result is to deny him the suffrage altogether. So to say is to confuse the privilege of membership in a party with the right to vote for one who is to hold a public office. With the former the state need have no concern, with the latter it is bound to concern itself, for the general election is a function of the state government and discrimination by the state as respects participation by Negroes on account of race or color is prohibited by the Federal Constitution" (295 U.S. 45, 54).*

In following the decision in the *Grovey* case the lower courts ignored the reasoning in the *Classic* case that in a state where choice at the primary is tantamount to election, the right to vote in the primary is derived not from the party but from the Constitution. In the *Grovey* case the question as to whether or not federal authority extended to primary elections was approached by a consideration of the relation between the Democratic primary elections and

* Similar reasoning appears throughout the *Grovey* decision: e. g., "Here the qualifications of citizens to participate in party counsels and to vote at primaries has been declared by the representatives of the party in convention assembled, and this action upon its face is not state action" (295 U.S. 45, 48).

the "Democratic party" in Texas. In the *Classic* case the Court viewed as controlling the fundamental relationship between the Democratic primary elections and the choice of office-holders. The Court was not concerned with who ran the machinery but with the practical operation of that machinery upon the expression of choice.*

The *Grovey* case was a complaint for damages in a state court based solely upon the Fourteenth and Fifteenth Amendments, and this Court, therefore, centered its attention upon the question of what constituted "state action" under those Amendments. Yet the language of the opinion is so broad as to create the impression that the effect of the primary in controlling the choice of office-holders has no bearing whatsoever upon the question of federal authority over the conduct of primary elections. The lower courts here gave this all-inclusive effect to the language of the *Grovey* case thereby ignoring the decision of this Court in the *Classic* case that the right to vote in such a primary is derived from the Constitution and protected by federal statutes not involved in the *Grovey* case.

B. *Grovey v. Townsend* and *United States v. Classic* present inconsistent theories of what constitutes "state action" in the conduct of the primaries.

The Louisiana and Texas election statutes are substantially alike. On the basis of the Louisiana election laws this Court in the *Classic* case concluded that the Democratic primary in Louisiana was "an integral part of the election machinery of Louisiana" and that the election officials who refused to count the ballots of qualified electors in the primary election in Louisiana were rightfully charged with violation of Sections 19 and 20 of the Criminal Code (18 U.S.C., secs. 51 and 52) because "misuse of power, possessed by virtue of State law and made possible only because the wrongdoer is clothed with the authority of State law, is action taken 'under color of' state law" (313 U.S. 299, 326). But in the *Grovey* case the action of officials conducting a primary election which was similarly created, required, regulated and controlled by the State was held not to be "state action." The essential inconsistency is that in the *Classic* case the Court decided the issue of state action by examining the relation of the state to the enterprise in which the election judges were engaged, while in the

* "The right of the people to choose (Congressmen), ... is a right established and guaranteed by the Constitution and hence is one secured by it to those citizens and inhabitants of the state entitled to exercise the right" (313 U.S. 299, 314).

Grovey case the Court disregarded this relationship and gave legal effect to the circumstances that the particular act complained of was not authorized by the state. If the *Grovey* doctrine had been applied in the *Classic* case it would have led to the conclusion that the election frauds were not "under color of state law" because they were not authorized by the state.

It is these conflicts between the theories of *United States v. Classic* and *Grovey v. Townsend* which should be resolved, and resolved in accordance with the sound theory in the *Classic* case. . . .

Government Correspondence and Testimony (1947–1949)

On behalf of the NAACP, Marshall corresponded with Truman administration officials and testified before the U.S. Congress in support of federal anti-lynching legislation and about other civil rights matters.

Marshall offered congressional testimony in favor of a civil rights bill in 1949. No major federal civil rights legislation had been enacted since 1875. It was not until 1957 that a federal civil rights bill was passed, and it was only in the 1960s that Congress followed up that initial effort with more comprehensive legislation.[13]

The material included here can be found in the Harry S. Truman Library, "President's Committee on Civil Rights" files.

[*On the letterhead of the NAACP Legal Defense and Educational Fund, Inc.*]

June 11, 1947

Mr. Robert Carr
President's Committee on Civil Rights
1712 G Street, N. W., Room 208
Washington, D.C.

Dear Mr. Carr:

This will reply to your telephone inquiry directed to Miss Baxter of our Research Department concerning the differences between the Case bill and earlier bills in the matter of the definition of a lynch mob.

As you are undoubtedly aware, the Case bill was the result of a conference sponsored by the N.A.A.C.P. Legal Committee, the National Lawyers Guild and the National Bar Association in Washington, on January 25, 1947. In preparing for that conference and in the discussions at the conference, every effort was made to draft a bill which would provide for federal action against individual members of mobs who inflicted or attempted to inflict bodily harm or death upon a person charged with or suspected of crime in an effort to prevent the administration of justice. Such changes as were made in the definition of the crime were made solely for the purpose of including within the purview of the Act more acts of violence of the general nature which has come to be known as lynching.

This is true of the definition of a mob which, as you have noted, has been changed from three persons to two persons, and the description of the reason for the lynching which was changed to include race, creed, color, national origin, ancestry, language or religion so as to spell out jurisdiction in cases involving attacks upon Jews, Mexican Americans, Catholics or other groups subject to intolerance.

Sincerely yours,
Thurgood Marshall
Special Counsel

—

June 18, 1947

Mr. Thurgood Marshall
Special Counsel, N.A.A.C.P.
20 West 40th Street,
New York, N.Y.

Dear Mr. Marshall:

Thank you for your letter of June 11th on the definition of lynching and the Case bill. I am afraid that there has been some misunderstanding about our telephone inquiry to Miss Baxter. Actually what we are seeking is the definition of lynching used by the N.A.A.C.P. in compiling statistics. We have been endeavoring to prepare for the Committee a statement of the statistical material on lynching with an appropriate explanation as to the varying definitions of lynching used by the different groups and the result and effect upon statistics.

If you can conveniently furnish me with a statement concerning the policy of your organization on this point I would appreciate it very much. I am sorry that there should have been any misunderstanding and I am very grateful for your cooperation in supplying us with material on the Case bill.

Sincerely yours,
Robert K. Carr

[*On the letterhead of the NAACP Legal Defense and Educational Fund, Inc.*]

July 3, 1947

Hon. Theron L. Caudle
Assistant Attorney General
United States Department of Justice
Washington, DC

Dear Mr. Caudle:

This will reply to your letter of June 24, 1947 informing us of the result of your investigation into the killing of William Rim Lockwood by Deputy Sheriff Willie Kirby in Macon County, Alabama.

In your letter you state that Kirby claimed that he shot Lockwood in self defense after being attacked by Lockwood with a knife. On the other hand you state that Mrs. Lockwood and her son claim that Lockwood was killed because he refused to say "Yes, sir" and "No, sir," in reply to questions. You state in your letter that since there are no other witnesses and the issue will be which of the two statements is a correct version of the affair, it is not believed that a successful prosecution could be maintained and the case has accordingly been closed.

I assume that it is also your conclusion that under the decision in the *Screws* case the facts would not warrant an attempt to prosecute even were Mrs. Lockwood's statements to be undisputed.

In reviewing this case, I am reminded of the case of Casey Lee Pointer in Cleveland, Mississippi, where the cold blooded killing of an unarmed Negro by two police officers was likewise found by your office to be one in which no prosecution could be successfully maintained.

It seems to me that these two cases are the type which should be brought to the attention of the President's Committee on Civil Rights to point out to them the need for adequate legislation to empower you to protect the ordinary Negro citizen in the South from wanton killing by police officers. May I suggest that the investigations of your office in these two cases be forwarded to the President's Committee as illustrative of the violations of fundamental human rights by police officers in the South which must be the subject of legislation enabling you to enter the cases.

Yours very truly,
Thurgood Marshall
Special Counsel

—

July 7, 1947

Mr. Thurgood Marshall
Special Counsel, N.A.A.C.P.
20 West 40th Street,
New York, N.Y.

Dear Mr. Marshall:

Thank you for your note of July 3rd and the enclosed copy of your letter to Assistant Attorney General Theron Caudle. I will see to it that this communication receives the attention of the members of the President's Committee.

Sincerely yours,
Robert K. Carr

Hearings Before a Subcommittee of the Committee on the Judiciary, United States Senate, Eighty-First Congress, First Session, on S. 1725, a bill to provide means of further securing and protecting the civil rights of persons within the jurisdiction of the United States, and S. 1734, a bill to establish a Commission on Civil Rights, and for other purposes, June 17, 22, 29, and July 14, 1949

STATEMENT OF THURGOOD MARSHALL, SPECIAL COUNSEL, NATIONAL ASSOCIATION FOR THE ADVANCEMENT OF COLORED PEOPLE, NEW YORK, N.Y.

MR. MARSHALL:...I want to say first of all that I am here on behalf of the National Association for the Advancement of Colored People. I am, personally, and we are always happy to appear before committees, because I believe, so far as I am concerned, whenever I have an opportunity to appear in court, before a legislative committee, it gives a new faith in the way of life, or whatever you want to call it.

The statement itself I think if I read it, it is not too long, will cover it.

There can be no question that the Thirteenth, Fourteenth, and Fifteenth Amendments need implementation. This type of legislation meets that need. At the outset, it should be made clear that this bill does not in any form or fashion deprive any State or political subdivision thereof of its lawful rights. It is only aimed at prohibiting unlawful acts. It does not interfere with any Federal- or State-protected right.

SENATOR WILEY: You are not talking about the substantive law changes?

MR. MARSHALL: Yes. It should also be pointed out that there is not a single provision, sentence, or word in this bill which is aimed at any particular section of the country. It will apply equally as well in Maine and Mississippi, California and Florida. No law-abiding citizen, whether he be a private individual or a governmental official, has any reason whatsoever to fear the enactment of this bill. On the other hand, the bill can have a deterring effect upon all private individuals and Government officials who have in the past or who contemplate in the future use of racial or religious prejudice as the basis for illegal action to deprive Americans of their federally protected rights.

Whatever progress has been made in recent years in the enforcement of federally protected rights has for the most part been brought about through the use of the Federal machinery. The progress that has been made in criminal actions to protect civil rights of Americans has been made by the United States Department of Justice in actions brought in the Federal courts. Progress in civil actions to protect and enforce civil rights has been made for the most part by private actions in Federal courts. Advances have resulted from interpretations by Federal judges, prominent among whom have been members of the bench from the South. Further progress has been halted by the limitations of the existing Federal statutes.

This bill does not propose any basic change in either the letter or spirit of the Declaration of Independence and Constitution of the United States. All it proposes to do is to recognize the inalienable right of all Americans to be free from racial and religious discrimination in the exercise of their civil rights. Surely there is no one at this late date who denies that all Americans are equal before the law. Surely there is no one at this late date who takes the position that our Government should not take any necessary steps to insure the fullest protection of this principle.

The need for this legislation and the purpose of the legislation is clearly set forth in section 11 of the bill. After pointing out the differences between our principles of government and our practices, the bill states:

> Congress recognizes that it is essential to the national security and the general welfare that this gap between principle and practice be closed; and that more adequate protection of the civil rights of individuals must be provided to preserve our American heritage, halt the undermining of our constitutional guaranties, and prevent serious damage to our moral, social, economic, and political life, and to our international relations—

and—

> The Congress therefore declares that it is its purpose to strengthen and secure the civil rights of the people of the United States under the Constitution, and that it is the national policy to protect the right of the individual to be free from discrimination based upon race, color, religion, or national origin.

The bill then sets forth in detail the purposes sought to be accomplished by this act.

The proposal for a Commission on Civil Rights in the executive branch of the Government should cause little opposition. In the first place, there is no question of the authority of Congress to establish such a commission. In the second place, the President's Committee on Civil Rights and its unbiased report did much to clarify the atmosphere and to separate fact from speculation. It gives to everyone a clear indication of the possibility for good inherent in such a commission if it had congressional sanction and approval.

The Civil Rights Division of the Department of Justice, which started with the administration of Attorney General Frank Murphy, has made some progress in efforts to protect the civil rights of Americans without regard to race, creed, color, and national origin. During the period this Division has been in existence, and especially during the administration of Attorney General Tom Clark, the main reasons more progress has not been made are (1) the inadequacies of the existing civil rights statutes; (2) the lack of full departmental status under an assistant attorney general; (3) lack of a sufficient number of agents for the Federal Bureau of Investigation; and, finally, the lack of sufficient funds to operate.

SENATOR WILEY: It is claimed by and large in the South that (1) there is violation of civil rights in relation to the lynching that takes place.

MR. MARSHALL: And a lot of other things.

SENATOR WILEY: And (2) the violation in relation to civil rights where the colored man is not permitted to vote.

MR. MARSHALL: That is another one.

SENATOR WILEY: And (3) what else?

MR. MARSHALL: (3) is what is going on in Birmingham right now; a Negro buys a home, pays for it, moves in it, and they throw a bomb in and blow it up.

SENATOR WILEY: And (4)?

MR. MARSHALL: (4) is just the complete denial of the feeling of violence and threatened violence. I do not think you included that in lynching, but that everlasting threat that, if you at any time stand up and insist that you are an American just like anyone else, you will either be lynched in the death portion of it or be maimed or beaten.

As to the other denial of civil rights down there, this bill does not, as I understand it, purport to protect all of the civil rights that are denied in the South. It is a pretty tough job.

SENATOR WILEY: Frankly, I am grateful to you for giving me these things. Is there any big stuff that you think of?

MR. MARSHALL: Offhand—and incidentally I am down here two-thirds of my time—I would say they are the major ones, the denial of opportunity of employment in Government agencies and things like that. This is all-inclusive, but those are the major ones.

SENATOR WILEY: What does the bill do, and how does it do it, to protect those rights?

MR. MARSHALL: Well, in the first place, we have some civil-rights statutes now; and, even with those that we have, the Department of Justice is blocked from the type of action that they could take under those statutes for departmental reasons. One is the Division is just in there as a division, does not have any money to operate on its own. It does not have status, and they do not have enough FBI men so that they can make the type of investigation necessary where they have a case…that a Negro has been denied the rights you have just mentioned. They cannot make a thorough enough investigation, and they cannot get enough departmental action to bring the case to trial.

SENATOR WILEY: The bill provides additional help.

MR. MARSHALL: It provides a moving arm for the Government to act with.

SENATOR WILEY: It gives additional help to the Attorney General's Department so that you feel that, even under the present statutes that exist, if they had that help, the Government could move in.

MR. MARSHALL: Move in better than they have been, but it would not settle it.

SENATOR WILEY: All right. Now, then, the bill changes the law so that I assume what it tries to do is to create jurisdiction in the Federal Government in relation to offenses that are debatable whether or not the Government could take jurisdiction.

MR. MARSHALL: If I might for just a moment say this, we take the position that this bill does not create any new right. It merely clarifies what was intended not only by the Constitution, Thirteenth, Fourteenth, and Fifteenth Amendments, but was also intended by the framers of the original civil-rights statutes.

For example, the changing of the language in there on each one of those sections, the ones you read where it is itemized, that was brought about by the decision in the case of *Screws against the United States* a couple of years ago in Georgia, came up from Georgia, where, after the case laid in court for at least 6 months, in the Supreme Court, and the majority opinion of the decision said that these rights, the old section 51 and section 52 of Title 18, which is now 241 and 242, that they did not itemize the rights that they were intended to be protected; and the Court said, the Supreme Court said, that those rights must be itemized so that, when you try man A for denying a right to man B, you must be able to say that man A deliberately took away a right that he knew he had.

SENATOR WILEY: What is that?

MR. MARSHALL: *Screws versus United States.* It is in here, sir.

SENATOR WILEY: If it is in there, all right.

SENATOR MCGRATH: 325 U.S. 91.

MR. MARSHALL: That was a decision where a policeman on the courthouse lawn beat a Negro's brains out, right on the lawn of the courthouse. And incidentally, as a result of the opinion in that case, he was subsequently tried and acquitted. And so that these rights here are not new rights in there.

I think the question was made in the interchange there; I think you said, sir, that those rights already existed. They do, but this is just Congress saying that these rights do exist so there will be no question from now on and we will know where everyone stands on it. And if I might say, sir, to my mind, I think it is a start that can be made. I for one am not in the group that believe that nothing can be done about this problem in the South. We have made progress. The criminal side has made progress in the cases in the Federal courts in the South. On civil cases we have made progress, with judges born and raised in the South, but we are now stymied because of certain blocks.

———

MR. MARSHALL: The proposal in S. 1725 and S. 1734 for the reorganization of the Civil Rights Division is, to my mind, so clearly necessary as to be beyond argument. The recommendation by the President's Committee on Civil Rights was based upon thorough study of cases referred to the Department by the organization I represent and other organizations, which basic civil rights had been denied Americans and in which the Department was hampered for the above reasons. My own experience with the Department bears out the need for the adoption of this section.

The adoption of this section of the bill will in itself be a demonstration to the world at large that our Government considers the protection of human rights, civil rights, and individual rights, of the highest importance. It will serve notice to those in this country who would deprive others of their basic constitutional rights that they will be subject to the same type of vigorous prosecution as has been exemplified by other divisions of our Department of Justice.

As I pointed out on the Commission on Civil Rights, there should be no argument in opposition to the creation of a joint congressional Committee on Civil Rights. There is most certainly more need for a joint congressional Committee on Civil Rights than there is for the continued existence of the Committee on Un-American Activities. Our Congress should be at least as interested in the state of civil rights in our country as it is in other matters which have heretofore been assigned to special committees. As a result of hearing by such a committee, research and investigations by its staff and Government agencies, Congress and each Member thereof, as well as our country and the world in general, would have the true picture of civil rights in this country. As to the actions of the committee itself, they will, of course, be subject to complete control by Congress.

Some 80 years ago the Thirteenth, Fourteenth, and Fifteenth Amendments to the Constitution of the United States were adopted. The true purpose of these amendments has never been in question. For example, in 1879 the United States Supreme Court in two cases made this clear.

The United States Supreme Court in the case of *Ex Parte Virginia* (100 U.S. 339, 344) declared:

> One great purpose of the amendment was to raise the colored race from that condition of inferiority and servitude in which most of them had previously stood into perfect equality of civil rights with all other persons within the jurisdiction of all the States. They were intended to take away all possibility of oppression by law because of race or color. . . .

The legislation you are considering today is necessary because the Fourteenth Amendment is in general terms and does not enumerate the rights its protects. As the Supreme Court has stated:

> The fourteenth amendment makes no attempt to enumerate the rights it is designed to protect. It speaks in general terms, and those

are as comprehensive as possible. Its language is prohibitory; but every prohibition implies the existence of rights and immunities, prominent among which is an immunity from inequality of legal protection, either of life, liberty, or property (*Strauder v. West Virginia* (100 U.S. 303, 310)).

However, despite the enactment of these amendments and their high purpose of removing from American life all discrimination and distinctions based upon race and color, no one can deny that this purpose has not as yet been accomplished. The primary duty of making this purpose a reality rests upon the Federal Government and specifically Congress.

The Supreme Court in a series of recent cases has made it clear that racial distinctions should be removed from American life.

Chief Justice Stone, speaking for a Court unanimous on this point, said in *Hirabayashi v. United States* (320 U.S. 81, 100 (1943)):

Distinctions between citizens solely because of their ancestry are by their very nature odious to a free people whose institutions are founded upon the doctrine of equality. For that reason legislative classification or discrimination based on race alone has often been held to be a denial of equal protection.

Mr. Murphy, in a concurring opinion, felt that racial distinctions based on color and ancestry—

are utterly inconsistent with our traditions and ideals. They are at variance with the principles for which we are now waging war. We cannot close our eyes to the fact that for centuries the Old World has been torn by racial and religious conflicts and has suffered the worst kind of anguish because of inequality of treatment for different groups. There was one law for one and a different law for another. Nothing is written more firmly into our law than the compact of the Plymouth voyagers to have just and equal laws (pp. 110–111).

The constitutionality of the existing civil-rights statutes was reaffirmed in the case of *Screws v. United States* (325 U.S. 91 (1945)). Further, in that case the present weaknesses of these statutes were pointed out, and the sections of this bill are in keeping with these suggestions. There can be no question of the constitutionality of the proposed amendments to the existing civil-rights statutes.

———

Section 242 extends the existing prohibition to those who bring about the denial of rights, privileges, or immunities secured or protected by the laws of the United States and increases the fine and imprisonment where the wrongful conduct causes death or maiming of the person so injured.

Section 242 (a) spells out some of the privileges and immunities referred to in section 242. The necessity for specifying these privileges and immunities was made clear by the decision In the case of *Screws versus United States*.

Section 594 of title 18, United States Code is amended so as to make it clear that it applies to intimidation for the purpose of interfering with the right to vote at either general, special, or primary elections. The constitutional right to vote without discrimination or intimidation has been recognized to apply to special and primary elections by the decisions in the cases of *United States versus Classic* and *Smith versus Allwright*.

Section 242 amends section 31 of title 8, United States Code, by making it clear that the provisions for civil action include those who are eligible to vote and clarifies the right protected to mean the right to vote in general, special, and primary elections.

Section 213 provides for civil, equitable, and declaratory relief to a person or persons injured as a result of action in violation of section 211. It also provides that sections 211 and 212 shall be enforceable by the Attorney General in the direct courts by actions for preventive or declaratory relief. That is a most important and essential provision, for it enables the Attorney General to proceed in a civil action in such a manner as to insure the protection of the civil rights threatened by illegal action. This section also provides that the district court, concurrently with State and Territorial courts, will have jurisdiction of proceedings under this section without regard to the jurisdictional amount.

Certainly there can be no question of the authority of Congress in this instance, for section 8 of article I of the Constitution of the United States specifically grants to Congress the power "to regulate commerce with foreign nations and among the several States, and with Indian tribes."

The case of *Morgan v. Virginia* (328 U.S. 373) recognized this principle and held inapplicable State statutes which sought to impose local segregation principles to interstate passengers on interstate carriers. In that decision the diversity of provisions for segregation in transportation among the several States was recognized; the lack of uniformity was emphasized. This provision of the bill prevents interstate carriers from imposing their own notions of racial segregation in an area in which it has already been declared unlawful for a State to impose such regulations. I cannot too strongly emphasize the need for this legislation because the enforcement of Jim Crow travel regulations, enforced under the guise of preventing friction, have as a matter of fact created more friction and violence than was expected. These regulations of segregation destroy completely the dignity of man and the basic principles of equality in our form of government.

The National Association for the Advancement of Colored People supports S. 1725 and S. 1734 without reservation....

This is not a question of one section of the country against another section of the country. It is not a question of one political party against another political party, because both major parties are committed to the civil-rights program in their platforms. This bill does not raise the question of one racial or religious group against another. Rather this legislation makes a serious effort to make possible the creation of a oneness of thought, oneness of principle, and oneness of the respect for our Constitution, our statutes, and our individual human and civil rights, the very basis of our democracy.

... At least two-thirds of my time is spent in the South and the Deep South. I think that progress is being made, but I think that if we are going to make real progress the Federal Government is the agency that has to stand out and make it clear as to what these rights are. Then I think the educational program that we all want can proceed. But it cannot proceed without what we consider a minimal program; as I understand it, this bill is just a minimal program....

2. "That Is Not What Our Constitution Stands For": 1950–1960

The 1950s began with Marshall victorious in two more cases he had argued before the U.S. Supreme Court: *Sweatt v. Painter*, 339 U.S. 629 (1950), and *McLaurin v. Oklahoma State Regents*, 339 U.S. 637 (1950). The result was a federal mandate for the racial integration of public graduate school education. The Supreme Court, however, declined to reach the question of whether to overturn *Plessy v. Ferguson*, the 1896 case that had given federal approval to "separate but equal" facilities. "Oh, boy, was that a disappointment," Marshall remembered. "I figured we'd just have to go back again and again, however many times necessary, to get the Court to one day recognize the psychological, social, educational, economic damages done to Black people when the state imposes the doctrine of *Plessy*."[1]

The new decade also saw the United States embroiled in another war, with North Korea. Marshall began receiving reports from Black servicemen about unfair treatment in the U.S. armed forces, and he visited South Korea in 1951 to investigate. President Truman had desegregated the military by executive order in 1948. But Marshall found that this order was slow to be implemented. He also found that Black soldiers were disproportionately charged with disobeying orders and were given longer sentences for misbehavior in combat than whites. His interactions with General Douglas MacArthur persuaded Marshall that the general was as "biased as any person I've run across."[2]

Pressing ahead, Marshall continued his work on the South Carolina case to desegregate public education in the lower grades. He knew that the school desegregation litigation, which would be consolidated under the name *Brown v. Board of Education of Topeka*, was the biggest case of his career, and he toiled doggedly at it. He consulted the brightest minds he could identify—professors, sociologists, anthropologists, psychologists—to synthesize an approach he felt would convince the U.S. Supreme Court that segregation was devastating to Black Americans and intolerable under the Constitution.[3]

In oral argument before the Supreme Court, with his opposing counsel the seventy-nine-year-old John W. Davis of South Carolina—who had reportedly argued more cases before the Court than anyone except the legendary Daniel Webster—Marshall emphasized the sociological evidence in the record showing that the humiliation of racial segregation hurt the development of Black children's personalities and destroyed their self-respect. Marshall told the Court, "That is not what our Constitution stands for."[4]

On May 17, 1954, in *Brown v. Board of Education*, a unanimous Supreme Court overturned *Plessy v. Ferguson*. Chief Justice Earl Warren announced, "In the field of public education the doctrine of 'separate but equal' has no place. Separate educational facilities are inherently unequal."

Marshall's joy over the decision was soon tempered. His wife, Buster, had been ill and mostly bedridden for some time, and Thurgood learned that she had cancer. He took care of her in the months before her death early in 1955. Deeply depressed, Marshall stopped working and went to Mexico for a time. Eventually he married Cecelia "Cissy" Suyat, who worked as a secretary at the NAACP; the couple then had two sons, Thurgood Marshall Jr. and John W. Marshall.[5]

Even on the evening in 1954 when he celebrated his win in *Brown v. Board of Education*, Marshall realized that the victory was partial: "I don't want any of you to fool yourselves, it's just begun; the fight has just begun," he said.[6] Obtaining the ruling that segregation in public education was unconstitutional was only the first step. The second was enforcing integration, especially in localities where segregation was deeply entrenched. The Supreme Court provided limited guidance in *Brown* II, 349 U.S. 294 (1955), ruling that integration proceed "with all deliberate speed." As school officials in many southern states dragged their feet, southern governors and legislatures vowed that segregation would continue.

In Little Rock, Arkansas, for example, a school board plan to start integration at just one school, Central High School, in September 1957, was thwarted when Governor Orval Faubus sent the National Guard to prevent

Black students from entering the school. Ordered by a federal judge to desist from using the National Guard to keep the students from attending school, Faubus obeyed, but unruly mobs of white segregationists encircled the school daily. As the situation became more violent, President Dwight D. Eisenhower sent federal troops to ensure that these rulings were respected.[7]

But when the Little Rock school board then went to court to request a two-year delay in desegregating the high school because more violence was threatened, the judge stunned Marshall by granting the request. Desegregation was put on hold while the case went through appeals to the U.S. Supreme Court, where Marshall argued that the Black students should be allowed to attend Central High without further delays. The Court ruled for the students in *Cooper v. Aaron*: "Law and order are not here to be preserved by depriving Negro children of their Constitutional rights.... The enunciation by this Court in the *Brown* case is the supreme law of the land."

During this time, Marshall worked on several cases in which state officials tried in various ways to stymie or delay racial integration and evade the law of the land, as well as cases in which state officials tried to shut down the NAACP's local operations. A partial list of Supreme Court cases Marshall argued or worked on includes *Lucy v. Adams*, 350 U.S. 1 (1955), holding that students could not be prevented from enrolling at the University of Alabama solely on account of their race or color; *Mayor & City Council of Baltimore et al. v. Dawson et al.*, 350 U.S. 877 (1955), upholding an order barring racial segregation at public beaches and bathhouses; *Holmes et al. v. Atlanta et al.*, 350 U.S. 879 (1955), reversing an order permitting Atlanta, Georgia, to allocate a city golf course to different races on different days; *Florida ex rel. Hawkins v. Board of Control of Florida*, 350 U.S. 413 (1956), ruling that the Supreme Court of Florida could not order a delay of the desegregation of the University of Florida's law school; *Gayle v. Browder*, 352 U.S. 903 (1956), upholding an order mandating the desegregation of the Montgomery, Alabama, bus system; *NAACP v. Alabama, ex rel. Patterson*, 360 U.S. 240 (1959), ruling that the state of Alabama could not require the NAACP to disclose its membership lists without a compelling justification; *Boynton v. Virginia*, 364 U.S. 454 (1960), overturning the conviction of a Black interstate bus passenger for refusing to leave a "whites only" restaurant in the bus terminal in Richmond, Virginia; and *Bush v. Orleans Parish School Board*, 364 U.S. 500 (1960), invalidating Louisiana legislation designed to prevent desegregation of New Orleans public schools.

Sweatt v. Painter, 339 U.S. 629 (1950)

With the NAACP Legal Defense and Educational Fund, Marshall took on case after case challenging Jim Crow: the "separate but equal" arrangements that consigned Black citizens to second-class accommodations. The plaintiff in this case, Heman Marion Sweatt, applied to the University of Texas Law School, whose president was defendant Theophilus Painter. The application was rejected under state law forbidding admission of Black students. Sweatt was offered a seat in a separate law school that the state had hastily established for Black students in a basement in downtown Austin, but he refused to attend that school.

The Texas state court that tried Sweatt's claims refused to compel the white law school to admit him, finding that the separate Black law school offered a substantially equal education. This ruling was upheld in state appeals, and Sweatt's appeal then came before the U.S. Supreme Court.

Included here are excerpts from Marshall's questioning of witnesses in the Texas trial court where the initial trial of the case occurred. One witness Marshall called was Donald G. Murray, whom Marshall and his mentor at Howard University, Charles Hamilton Houston, had represented in the 1936 state court lawsuit that enabled Murray to become the first Black student to attend the law school at the University of Maryland.

In Sweatt's case, Marshall developed a record in the Texas trial court showing that the separate Black law school did not offer an education substantially equal to what was offered white law students. This record was the foundation for the U.S. Supreme Court's landmark ruling that the equal protection clause of the Fourteenth Amendment required the previously all-white University of Texas Law School to admit Black students.

Years later, in 1992, Marshall reminisced:

> Do you remember Heman Sweatt? He was an ordinary man who had an extraordinary dream to live in a world in which Afro-Americans and Whites alike were afforded equal opportunity to sharpen their minds and to hone their skills. Unfortunately, officials at the University of Texas Law School did not share his vision. Constrained by the shackles of prejudice, and incapable of seeing people for who they were, they denied Heman Sweatt

admission to Law School solely because his color was not theirs. It was a devastating blow and a stinging rejection, a painful reminder of the chasm that separates White from Negro.

But Heman Sweatt held on to what racism tried to snuff out: a sense of self and a recognition of place; a determination to attain the best and a refusal to settle for anything less. Heman Sweatt knew what Whites and Segregationists tried to forget, that none of us Afro, White or Blue, will ever rest until we are truly free.[8]

Supreme Court of the United States
October Term, 1949
Heman Marion Sweatt, Petitioner, vs. Theophilus Shickel Painter, et al.
On Writ of Certiorari to the Supreme Court of the State of Texas

TRANSCRIPT OF RECORD, WITNESS EXAMINATION
Excerpts from witness examination in the District Court of Travis County, Texas, beginning May 12, 1947, with Thurgood Marshall appearing for relator Heman Sweatt and Price Daniel, Texas attorney general, representing the state of Texas.

Direct examination: Robert Redfield

Questions by MR. MARSHALL:
    Q. Give the Court your full name, sir.
    A. Robert Redfield.
    Q. And your present occupation?
    A. I am now Professor of Anthropology and Chairman of the Department of that name at the University of Chicago.
    Q. Will you review briefly your past qualifications, and your training, and the positions you have held, and the general work you have been doing?
    A. After taking a Bachelor's Degree, I went to the University of Chicago Law School and took a degree of J.D. I was admitted to the Bar of the State of Illinois, and two years thereafter returned to academic life, where I received training in Anthropology and Sociology, and special work in the problems

between the racial and color groups. I received a Doctor's Degree in 1928.

Except for periods when I have been giving instruction at other universities in the United States, I have been employed at the University of Chicago as a teacher, and doing research work, and as an educational administrator.

I have also been in charge of the research program for Carnegie Institute at Washington, and at the present I am in that capacity. Last October I gave up the position of Dean of Social Sciences at Chicago University, a position I held for 12 years.

Q. How long have you been studying in the field of racial differences?

A. About 20 years.

Q. And in that period of time have you considered the question of alleged racial differences in school students?

A. I have considered many aspects of the problem of differences between national groups, including school students.

Q. And have those studies included the comparison of students of both races, studying under the same circumstances?

A. I have followed the literature in that field, as well as, of course, making my common-sense observations as a teacher and administrator.

Q. Well, Dr. Redfield, as a result of your studies, are you in a position to give your opinions on the general subject? I will give you more specific ones later, but I wish on the general subject of, one; the inappropriateness of segregation to the purposes of education, the inappropriateness of segregation in education to the interests of public security end of it, and to the general welfare of the community.

MR. DANIEL [*Price Daniel, Texas attorney general*]: Your Honor, we object because this lawsuit involves only education in law and procedure. We object to any questions or opinion evidence that may be offered as to general surveys, not limited to law schools, which are composed of those who have completed certain preliminary work in other fields, and we object to the testimony that has been called for by this question, to the question, and to any other questions along that line.

MR. MARSHALL: May it please the Court, this case has narrowed down to one issue. I think the pleadings did considerable toward the end of narrowing it down. In the first place, in our original petition we claimed that the refusal to admit the relator [*i.e., Heman Sweatt*] was in violation of the 14th Amendment, and in all of the pleadings filed by the State of Texas, no question has ever been raised as to the qualifications of relator other than his race or color, so that is out of consideration.

The defense of respondents is summed up in their first supplemental answer...in this statement. I am quoting.

> "The Constitution and laws of the State of Texas require equal protection of law and equal educational opportunities for all qualified persons, but provide for separate educational institutions for white and Negro students."

And then follows the allegation that the refusal to admit the relator in this case was not arbitrary at all, and was not in violation of the 14th Amendment, but was in keeping with the segregation statutes of the State of Texas, and in that way joined issue; and in the second supplemental petition we alleged:

> "In so far as respondents claim to be acting under authority of the Constitution and laws of the State of Texas their continued refusal to admit the relator to the Law School of the University of Texas is nonetheless in direct violation of the 14th Amendment to the Constitution of the United States."

If there can be any doubt as to our position in the case, in the fourth paragraph in the same pleading in the supplemental petition, we state:

> "In so far as the Constitution and laws of Texas relied on by respondents prohibit relator from attending Law School of University of Texas because of his race and color such constitutional and statutory provisions of the State of Texas as apply to relator are in direct violation of the 14th Amendment to the Constitution of the United States."

So, I think that the lines are drawn in this case, and the direct attack has been made that the statutes requiring segregation, the general statutes which prohibit this relator from attending the University of Texas, we claim are unconstitutional, and we have the right to show their unconstitutionality.

How do we propose to do so? Several ways....

There are several ways of going about proving the unconstitutionality of statutes. They haven't shown any line of reasoning for the statutes. I imagine they are relying on the presumption that the statutes are constitutional. If they are relying on that we have a right to put in evidence to show that segregation statutes in the State of Texas and in any other state, actually when examined, and they have never been examined in any lawsuit that I know of yet, have no line of reasonableness. There is no understandable factual basis for classification by race, and under a long line of decisions by the Supreme Court, not on the question of Negroes, but on the 14th Amendment, all courts agree that if there is no rational basis for the classification, it is flat in the teeth of the 14th Amendment.

THE COURT: I will let you offer your testimony. . . .

MR. DANIEL: Do I understand they will be limited to surveys on law students, or education in general?

THE COURT: Of course, it is like throwing a rose into a group of flowers. The odor is there. We are presumed to act only upon what is admissible testimony, in the last analysis, anyhow, so I am going to hear it, and if in my opinion it is material and admissible testimony, I will consider it. If it isn't, I will not.

MR. MARSHALL: Thank you, sir.

THE COURT: It will be in the record.

———

By MR. MARSHALL:

Q. Dr. Redfield, as to the question of the relationship of segregation to the purposes of education, will you first give us what are the overall acceptable purposes of education as construed by educators in the field? What is the main purpose of public education?

A. No two men, of course, will state this the same way, but I should say that the main purposes of education are to develop in every citizen in accordance with the natural capacities of those citizens, the fullest intellectual and moral qualities, and his most effective participation in the duties of the citizens.

Q. Dr. Redfield, are there any recognizable differences as between Negro and white students on the question of their intellectual capacity?

MR. DANIEL: Your Honor, we object to that. That would be a conclusion on the part of the witness. It covers all Negro students and all white students. It isn't limited to any particular study or subject or even show what it is based on.

THE COURT: I suppose his qualifications he has testified to would qualify him to draw his conclusion.

MR. MARSHALL: We will follow with what he bases it on.

A. If Your Honor will allow me I will present the answer in that form.

The Court: Yes.

A. We got something of a lesson there. We who have been working in the field in which we began with a rather general presumption among our common educators that inherent differences in intellectual ability or capacity to learn existed between Negroes and whites, and have slowly, but I think very convincingly, been compelled to come to the opposite conclusion, in the course of long history, special research in the field.

The general sort of situation, Your Honor, which brings about this opposite conclusion, the conclusion that I may state now, significant differences as to intellectual ability, or as to ability to learn, if any, are probably not present between the two groups. We have been brought to that conclusion, Your Honor, by a series of studies which have this general character.

Samples from the two groups, Negroes and whites, are placed in as nearly identical situations as possible, and given the limited tasks to perform, tasks which are understood to be relevant to the intellectual faculties, or the capacity to learn. Then these samples are measured against each other as to the degree and kind of success in performing these limited tasks. That is a general description of the material which leads to the conclusion I have stated. Perhaps at this point it is sufficient to say that the general conclusion to which I come, and which I think is shared by a very large majority of specialists—

MR. DANIEL: We object to that as hearsay, Your Honor.

THE COURT: I think so.

A. The conclusion, then, to which I come, is differences in intellectual capacity or in ability to learn have not been shown to exist as between Negroes and whites, and further, that the results make it very probable that if such differences are later shown to exist, they will not prove to be significant for any educational policy or practice.

By MR. MARSHALL:

Q. As a result of your studies that you have made, the training that you have had in your specialized field over some 20 years, given a similar learning situation, what, if any differences, are there between the accomplishment of a white and a Negro student, given a similar learning situation?

A. I understand, if I may say so, a similar learning situation to include a similar degree of preparation?

Q. Yes.

A. Then, I would say that my conclusion is that the one does as well as the other on the average.

Q. Well, in your experience, your studies in this particular field, what is your opinion as to the effect of segregated education; one, on the student—I will give them all to you, and then you can take them separately—two, on the school, and three, on the community in general. Will you give your opinion?

A. My opinion is that segregation has effects on the student which are unfavorable to the full realization of the objectives of education. First—for a number of reasons, perhaps. I will try to distinguish.

Speaking first with regard to the student I would say that in the first place it prevents the student from the full, effective and economical coming to understand the nature and capacity of the group from which he is segregated. My comment, therefore, applies to both whites and Negroes, and as one of the objectives of education is the full and sympathetic understanding of the principal groups in the system in which the individual is to function as a citizen, this result which I have just stated is unfortunate.

In the second place, I would say that the segregation has an unfortunate effect on the student, which I might now anticipate, since, to my opinion, it has an unfortunate effect on the general community, in that it intensifies suspicion and distrust between Negroes and the whites, and suspicion and distrust are not favorable conditions either for the acquisition and conduct of an education, or for the discharge of the duties of a citizen. You asked me, did you not, as to the class, and the community?

Q. The school was the second, and the community was the third.

A. I think I have perhaps indicated the difficulties with reference to the school. The schoolroom situation provides less than the complete and natural representation of the full community. That is the general view of educators, or it is my view, I should say. It is my view that education goes forward more favorably if the community of student, scholar and teacher is fairly representative of the total community. Rather, the highly specialized and the development of the suspicion and distrust which the segregated situation brings about is correspondingly unfavorable in the school.

With respect to the general community, I suppose there isn't a great deal to add, but if I am still answering your question, I might say this. In my opinion, segregation acts generally on the total community in an unfavorable way for the general welfare, in that it accentuates imagined differences between Negroes and whites. These false assumptions with respect to the existence of those differences are given an appearance of reality by the formal act of physical separation. Furthermore, as the segregation, in my experience, is against the will of the segregated, it produces a very favorable situation for the increase of bad feeling, and even conflict, rather than the reverse.

Q. Dr. Redfield, what has been your personal experience concerning the admission of minority groups to educational facilities to which they had previously been denied admission?

A. Well, as I have indicated, my principal experience has been…in the University of Chicago, and in its related educational institutions. The situation there generally is that no segregation is practiced in any of the educational facilities of the University, neither in the classroom nor in the dormitory, or in eating facilities or anywhere else in the educational facilities—while the same city or community in which the University lies is one in which segregation or exclusion is practiced as a matter of custom, but not as a matter of law, in a very wide variety of situations, and facilities open to the general public.

In giving that background, I come to the question of what my experience has been with Negroes theretofore denied some educational facilities, and I have had experience with one or two such situations in the University of Chicago and its affiliated institutions, and that in each of the cases that I can recall the result has been, in my opinion, highly beneficial to education and to the University community.

Q. Were there any ill effects at all?

A. I don't know of any.

Q. Do you know of any good effects?

A. Yes. Perhaps I should mention a case. The students were denied admission, Negro students were discouraged from admittance is perhaps a more accurate statement, to the laboratory school of the University.

They were discouraged admission for a great many years. Then it was made apparent that they would be welcome, and they began to come, and there was an opposition from a minority of the academic community to the step. Many evil consequences were told. None of those consequences took place, but, on the other hand, there was an improvement in the community in that there was a representation of the national community which is favorable to education, and the relations between the white and the Negro groups were improved in parent-teacher and endeavor.

Q. Thank you, Doctor.

—

Redirect examination

Questions by MR. MARSHALL:

Q. Dr. Redfield, you testified on cross examination that your opinions were based on your own studies, but mostly on other studies that have been made. I want to ask you as to whether or not the studies you are speaking of made by other people were scientific studies or not?

A. They were.

Q. And I want to ask you as to whether or not they were mostly published scientific studies?

A. They were.

Q. Generally recognized in your field as authorities?

A. Yes, they were.

Q. Do you know of any recognized scientific study that recognizes any inherent racial difference among the races, as to capacity to learn?

A. A man named Portees in Australia published some papers which I have read, on the Australian aborigines, which reach the conclusion that there are inherent differences between the races. I am sure there are other papers that reach a similar conclusion. They are all specific studies, and the conclusions are drawn on differences in achievement in the races, and the case of Portees is one. John Ferguson is publishing one, but there are very, very few that would draw the opposite conclusion to the one that I have stated concerning the inherent difference.... The important thing is there are different studies, and it has taken them a long period of time to reach the conclusion I have offered.

Q. Isn't it true the majority of scientists in your field are in agreement there is no inherent racial difference?

A. Yes.

Q. Isn't it true that such studies as the Kleinberg study in 1935, and others, are specific factual studies which show that a given fact situation, there is no difference?

MR. DANIEL: We object to that because it is leading.

THE COURT: Of course, it is leading.

MR. MARSHALL: Your witness.

—

Direct examination: Charles H. Thompson

Questions by MR. MARSHALL:

Q. Will you give your full name?

A. Charles H. Thompson.

—

Q. Your present position?

A. I am Dean of the Graduate School of Howard University.

Q. That is in Washington, D.C.?

A. Yes.

Q. First of all, where were you born?

A. I was born in Jackson, Mississippi.

Q. Will you trace your educational qualifications?

A. Yes. I attended an elementary school, private Baptist school in Kosciusko, Mississippi, and graduated from what I thought was a high school; and I attended Wayland Academy, of Virginia Union University, in Richmond, Virginia, starting in 1911, and finishing the academy there in 1914, and subsequently attended college until 1917, and went to Chicago, and spent a year there and got the degree of Bachelor of Philosophy in June, 1918, and then I went overseas in World War I and spent eleven months in France, returned and went back to the University of Chicago, where I took my Master's Degree in 1920.

In 1920–21 I taught at the Virginia Union University in Richmond, Virginia. At the end of that year I went back to the University of Chicago to work toward a doctorate in psychology. In 1922 I went to the State Normal School in Montgomery, Alabama, and spent two years as instructor in teacher training in that institution.

In 1924 I went back to the University of Chicago and completed the training for the doctorate, and received my Doctor's Degree in 1925. On completion of my doctorate at the University of Chicago I went to the Sumner High School in Kansas City, Kansas, and taught psychology and economics in the Junior College for one year.

Q. Dr. Thompson, on your master's, what was your particular study in your thesis?

A. I made a study of comparative learning abilities of Negro children in the City of Chicago.

Q. Getting back to the positions you have held since you obtained your doctorate, after leaving Sumner High School in Kansas City, where did you go?

A. To Howard University, as Associate Professor in Education, in 1926. In 1929–1930, I was made Professor of Education. In 1931 and 1932, I was Acting Dean of Education at Howard University.

In 1932 I was made Director of the Bureau of Educational Research and editor of the *Journal on Negro Education*, and in 1938 I was made Dean of the College of Liberal Arts, which position I held until 1943. Beginning January 1, 1944, I have since been Dean of the Graduate School of Howard University.

Q. Up to the present time?

A. Yes.

Q. Explain to the Court what is the *Journal on Negro Education*.

A. The *Journal on Negro Education* is a scholarly magazine in the field of education, which deals primarily with the education of minority groups, and particularly, the Negro group.

Q. And how wide is the circulation of that?

A. It has average circulation of a scholarly journal.

Q. Is it a magazine of general circulation, or a magazine usually circulated among people in the educational field?

A. Primarily the latter.

Q. What then is the Bureau of Educational Research that you are Director of?

A. The Bureau of Educational Research is an organization which was set up to make investigations of various types of educational problems, primarily problems dealing with minority groups, particularly Negroes in America.

Q. Have you published any scientific articles?

A. Yes.

Q. In what publications, as far as you can remember?

A. A number of publications. The *Annals of the American Academy on Political and Social Science*, *Educational Administration and Supervision* and several others that I do not recall at the present time, *School and Society*.

Q. Dr. Thompson, have you done any scientific work, research on the question of the comparative educational facilities for white and Negro students in segregated school systems?

A. Yes, I have.

Q. About how long have you been working on that?

A. Oh, as I indicated a moment ago, I became interested in the problem when I was working for my Master's Degree at the University of Chicago. In 1928, I believe I published the first results of an investigation that I made on the educational achievements of Negro children in separate schools. That was published in the annals to which I referred, in 1928, and since then I have published a lot of things, a list of which I do not have at the present time.

Q. Dr. Thompson, are you familiar with other recognized scientific studies in the field of the comparison of education of Negro and white students in separate schools?

A. I am.

Q. Have you worked at all with the United States Department of Education in recent years?

A. On several occasions.

Q. Can you briefly give those occasions, and what type of work it was?

A. The first contact with the Bureau was around 1931 or 1932. That wasn't on one of these comparative studies. It happened to be a study of the products of graduate schools of the country. The second contact was a commission called the Wartime Educational Commission. The most recent contact I have had was as advisory member of the National Survey on Higher Education of Negroes, published in 1942.

Q. Was that published by the United States Government Printing Office?

A. Yes, it was.

Q. As an official document?

A. It was.

Q. By the way, while discussing the Government, do you at the present time hold a position on any official commission of the Federal Government?

A. I don't know whether you would call it United States Educational— United Nations Scientific Educational Organization. I am on the National Committee for the United Nations Scientific and Cultural Organization, which is under the sponsorship of the State Department.

Q. That represents the United States Government?

A. Yes.

Q. In the United Nations organization on education?

A. Yes, commonly known as UNESCO.

Q. Are there any people from Texas serving on that Commission with you?

A. I think Professor Dobie, at the University of Texas, and Dr. Evans, of the Library of Congress, is on that Commission.

Q. Do you have any official connection—what is the National Educational Association?

A. That is an association of teachers in the United States, public and private.

Q. And do you hold any official position in that organization?

A. I am the consultant to the Educational Policies Commission of the UEA.

Q. What is the Educational Policies Committee?

A. That is very much as its name suggests, to study and make recommendations concerning educational policies for development of education in the United States.

Q. Do you know of the Association of American Colleges?

A. Yes.

Q. What is that?

A. That is an association of some five or six hundred liberal arts colleges in the United States which have come together in an association for their mutual benefit.

Q. Do you hold any official position in that organization?

A. Yes, I happen to be a member of the Committee on Teacher Education of that organization.

Q. Do you know anything about *The Nation's Schools*, a magazine, and if so, what is it?

A. *The Nation's Schools* is a magazine in the field of education that deals largely with administrative and supervisory problems, broad policy problems.

Q. Do you hold any position in that organization?

A. I happen to be consulting editor of that magazine.

Q. Do you hold any position with the *World Book Encyclopedia*?

A. Yes. I have forgotten my exact title. I suppose it is consulting editor. What I do is edit all of the material concerning Negroes which goes into that encyclopedia.

Q. What is the Southern Association of Colleges and Secondary Schools?

A. The Southern Association of Colleges and Secondary Schools is an organization composed of a number of white secondary schools and colleges in the southern area. It is an accrediting agency for this region, and I presume there are other things that go on in it that I don't know of.

Q. Does that Association accredit white schools in the Austin area?

A. It does.

Q. Colleges and secondary schools?

A. Yes.

Q. Does it also accredit Negro separate schools in the same area?

A. Yes.

Q. Do you hold any official position in connection with the accreditation of these schools?

A. During the past year and a half I have been an inspector of Negro colleges for the Southern Association Committee which accredits Negro schools.

Q. What were your duties in that position?

A. My duties were to go around with a committee, generally of three, to inspect designated institutions, and to make a report as to whether or not they were living up to standards, in the case of schools already in, and in the case of schools that were trying to get in, to find out whether they met the standards.

Q. How many such schools have you inspected in the last year and a half?

A. Six or seven.

Q. Six or seven?

A. Yes.

Q. Were you requested by the relator in this case to make certain studies concerning higher education for Negroes in Texas?

A. I was.

—

Q. As a result of that request what did you do?

—

A. The first thing I did on the study was to exhaust all of the sources that were available to me in the Bureau of Educational Research at Howard University. That was number one. Number two, I exhausted all of the resources in the United States Office of Education, particularly the Statistical Division. By exhaust, I got all of the material and made a study of it, as far as possible, up until about May first, when I got on the train to come to Texas. I have been here since, the last 10 or 12 days; in fact, I got in Austin Tuesday a week ago. I have been attempting since being in Austin to exhaust all possible sources of information relative to the education in Texas.

Q. Where did you go for this information? What I am driving at, what type of information did you examine?

A. First, I went to the Department of Education.

Q. Is that the State Department of Education of Texas?

A. That is the State Department of Education of Texas, to the office of the Executive Secretary of Scholarship Commission. I have forgotten the gentleman's name, but his secretary was there, and she gave me the information which I desired.

Then I went over to the Capitol Building... to the State Superintendent's Office, with the intention of talking to the State Superintendent but he was busy and I found I could get the information I wanted from the statistical department in the Superintendent's Office,... and I went to the Division of Higher Education to see if I could get catalogues or audit reports of State supported institutions in Texas, and found I couldn't get them from that office, but I was directed to the State Auditor's Office, where I went and got all of the available latest reports for all of the higher institutions, State supported, in the State of Texas.

Then I went out to the University of Texas for two reasons. First, to get some information, and, second, to see it and to look over the general plan. I went to the Registrar's Office to get some catalogues, which I did, on various schools. I didn't get all of them that I need, but sufficient. Then I went over the grounds of the University of Texas. I started on foot, and it was very hot, and I got a taxicab and drove all around the place to get an idea of what it looked like. Then I began work on the material. While I am talking about where I went—

Q. Didn't you also go some place else in Texas?

A. The next place I went was to Prairie View State College [*the only state college open to Black Texans at the time*], where I spent five or six hours going through that plant, talking with the principal and teachers, looking at the equipment in the various buildings and that sort of thing. I spent a very profitable five or six hours at Prairie View. I hadn't been to Prairie View before, and I was very anxious to get all I could from that institution.

Q. Dr. Thompson, in these studies that you made of the information that you did not have in your own mind, but that you obtained from other documents and records, will you give the Court as many of those documents and records as you can remember, as to whether or not they were official or private documents? [*Dr. Thompson recites an extensive list of documents, omitted here, including State Auditor's reports for 1945 and 1946, catalogues of all Texas-supported institutions of higher learning, and surveys and statistics compiled by the U. S. Office of Education from 1937 through 1946.*]

Q....Now, Dr. Thompson, as a result of your experience over twenty-some years in the field of comparing the education in segregated school systems, and as a result of the materials that you have gone into and examined, are you prepared to testify as to the comparative value of the public education in college, graduate and professional levels, in the State of Texas, with statements as to the official documents from which you obtained information that you do not have in your own mind?

A. I do—I am.

Q. As a result of your past experience, your research among recognized scientific sources of information, and your personal observation and examination of official documents and records while in Texas, have you made a comparison of the provisions for and the quality and quantity of education offered at Prairie View for Negroes with that offered at the University of Texas and other schools offering college, graduate and professional training for white students in the State of Texas?

A. I have.

Q. First of all, will you name the State supported institutions of Texas above the high school level to which Negroes are admitted?

MR. DANIEL: Your Honor, I would like to interpose our objection to that question. It seems to be the phase where he is about, after having qualified, to testify as to the schools for the purpose of making a comparison in the field of higher education. I would like to make the objection to that question and to the testimony along that line concerning higher education that has been furnished in Texas in the past in other schools other than the two schools that we now have for consideration in this case. The relator's petition asserts an individual right, as held by the Supreme Court in the *Gaines* case, the right that he has to enter the State supported white school, is an individual right which he has, unless the State furnishes a separate school with substantially equal facilities for the training he desires.

In his petition here, he makes no allegations whatever that would put us on notice that he intends to put into this case evidence as to all of the other schools, schools he doesn't seek to enter. Whatever the comparative value or the comparative value may have been in the past as to those schools, has no bearing whatever as to his individual right to a legal education, what he is seeking by this suit, and we say that certainly that line of testimony is not admissible. It is irrelevant and immaterial in this case. We will not object to any part of that testimony bearing on the schools that we have directly involved in this case, but as to the other schools, and what has gone on in the past, and not concerned with what we have at the present, we feel is irrelevant and immaterial in this case. It is today, and what we have for the relator today that answers what he has alleged that he is entitled to as an individual right in this case.

THE COURT: Unless it has a final bearing on this case it would not be considered.

MR. MARSHALL: But I can proceed, sir?

THE COURT: Yes.

By MR. MARSHALL:

Q. Will you name the State supported institutions of Texas above the high school level to which Negroes are admitted?

A. Prairie View University.

Q. Would you say—do you know of any others?

A. I don't know of any other school, no.

Q. Any other public supported school?

A. No.

Q. Will you name the State supported institutions maintained by the State of Texas above the high school level to which white students are admitted?

A. I take it that you mean the four year institutions, rather than—

Q. I do mean four year institutions.

A. Well, there is the University of Texas, and all of its branches; the Texas A. & M., and its several branches, including the Agricultural School at Tarleton, and Prairie View, by the way, is a branch of A. & M., and Texas State College for Women at Denton; Texas Technological College at Lubbock; the Texas College of Arts and Industries, and then there are seven teachers colleges.

Q. There are seven teachers colleges?

A. There are seven teachers colleges, North State Teachers College, and East State Teachers College, West, Southwest Teachers College, the Sul Ross State Teachers College, and Sam Houston State Teachers College.

Q. Making a total of how many?

A. That ought to be twelve, the way I named them.

——

Q. What are the—and I am speaking now, I am asking you to answer this from your experience in this particular field, and among your associates in that field and the studies that have been made in that field—what are the recognized criteria for comparing education offered in different schools?

A. Well, the adequacy of, at least, the following things which I shall mention: Number one, physical facilities, plant assets, and the general total assets of an institution. The physical facilities, such as buildings, equipment, et cetera. The total assets of the institution would include not only that, but endowments and other items involved. Number two, the amount of current educational funds at the disposal of the institution. Three, the curriculum, courses of study offered, or the course, as the case may be. Four, the faculty. Five, the library. Those are the five generally recognized criteria. I might add, the standing of the educational institution in the educational world and in the community. I don't know whether accreditation would cover it or not, but we will say those five or six.

Q. Now then, in appreciating and comparing one school with another, or one school with a group of schools, do you use any one of these as the most important, or any group of them as the more important, or how are they considered in relative value, the six items you have mentioned?

A. I don't know how you would make any relative value. They are so interdependent it would be difficult to divorce one from the other. You can't have a curriculum without a building and equipment.... You can't have one of these without the other. They are interdependent.

Q. The first of the criteria mentioned was physical plant. Will you compare the physical plant at Prairie View with that of the University of Texas and other colleges and universities, public supported, that you mentioned above, which are offered to white students?

MR. DANIEL: We wish to renew the objection directly to that question. That has no bearing on any issue in this case.

THE COURT: I am going to hear it. I am unable yet to relate it to this.

——

A. I have made a study of the plant assets, and the total institutional assets of the eleven institutions that I have mentioned, with the exception of the Texas Technological College. I have used as sources for my information the audit reports of the State Auditor of these institutions, S. B. 140, and the U.S. education bulletins to which I have just referred. Now, in 1945–46 these institutions, with the exception of Texas Technological College, had plant assets worth approximately $72,000,000.00. Probably before I go into that, Your Honor, I might state the basis upon which I am determining adequacy and the general criteria of measurement, if you please.

THE COURT: All right.

A. Beginning with the second Morrill Act—

Q. What is the second Morrill Act?

A. That is the land grant college act in 1867.

Q. Of the United States Congress?

A. Of the United States Congress. There were four Negro schools under the act of 1862 which received some money, some of the land grant money. Then in 1890, when the second Morrill Act was passed, it made provision for all of the Negro schools to receive—all of the Negro land grant schools—to receive a portion of the money, the act reading something like this; that a just and equitable distribution shall be made. That phrase has been in the subsequent amendments, the Nelson amendment in 1922, and Section 2 of the Bankhead-Jones Amendment of 1925. In making out the just and equitable distribution, the administrators of that fund have set up a formula as follows, or substantially as follows: That where you have separate schools and there is to be a division of these funds, that the Negro school or the school separated, or the schools separated, because in some states they have separate schools for several races, they would receive an amount at least, or a proportion, at least equal to the proportion which they are of the total population.

Q. Is that formula used by the U.S. Department of Education?

A. That is in the case of the distribution of those funds.

Q. As to the U.S. Department of Education and other studies that have been made, and all of the comparisons that you have studied during your years of experience, isn't that the formula that is generally used by the people in your field?

A. Among the majority, I think. I don't know all of them, but I think the majority accept that.

Q. Is that a formula in comparing Negro and white schools where they are separate?

A. Where money is involved.

Q. Where money is involved. Get back to the plants.

A. To explain further the formula, in the State of Texas there are roughly five and a half million white people, and, roughly, one million Negroes. Just for purposes of illustration, suppose that $11,000,000.00 were appropriated to the white schools, that would mean two dollars for each white person in the population. Therefore, I would say it was two dollars per capita total population for the whites. If in the Negro schools one million dollars were appropriated, and there were one million Negroes, that would be one dollar per capita. That is one way I will use the formula in giving the statistics. The other way is this; the Negroes in the State of Texas constitute 14.4% of the population. Let's assume that ten million dollars were appropriated for the higher institutions in the State of Texas, Negro and white.

On the basis of this formula, it would be expected that the Negroes would receive at least $1,440,000.00, being 14% of ten million dollars. I shall use from time to time that formula in those two ways, if I may.

Q. I want to get back to the plant. I think you testified there were some $72,000,000.00 worth of assets?

A. Yes; I had better be exact about that.

Q. First, let's have that, will you? While the Attorney General is looking at them I want to ask you a few questions.

MR. DANIEL: Those are just his notes?

MR. MARSHALL: Yes.

MR. DANIEL: You are not going to introduce them?

MR. MARSHALL: No.

MR. DANIEL: He can read them better than I can.

THE COURT: He can use them to refer to.

By MR. MARSHALL:

Q. Using that group of papers you have in your hand to refresh your recollection, and to testify to, to go back to the comparison of the physical plant at Prairie View with these other schools—

A. All right. Now the plant assets of all of the institutions studied, the four year institutions, minus the Texas Technological Institute, the plant assets of all of those institutions in 1945–1946 amounted to a total of $72,790,097.00.

Q. What was it at Prairie View, according to the same report?

A. Prairie View's plant assets were stated as being $2,170,910.00. Now, recently S. B. 140 has appropriated $2,000,000.00 for plant, so adding that to the Prairie View item, you would get a total appropriation for, or total plant assets for Negro education or higher education as being $4,170,910.00.

Q. May I ask one question there, Dr. Thompson? In arriving at any figure on the physical plant and the assets, is it not proper to include money that has been appropriated and available, even though it hasn't been spent yet?

A. Yes, that is the reason I call it plant assets, rather than physical plant. Under that formula, of $72,790,097.00, which represents the plant assets of the total institutions, if the formula had operated, that is to say, if Negro institutions had gotten 14.4% it would have totaled $10,481,773.00. Instead, however, they got a little over four million dollars. In other words, they got six million— or they didn't get six million, three hundred and ten thousand, seven hundred and sixty-three dollars which they would have gotten under the formula.

Now, to put it another way, and probably a little clearer, on a total per capita population basis, there were invested in plant assets of white institutions $12.88 for every white person in the State of Texas. There were invested in the Prairie View—in the plants of Negro institutions—$4.71 for every Negro in the population in Texas.

———

By MR. MARSHALL:

Q. Dr. Thompson, from your experience over a period of years of comparing the educational facilities available to white and Negro students in segregated public school systems, and the recognized treatises you have read on that subject, and I mean scientific treatises, as a result of your work in inspecting colleges and the knowledge you have obtained therefrom, what is your opinion as to the equality of educational facilities offered by the State of Texas to its white and Negro students, limiting your opinion to college, graduate and professional training?

MR. DANIEL: We object to that, Your Honor. It has no bearing in this case. His question should be limited to the schools involved in this case, if it is to have any material bearing at all on the case.

THE COURT: I believe I will hear it.

MR. DANIEL: Note our exception.

—

A. The answer is that Negroes are seriously disadvantaged both from the point of opportunities and relative accomplishment. In the first place—

MR. DANIEL: Now—

THE COURT: That answers it.

MR. MARSHALL: That answers it.

Q. Now, is that based—I want to ask whether or not your answer includes the studies you have made in Texas or not, that you have testified about?

A. Yes.

Q. It does include that?

A. Yes.

Q. Now, will you explain to the Court your reasons for your opinion which you have just given?

A. Well, I have three reasons. In the first place, twice as many white students are provided opportunity in the public higher institutions in Texas as Negroes, and I would like to quote, if it is permissible, from a study, "11 Senior Colleges for Negroes in Texas," which was made at the direction of the Biracial Conference on Education for Negroes in Texas, Professor T. S. Montgomery, of the Sam Houston Teachers College, Chairman of the Committee for Study, Dean B. F. Pittenger of the School of Education of the University of Texas, Chairman of the Steering Committee. The study was made and printed about—at least printed, in 1944, presumably made between 1942 and 1944.

—

A. Now, this report states the following, and I quote:

—

"Texas provided through State-supported senior institutions of higher education for 66.8% of white students enrolled in senior colleges, but for only 31.8% of her Negro students in senior colleges. The ratio of the percentage that the Negro students in the State college are of all Negro college students to the percentage that the white students in State-supported senior colleges are of all white senior college students, is 1 to 2.1. In other words, the State is bearing twice the burden of providing opportunity for higher education for whites than [the State] is providing such opportunities for Negroes.

A disproportionate burden is placed on private effort in providing opportunity for higher education for Negroes."

On page 25:

"The ratio of the number of white students to Negro students in State-supported colleges per thousand of youth of each race, age 15 to 20 is 5 to 1. On this basis the State is providing five times as much opportunity for higher education in State-supported colleges for white youth as it is for its Negro youth."

MR. DANIEL: Give us the date of that report.

A. It is dated April, 1944. Now, in the second place, I said that the differences in financial support resulted in differences in educational accomplishment. In the last census, which was the sixteenth census, in 1940, for the first time the U.S. Bureau of Census attempted to find out the educational level of the population; so that they obtained from all persons 25 years old and over certain information concerning how much education you have had, how many years, et cetera. It was found in the State of Texas that 218,225 persons, or 8% of the population 25 years old and older, have from one to three years of college. That is white. In the case of Negroes 11,704, or 2.5%. Over three times, to be exact, 3.2 times as many whites had one to three years of college as Negroes.

Those who had had four years or more of college among whites constituted 5%. Among the Negroes, 1.2%....

MR. DANIEL: I would like to know where you are getting those figures.

A. The U.S. Census Report for the State of Texas.

MR. DANIEL: Do you have them for the northern states also in that book?

A. That is Texas.

MR. DANIEL: That is all right. I will ask you about it later.

A. I said a moment ago that the Negro was disadvantaged in this respect, particularly from the point of view of college because, as we all know, an individual has to have two or three years of college before he can get in a law school or medical school or dental school, to say nothing about other areas in which college training is necessary. Now, in the third place, a similar situation exists on the professional level.

Take the matter of doctors. In Texas there were 6,076 white doctors, 164 Negro doctors. In other words, there were of the white doctors 1 to every 903 of the white population in Texas, and one Negro doctor to every 5,637 of the Negro population.

Thus, on the basis of population, there are more than six times, in fact, 6.24 times as many doctors in proportion to the white population as there are Negro doctors in proportion to the Negro population. For the sake of comparison, in Tennessee, where the Meharry Medical School is located, to which Negroes are admitted, there are almost three times, in fact, to be exact, 2.8 times as many Negro doctors in Tennessee as there are in Texas, where Negroes have no medical school to which they can be admitted.

Take the matter of dentists—

By MR. MARSHALL:

Q. First, one question there. State whether Meharry Medical College is a fully accredited medical college or not.

A. It is.

Q. Go right ahead.

A. Take the matter of dentists. The number of male dentists in the State of Texas, white, are 1,901; Negro, 81. The ratio of white dentists to white population is 1 dentist to every 2,886 of the white population, one Negro dentist to every 11,412 of the Negro population. There are almost four times, to be exact, 3.9 times as many white dentists in proportion to the white population as there are Negro dentists in proportion to the Negro population. Again, taking Tennessee for comparison, in Tennessee where the Meharry Dental College is located to which Negroes are admitted, there are twice as many Negro dentists as there are Negro dentists in Texas, where Negroes have no dental school to which they can go.

In the District of Columbia, where the Howard University Dental School is, there are almost four times as many Negro dentists in proportion to the Negro population as there are Negro dentists in proportion to the Negro population in Texas.

Q. What about engineers, Dr. Thompson?

A. In the case of engineers in Texas, there are 8,961 white engineers in Texas. In the case of Negroes, there are 6 Negro engineers in Texas. The ratio of white engineers to the white population is one to every 612 of the white population. The ratio of Negro engineers and Negro population is one Negro engineer to every 154,065 Negroes. In other words, there are over 250 times as many white engineers in the State of Texas in proportion to the white population as there are Negro engineers in proportion to the Negro population.

Now, finally, take the matter of lawyers. In Texas, and all of these figures are from the 1940 Census.

Q. That is the latest census?

A. That is right. In Texas there were 7,701 white lawyers. There were 23 Negro lawyers. The ratio of white lawyers to the white population was one white lawyer to every 712 of the white population, one Negro lawyer to every 40,191 of the Negro population. In other words, there were 56 times as many white lawyers in proportion to the white population as there were Negro lawyers in proportion to the Negro population.

Q. Dr. Thompson, getting to the next point of comparison between Prairie View and the other schools, will you compare the curriculum at Prairie View, first, with the curriculum at other schools?

A. May I make this introductory statement about the curriculum? The curriculum and faculty and library are the very heart of an institution. However, you must have sufficient financial resources in order to have an adequate curriculum or adequate library or adequate faculty.

Q. When you say you have to have sufficient funds to have an adequate faculty, are you or not speaking from your experience in getting a faculty for the graduate school at Howard?

A. I am.

Q. You have been in that field for quite a while, and know quite a bit about that?

A. About 15 or 20 years.

Q. Let's compare the curriculum.

A. First, let's take the undergraduate curriculum.

Q. What is this testimony based on?

A. This is based on the National Survey of Higher Education for Negroes, which was a U.S. [Government Printing] Office publication, and also upon the catalogue study of Texas A. & M., University of Texas, and Prairie View.

Q. Go right ahead.

A. The National Survey of Higher Education for Negroes, to which I have just referred, in the making of this survey, found out in Texas that there were

106 undergraduate fields of specialization in the white State supported institutions, and 49 in the Negro institution, Prairie View. In other words, there were about twice as many fields of undergraduate specialization in the white institutions as in Prairie View.

Now, I have made an analysis, or used the sources, the Texas A. & M. Catalogue and the University of Texas Catalogue; the Texas A. & M. Catalogue states, and that is for 1946–1947, page 10, general information; there are 45 departments of undergraduate specialization.

Prairie View University has 13 departments of specialization. In other words, A. & M. has more than three times as many. In the case of engineers, engineering is offered in four white technical schools with eight different curricula leading to engineering degrees. No such curricula was offered at Prairie View, except that you might call mechanical arts education, or industrial education, engineering.

There are, however, a number of sub-collegiate, or high school trade courses given at Prairie View, such as broom making and mattress making; auto mechanics, carpentering, laundering and dry cleaning, plumbing, shoe repairing, tailoring and the like.

Q. Dr. Thompson, in your experience in the field of education, do you know of any other university in the country that will give credit toward a degree in liberal arts college for broom making and mattress making? I am talking about universities, not colleges or institutes. Do you know of any recognized, accredited university?

A. No, I don't know of any. I am trying to think. There are several institutions which give similar courses. I don't know of any other institution that gives broom making and mattress making.

Q. Isn't it true that those are the subjects that are usually taught in the high schools or lower vocational schools?

A. That is correct.

Q. For example, do they teach any of the subjects you have mentioned at Howard?

A. No.

Q. Do they teach—did you find in the catalogue of either A. & M. or the University of Texas, or any other of the schools you have talked about broom making and mattress making?

A. No, I did not.

Q. Auto mechanics or carpentering, or any of those?

A. No.

Q. You can go ahead, if you will, Dr. Thompson, to the graduate level of curricula.

A. Yes. I might mention in connection with the undergraduate field, if I may, because it connects up with the graduate field—

Q. Go right ahead.

A. The chemistry department, the chemistry department, which is a very important department in a land grant institution; the chemistry department at Prairie View is not accredited by the American Chemical Society. I did find they were approved at Texas A. & M. and the University of Texas.

Q. What effect does that have on a student who wants to do graduate work?

A. It means if he wants to do it in chemistry he has to be conditioned a year or a half year; for example, a student coming to us without physical chemistry, which is a thing not given in one of these departments, would have to take a year of that before he could begin his graduate school in chemistry.

Q. You are speaking of Howard Graduate School?

A. Yes, sir.

Q. Is that true in all of the other schools that you know of?

A. I should imagine so. I know it is true in some. I don't know about all of them. The graduate school is of recent origin. It began about the date of the *Gaines* decision, which was around 1938. In the fall of 1946 nine state Negro colleges in eight southern states gave graduate work in at least one field.

In Texas, Prairie View and the Houston College were the Negro institutions giving graduate work. They had a combined enrollment at Prairie View for the regular term and summer of 1946 of 229; Houston College, 308, making a total of 537 students. Graduate work is given in all of the white four year State high institutions in Texas.

The regular term enrollment in white State graduate schools in 1945 was 2,358. Thirteen white State institutions gave 2,846 Master's Degrees and 212 doctorates during the period 1940 to 1945. That is from the Director of Colleges, universities offering graduate work relating to Master and Doctor Degrees, 1940 to 1945, U.S. Office of Education.

Prairie View gave during this same period 103 Master's Degrees and 55 Negro students got Master's Degrees on the out of state scholarship fund, and six doctorates on the out of state scholarship fund between 1939 and 1943, making a total of 159 Negroes who got graduate degrees during approximately a five year period, as contrasted with some 3,000 white students who got graduate degrees in the same period. Now, in general, the range of offerings in white graduate schools, whether in Texas or in other southern states, is wider than in the Negro graduate school. The National Survey of Higher Education for Negroes, to which I have referred, a U.S. [Government Printing] Office publication, indicated in 1942 that the Texas state supported higher institutions for whites offered graduate work in 65 fields, and 5 for Negroes.

At the present time Prairie View offers graduate work in 13 fields, and the Texas A. & M. 45 fields. The University of Texas gives 10 different types of graduate degrees in 40 fields. Prairie View gives a Master's Degree in 13 fields. . . .

The University of Texas and A. & M. College of Texas, between the period of 1940 and 1945 gave 212 doctorates. Now, if a Negro wishes to obtain a Doctor's Degree in the State of Texas, the only recourse he has in so doing is through what is admittedly an inadequate scholarship fund.

—

A. All right. Now, in order for a Negro to be eligible for an out of state scholarship to do graduate or professional work, he must be a resident of Texas; he must have resided in the State of Texas for eight years. In order for a white student to do graduate work, all he has to do is be white, and maybe a resident of Texas, because out of state students are admitted in the graduate school at the University of Texas. The out of state scholarship fund provides $100 a semester in all fields except medicine, where it is $150 a semester.

It provides round-trip to the school of the student's choice at three cents a mile, less the following items: the tuition fee paid to the University of Texas, which is stated as $25 a semester, less the round-trip fare from the student's home to Prairie View. The student may also get ten percent of the total award. In other words, a student may get a maximum of $165.00 for tuition for the regular year, that is, two semesters, and three cents a mile for transportation, less the round-trip from Prairie View.

Now, I have an illustration that was given on the Scholarship Committee Report of a student who wished to attend Columbia University, taking fifteen percent. The tuition was approximately $407.00, the railroad fare was $96.00. That student received from the scholarship fund $165.00 for tuition and $70.00 for railroad fare, making something like $235.00 out of a total which he would have to pay, merely for railroad fare and tuition to go to Teachers College, Columbia University, of five hundred and eight dollars and some cents, making the student pay $237.00 himself.

Now, the cost per student at the University of Texas in 1945–1946, at the Main University was $511.00. At the Texas A. & M. College, after eliminating the funds for cooperative extension, the cost of instruction per student was $734.00 for the same year. The State spends $200 to $500 more in these institutions to educate a white graduate student than they spend on the Negro student who wishes to do graduate work on a scholarship.

Q. Dr. Thompson, how important is the question of opportunity to do research in a well recognized and well organized university?

A. It is very important indeed.

Q. Have you made any comparison as to the research opportunities available at Prairie View with the other colleges you have mentioned?

A. Yes, I have.

Q. What is the result of your study, please?

A. The results show, taking a sample of five white high institutions of four years, shows that they expended in 1945, 1946, $2,753,809.00 for separately organized and budgeted research. Prairie View received for that year, 1945–1946, nothing, as in previous years, for separately budgeted and organized research.

On the basis of the formula which I described this morning, Prairie View or Negro higher education would have received $396,547.00. In 1946 Prairie View was voted $10,000.00 by the Texas A. & M. Board of Directors of the Experiment Station to set up a sub-experiment station at Prairie View to be known as Sub-Experiment Station No. 18. This is all of the money that Prairie View has received, to my knowledge, for research.

The Federal Government in 1945 made an appropriation, or gave Texas A. & M. College $251,288.00 for experiment station research. In taking into account the amount of money that the State puts in, if the formula had operated, Prairie View or Negro higher education would have received $36,185.00.

Q. The question was raised as to how much did they receive, Prairie View?

A. $10,000.00 in 1946 for the special purpose of setting up that Sub-Experiment Station No. 18.

Q. That came from Texas A. & M.?

A. That is right.

Q. Have you compared the professional curriculum of Prairie View with other schools?

A. I have.

Q. What are the results of your studies on that?

A. Well, in medicine, I might state, as a general background, that there are three Class A medical schools in the State of Texas; two private, Baylor and Southwestern, and one public, the medical branch of the University of Texas. The University of Texas catalogue, 1945–1946, lists 353 students. They receive from the State for current expense, not counting the amount of money that went to the three hospitals which are used for clinical purposes, $694,165.00 for the year ending 1946. In other words, there was a cost per student of around $1,800.00 or $1,900.00. Now, a Negro student who wants to take medicine in the State of Texas, his only recourse is to the scholarship fund, which I have mentioned previously. Even if the student attended McGill University in Montreal, Canada, and I pick that because it is the farthest away and it would cost more for travel, he would get less than $500.00 for mileage. McGill is 2,100 miles. The State spends more to educate a white medical student in the University of Texas than they spend on a Negro student through the scholarship fund, and there are six times as many white doctors in the State of Texas in proportion to white population as there are Negro doctors in proportion to the Negro population.

Now, taking the matter of dentistry, the State pays around $1,500.00 per dental student. A Negro who wishes to study dentistry can not get more than $400.00 from the scholarship. Thus, the State spends a thousand to eleven hundred dollars more for the dental education of a white student than for a Negro student through the scholarship fund, which probably explains why there are almost four times as many white dentists in proportion to the white population than there are Negro dentists in proportion to the Negro population.

Q. Without comparing the curricula at all, or other items, how many accredited law schools do the records show there are in Texas?

A. Three—let's see. Yes, three, Baylor and S. M. U. and a public law school, the University of Texas.

MR. DANIEL: Accredited by whom?

A. The American Bar Association.

By MR. MARSHALL:

Q. Now, getting to the fourth point of the criteria to compare schools, public education in general, did you compare the faculty at Prairie View with the faculty at these other schools you have testified to?

A. I have.

Q. What do the results of your examination show?

A. I might say that the basis of my examination is twofold. Number one, salary; number two, training. Obviously, to have a good faculty and to hold it, you have got to pay them attractive salaries and give them satisfactory working conditions. That is why I took salaries from the point of view of training. I wanted to see whether or not the training at Prairie View seemed to be, or some of the members, at least, seemed to be equal to the training of some of the white teachers in some of the white State teachers colleges and other higher institutions, which got high salaries.

Now, as to salaries, the salaries in general at Prairie View are too low, in general, to attract and hold a sufficiently large number of good teachers, or even to meet the competition from other Negro colleges, as I will point out in a moment.

Q. Do you, as Dean of the Graduate School of Howard University, have any knowledge as to the necessities of this Negro university as to faculty members?

A. Very definitely so.

Q. Is the item of salary an item that is at least a part of the consideration?

A. A very large part.

Q. Go right ahead.

A. Now, I would like to refer again, if I may, to the study that I referred to, Senior Colleges for Negroes in Texas, in which two statements, at least, were made concerning salaries. Page 36, the first statement, and it is as follows, and I quote:

"With reference to Prairie View, further study was made to determine the number of faculty members who had accepted offers from institutions outside of Texas. Investigation disclosed that twenty-five 'well prepared and able teachers' were lost to other institutions within the past five years because of the inability of Prairie View 'to match their salary offers.' Of the twenty-five faculty members lost, eleven held the degree of Doctor of Philosophy."

The next quotation, page 39:

> "In no professorial rank is the median salary in Prairie View equal to the lower limits of the range in State supported white colleges. The median salary of a full professor in Prairie View is $2,025.00, while the lowest salary paid a full professor in a State supported white college is $2,700.00. The corresponding figures for associate professor are $1,530.00 and $2,000.00; for assistant professor, $1,520.00 and $1,800.00; and for instructor, $1,170.00 and $1,500.00."

Now, not only was that statement true in 1942 or 1943, when it was gathered for this study; the same is true in 1946 and 1947. Except for one white teacher, in thirteen white State supported higher institutions, holding comparable positions in comparable departments, the highest salary paid a full professor in Prairie View is lower than the lowest salary paid a white professor in any one of these thirteen institutions, on a nine months basis.

Again, the principal—

MR. DANIEL: May I interrupt there? May I get this down to date? What is the date of it?

A. 1946 and 1947.

MR. DANIEL: And the data you read a minute ago was—

A. From this book in 1944, which was in 1942 or 1943. The principal of Prairie View in 1946–1947 got a salary that was $1,000.00 less than the lowest paid head of any four year State supported institution in Texas.

By MR. MARSHALL:

Q. In going through the records of these several institutions, did you find any other institution in Texas giving college and graduate work that has a principal at the head of it?

A. No, I haven't.

Q. Have you ever heard of any University in the United States giving graduate work that is headed up by a person with the title of principal?

A. No, I haven't.

Q. What is the usual title?

A. President or chancellor, or something of the sort.

Q. Go right ahead.

A. Now, Prairie View's faculty as a whole obviously—I won't say obviously—Prairie View's faculty as a whole isn't adequately trained. However, there are some adequately trained teachers at Prairie View, and naturally they should be paid accordingly. Let's look at the training for the moment. In 1940–1941, and this is found in the National Survey of Higher Education for Negroes, page 31,—page 14, 8.33% held the Doctor's Degree, 45.5% held the Master's Degree. In 1942–1943,—this is from the Senior colleges, this study here, Senior Colleges for Negroes in Texas, in 1942–1943, 6% had the Doctor's Degree and 52% had the Master's Degree. In 1945–1946, according to the Prairie View catalogue, and the degrees listed therein, 9.3% had a Doctor's Degree, 52.3% has the Master's Degree. I said a moment ago that Prairie View would obviously have to raise salaries considerably in order to meet the competition of other Negro colleges. There are some four or five Negro colleges, to my knowledge, that pay as much as $5,000.00 for a full professor.

Q. Isn't it also true that in recent years Negroes have been given opportunities to teach in colleges that are not designated as Negro universities?

A. That is true. There are some fifty or sixty Negroes now teaching in northern institutions.

Q. So that you have additional competition now?

A. That is right.

Q. You go right ahead.

A. The library, obviously, is very important. It is the life-blood of graduate work. The present library holdings of Prairie View are 25,000 titles, 465 serials.

Q. I think we know what titles are. What are serials?

A. Any sort of thing that runs in serial magazines and proceedings which run in serials. Leaving out of account the library at the University of Texas, which is one of the best university libraries in the South, it certainly has the largest collection of any university in the South, and taking the State Teachers Colleges libraries, the holding of white State Teachers Colleges libraries in Texas are larger than Prairie View. For example, the holdings of twelve white, four year schools, that is, teachers colleges and four schools in 1945, ranged from 28,357 in the Texas College of Arts and Industries, to 750,974 in Texas University.

North State Teachers College had more books, 144,426, than all the Negro public and private colleges in the State of Texas in 1945. The number of books that the Negro colleges in Texas was supposed to have in 1945 was one hundred and ten thousand and something.

Now, East State Teachers College, with 1205 students in 1945–1946, had library holdings of 81,974 volumes in 1945, as compared with Prairie View in 1947 with 1619 and 25,000 volumes.

The Southwest State Teachers College, with a student body of 957 students, had 56,612 volumes in the library in 1945. The Sam Houston Teachers College, with 1401 students in 1945–1946 had 63,100 volumes in the library in 1945.

Q. Dr. Thompson, from your experience as Dean of the Graduate School of Howard University, is it one of your responsibilities to ascertain as to whether or not that library is kept up to standards for accredited graduate schools?

A. That is true.

Q. And in your position as inspector for the Southern Association of Colleges and Secondary Schools, is it one of your jobs to inspect, as to the adequacy of libraries in the colleges?

A. Yes.

Q. On the basis of your experience in those two fields over a period of years, what is your opinion as to the adequacy of the facilities which you saw and inspected at Prairie View last week?

A. Well, frankly, they are inadequate.

Q. Did you see the library at the University of Texas, for example?

A. I didn't go in it.

Q. Are you acquainted with the number of books in it?

A. I am acquainted with the holdings.

Q. How does Prairie View library, regardless of the number—just the number of books—is there any semblance of equality between the two?

A. There would not appear to be.

Q. And the figures you have given on the books are figures that are used in that opinion of yours; is that correct?

A. That is right.

Q. Do you believe that Prairie View's library is adequate to maintain a graduate school?

A. In fact, Prairie View doesn't have a first class undergraduate library. That isn't only my opinion, but the opinion of this survey committee. They quoted the late Dr. Bishop, who was one of the outstanding librarians, who was last at Michigan, if I may quote that, page 64, and this is the quotation:

"A well selected library of 50,000 volumes will perhaps suffice for the needs of sound teaching in a college of not more than 500 students. This number does not include duplicates."

Q. Does Prairie View have anywhere near that amount?

A. They have 25,000 volumes.

Q. And how many students?

A. 1619, I think I mentioned that a moment ago, 1619 students.

Q. Dr. Thompson, in the earlier part of your testimony, I think your last criteria was the one of—I don't think this is the exact phrase for it—accreditation or standing in the scholarly world. Did you check on the accreditation of Prairie View with the other public supported schools in this state?

A. I did.

Q. What was the result of that study?

A. Well, the results that I found are as follows: I might explain, in order to explain what the results mean, the highest accreditation which any college can get in this country is to get on the approved list of the Association of American Universities. The highest accreditation that a university can get is to be a member of the Association of American Universities. There are three white State schools on the approved list of the Association of American Universities; Texas A. & M., North Texas State Teachers, and Texas College for Women.

Q. What about the University of Texas?

A. The University of Texas is a member of the Association of American Universities.

Q. Is Prairie View a member?

A. No, Prairie View is not a member.

Q. Is it accredited by that association?

A. No.

Q. Well, did you—about how much accreditation did you find Prairie View to have?

A. Prairie View is accredited by the regional association in this area, the Southern Association.

Q. Does it carry any other accreditation that is recorded in the legal proceedings, that you know of?

A. Not that I know of, except the State accredits the institution, of course.

Q. Well, now, what about for example the Medical School of the University of Texas? Is that accredited or not?

A. Yes.

Q. What about the—it is already in about the Law School. What about the School of Engineering?

A. The School of Engineering is accredited by the Engineering Council for Professional—I will give you the name of it—Engineering Council for Professional Development.

Q. Dr. Thompson, as a result of your study that you have made of Prairie View with the other schools and universities in this state that are publicly supported, can you compare favorably—can you compare Prairie View favorably with any one of them?

A. I don't think so, at present. I can't think of any institution that it would compare—would you define "compare favorably" for me, so that I may be sure to know what you are talking about?

Q. Pick the smallest State teachers college in Texas—your mind. Tell the Court whether or not there is any State supported school in the State of Texas that will give a Negro the equivalent of the education that can be obtained by a white student in the smallest of the teachers colleges in Texas.

A. I doubt if I can answer that.

Q. I will ask you this. In your criteria you used to compare the schools, how do you compare Prairie View with the University of Texas?

A. There is no comparison there. I can answer that.

Q. What do you mean, there is no comparison?

A. I mean that Texas University is a university. Prairie View is the university—I don't know how else to say it. It is a poor college.

Q. And it isn't—and is it or is it not a university in the field of general educational policies?

A. You mean on paper?

Q. No, as it exists today. Is it or is it not a real university?

A. No, it is not a real university.

Q. Can it give to the Negro student the type of education that is given to the white student at the University of Texas?

A. Not at all.

Q. Can a graduate student attending Prairie View University get the type of education that a graduate student at the University of Texas can get?

A. I doubt it very seriously.

Q. In your experience in your field of education, and as Dean of the Graduate School, is it possible to put graduate work, adequate graduate work training on to a school that gives inferior undergraduate training?

A. If I may turn the question around, I would say it is highly undesirable. It is possible to put it on there and have just as poor graduate work as you have undergraduate work...

Q. Would it inevitably follow that the graduate work would be inferior?

A. I think so.

Q. Your witness.

—

Redirect examination
Questions by MR. MARSHALL:

Q. Dr. Thompson, you were questioned about this conclusion in this study of senior colleges for Negroes in Texas that "even if Negroes were admitted they would not be happy in the conditions in which they would find themselves." You have already testified you were born in Mississippi. Is that right?

A. That is right.

Q. Subsequent to that time you went to the University of Chicago, after attending a Negro school in Richmond, Virginia; is that correct?

A. That is correct.

Q. And the University of Chicago has all races; is that correct?

A. Yes, sir.

Q. You were in classes with other students of other races?

A. That is correct.

Q. What I want to ask you is, did you find that you "would not be happy in the conditions in which you found yourself?"

A. No, I wasn't more unhappy; in fact, I was happier at the University of Chicago than I was at Virginia Institute.

Q. You can testify to that of your own knowledge, can't you?

A. That is correct.

Q. The faculty at Howard University, is it restricted to one race, or is it all races?

A. All races.

Q. Is there any unhappiness among them?

A. Well, I don't suppose any more than the average faculty, in any university.

—

Q. What is your experience at Howard University as to students who come from most of the separate Negro schools in the South, as to their ability to shape up?

A. They have pretty weak backgrounds, on the whole. I mentioned a case this morning, in the case of chemistry, where one of the chemistry departments of the Negro college doesn't have physical chemistry. They come to Howard University to take graduate work, and they have to take a year of physical chemistry before they can begin the graduate work. You face deficiencies in any of them.

Q. Isn't it true that many of the Negroes from southern schools are ineligible to attend a northern university; isn't that true?

MR. DANIEL: You are asking a leading question. We ask that you not lead him.

By MR. MARSHALL:

Q. Are there any Negro schools in the South that are unaccredited?

A. Yes.

Q. Can you get into an accredited university in the North if you come from an unaccredited school?

A. You can get in, but you are conditioned.

Q. Does a condition mean that you have to do more work?

A. Yes. My own personal experience bears that out. I got a Bachelor's Degree at Virginia University, and when I went to the University of Chicago, I had to do more work to get another Bachelor there.

Q. And you had already been to some kind of an academy in Mississippi, hadn't you?

A. That is right.

Q. Now, as to your experience in examining the relationship between the education in white and colored schools, on the question that was asked you on cross-examination as to one applicant to a law school, I want to ask you if, in your opinion, what, in your opinion, would be the same viewpoint of a governmental agency as to that one pupil applying for a law school—

MR. DANIEL: We object to that. That would be a conclusion of the witness.

THE COURT: I don't see what a governmental agency would have to do with it.

MR. MARSHALL: I am speaking of the University of Texas, with the University of Texas, with one Negro student applying for the law school, and the duty of the University to conserve the funds of the taxpayers.

A. I believe it would be the same answer that I gave the Attorney General when he asked me the same question a while ago in a different form. It seems reasonable the student should be admitted to the University of Texas.

Q. The question was asked whether or not Meharry was a Negro school. You testified on direct examination as to both Meharry and Howard. I now ask you whether or not Howard is a mixed school, or a Negro school?

A. Howard University has no restrictions as to race. In fact, we have all types of races at Howard. At least, they have had during the 20 years that I have been there.

Q. Getting back to this question of comparing the schools, the population of schools, is the population of the school—what determines the number of students a school can accommodate?

A. Well, there are a number of things. Of course, your physical plant, the things I enumerated this morning, physical plant, the number of teachers you can get, the number of facilities that you can offer.

Q. Even assuming that they are doing no better job than they are doing right now, could Prairie View accommodate any more students?

A. I doubt it. I was there last week, and I understand they are overcrowded.

Q. As to library facilities, you did compare Meharry as to individual schools and student body?

A. Meharry?

Q. I mean Prairie View.

A. Yes.

Q. And are you familiar with the approximate size of the State of Texas—are you not?

A. I thought I was until I came here. I doubt it.

Q. What relationship to the number of students attending college is it to the fact that in one instance you have eleven schools scattered all over the state and in the other instance you have one school at the far—one of the far sides of the state?

A. Of course, geographically, it would be difficult, if Negroes lived on the other side of the state, and would have to come to the other side of the state.

Q. Does that have some determinative bearing as to the number?

A. It probably would.

Q. That is all.

—

Direct examination: Donald G. Murray
Questions by MR. MARSHALL:

Q. Give your full name.

A. Donald G. Murray.

—

Q. Your present occupation?

A. Attorney.

Q. Where did you go to college?

A. Amherst College.

Q. Where is that?

A. Amherst, Massachusetts.

Q. When did you finish Amherst?

A. 1932.

Q. And did you apply for admission to the University of Maryland Law School?

A. I did.

Q. First; and what happened to your application?

A. It was refused.

Q. On what grounds?

A. On the grounds it was against the policy of the State of Maryland to admit Negroes to the University of Maryland Law School.

Q. What happened thereafter?

A. I consulted briefly with attorney Thurgood Marshall.

MR. DANIEL: We object to that as being irrelevant and immaterial, as to how he got in the school.

THE COURT: Tell me your purpose of it. I don't quite see.

MR. MARSHALL: The whole purpose of it is that in the State of Maryland they have segregation statutes similar to the State of Texas. He was refused admission, and a lawsuit was filed, and they said if he was admitted to the school it would wreck the University, and he was admitted, and everybody got along fine.

THE COURT: How is he going to prove what the State said except by hearsay?

MR. MARSHALL: We have here a document from the Court of Civil Appeals, and motion to advance a case, signed by the Attorney General, and the Assistant Attorney General, from the State of Maryland. That is the only piece of evidence we are going to introduce in evidence as to what the State of Maryland said.

———

By MR. MARSHALL:

Q. Was a lawsuit filed as a result of your case?

MR. DANIEL: We object to that.

THE COURT: It is on his bill.

MR. DANIEL: The records would be the best evidence.

THE COURT: He can say whether it was filed or not.

By MR. MARSHALL:

Q. Did the Court of Appeals of Maryland in a decision reported in the official documents of the Court of Appeals of Maryland, and reported in the Atlantic Reporter, the title of which was *Pearson against Murray*, decide upon the case of which you were speaking?

A. Yes, it did.

Q. Now, I ask you as to whether or not you were admitted to the University of Maryland prior to the decision of the Court of Appeals of Maryland?

A. Yes, I was.

Q. And prior to the decision of that case, I will ask you, did the Attorney General in Maryland, Herbert R. O'Conor, and the Assistant Attorney General, Charles T. LeViness, III, file a certain document with the Court of Appeals of Maryland concerning your case?

A. Yes, they did.

———

Q. I show you this document entitled Raymond A. Pearson, President, and other names, versus Donald Murray, in the Court of Appeals of Maryland, with the certification from the archivist of the State of Maryland, and ask you if you can identify it?

A. Yes, I can.

Q. What is it?

A. It is the notice to advance the hearing in the Court of Appeals of Maryland on the case *Pearson, et al. vs. Murray.*

———

(Thereupon counsel for relator had the Reporter mark said instrument above referred to as Relator's Exhibit No. 7, and same was admitted for the purpose of the Bill of Exception as such exhibit.)

MR. MARSHALL: Thank you, sir.

Q. Mr. Murray, the sum and substance of the relator's Exhibit No. 7 is the request to the Court of Appeals of Maryland to advance the hearing in this case from the October term on the theory that if you were admitted that dire results would come about at the University of Maryland; is that not correct?

A. That is correct.

Q. You were admitted in September, 1935, were you not?

A. That is correct.

Q. Will you tell briefly to the Court what, if anything, happened to bear out the predictions of the Attorney General of Maryland?

A. Absolutely nothing happened.

Q. Were you ostracized in any way?

A. No, I was not.

Q. Were you segregated in any way?

A. No, I was not.

Q. Were you mistreated in any way?

A. No, I was not.

Q. What was your experience, briefly?

A. My experience, briefly, was that I attended the University of Maryland Law School for three years, during which time I took all of the classes with the rest of the students, and participated in all of the activities in the school, and at no time whatever did I meet any attempted segregation or unfavorable treatment on the part of any student in the school, or any professor or assistant professor.

Q. Where is the University of Maryland Law School located?

A. Baltimore, Maryland.

Q. Are the public schools there mixed or separate, according to race?

A. Separate.

Q. Are housing conditions mixed or separate?

A. Separate.

Q. Are eating facilities mixed or separate?

A. Separate.

Q. With the exception of the separation of races on buses and trolley cars here in Austin, do you find any item of segregation that is not present in Baltimore, Maryland?

A. As far as I have observed, I have observed none.

Q. Attorney General Herbert O'Conor signed this motion to advance, did he not?

A. Yes.

Q. Who gave you your diploma when you graduated from the University of Maryland?

A. Governor O'Conor.

Q. The same man?

A. Yes.

Q. And Charles T. LeViness, III, signed that motion as Assistant Attorney General?

A. Yes.

Q. Who gave you your first job when you left the law school?

A. Charles T. LeViness, III.

Q. How did that come about?

A. I applied for a position as inspector with the Board of Liquor License in Baltimore City. At the time Mr. LeViness was the Chairman of that Board, and in charge of the hiring of applicants. I applied and was accepted and worked for about eight months with him.

Q. And then you went to the Army?

A. No, I went in private practice.

Q. Do you know of your own knowledge whether other Negroes have attended the University of Maryland since your time?

A. Yes, I do.

Q. About how many are in there now?

A. Nineteen.

Q. Has there been any trouble of any kind since you have been there that you know of?

A. Not that I know of.

—

Direct examination: Malcolm Pittman Sharp
Questions by MR. MARSHALL:

Q. Will you give your full name, please?

A. Malcolm Pittman Sharp.

—

Q. What is your present occupation?

A. Professor of Law, University of Chicago.

Q. Will you state briefly your legal education and your qualifications in general, in the field of law?

A. I received my A.B. at Amherst in 1918, A.B. in Economics at the University of Wisconsin in 1920, L.L.B. at Harvard Law School in 1923, Doctor's Degree, Harvard Law School, in 1927. I did some teaching while I was still in college. Then I have been teaching law since 1925, at Iowa, Wisconsin, and the University of Chicago; a member of the New York Bar—counting a period for establishing residence, I practiced in New York City for about two years, served in various advisory capacities in Wisconsin and Washington during the past years.

Q. And are you a member of the Association of American Law Schools?

A. I am.

Q. And have you recently held any position on any committees of that association?

A. I was Chairman of the Curriculum Committee that reported in 1942. Our work was somewhat disorganized by the war.

Q. What was the purpose of that committee?

A. The committee is appointed annually to consider the curriculum of member schools, recommend changes, improvements, make suggestions to member schools.

Q. Now, as a result of your studies and your teaching experience, along with your experience in the Association of American Law Schools, would you state briefly the recognized purposes of a law school as of today?

A. The purpose of a law school is, of course, first, to train for practice of the profession in the familiar way.

The second purpose has been becoming more and more important, as all of the leading schools have recognized, training for positions of public service, as lawyers are called on to fill, to a marked extent, administrative agencies, the bench, legislative positions. The schools are paying more and more attention to training for that purpose. Of course, the training of teachers and scholars in the field.

Q. In the several items you have mentioned, what type of student body do you need in order to best accomplish that purpose?

A. You need more than anything else, what I should call, a stimulating student body.

Q. What is that?

A. Where competition is great, lively; people from all walks of life. It is more important than your faculty. The most important thing a faculty does, perhaps, is to attract a stimulating, large student body.

Q. Speaking of the student body, your testimony is that you need all walks of life. Are there any other factors you need as to individual students?

A. You need to be well prepared, I should say, in so far as the group of students came from educational institutions whose standards were not up to the best that the others have. They would be a less stimulating group, to that extent. Their native capacity, and their training would not have been up to that of the other students.

Q. What method do you use in teaching in the University of Chicago?

A. We use the case method.

Q. Will you explain that briefly?

A.... The case system is designed to, in the first place, to bring out clearly the rules of law, partly by making discussions clear, working over discussions in class room; partly by practicing the application of the principles applied to cases.

I should say those particular advantages in a controlled situation starts the students off to what they are to do all through their careers at the bar. Of course, with practical problems, they have, perhaps they have heard of them in law school, and developed capacity for judgment, which is the mark of a good lawyer. I think in these days a very important addition to the case system is the seminar system which has been considered, and again, we give the students a chance to develop, present their own individual work, differ perhaps, and present it to the class mates for criticism, and hashing over in small groups.

Q. Do you believe the seminar method can be used in a first year law class?

A. I think it can be.

Q. Under what conditions?

A. This is a rather odd notion of my own. As a matter of fact, I think not many law teachers would agree with me, but we have had some success in our tutorial work in our first year students, not for the first year students to work right away at problems, if you are talking about the familiar first year class. The use of the case system would be better than the most likely alternative, lecture. Seminar is theoretically possible for first year students, but as far as I know, it isn't used anywhere, and I haven't heard that that was suggested here in connection with the proposed new school [*the "Negro Law School" that had been hastily assembled as Texas attempted to provide "separate but equal" access to law school for Heman Sweatt*].

Q. Dr. Sharp, the other question I wanted to ask was—first, I will ask you, is it possible to use the case system in a one-man class, with one man and a professor?

A. Well, as a matter of words, but it wouldn't be what I call the case system.

Q. And is it—which system is the recognized system for teaching a law school today?

A. The case system.

Q. And as used in the progressive law schools of the country today, is it possible to use that same system with a one-man class?

A. Not really, no, I think not.

Q. Doctor, as a matter of fact, wouldn't it come mighty close to the lecture method?

A. I think there would be a great danger that it would.

Q. Do you believe that—well, in your experience—let me ask you this question. Assuming that the proposed Negro Law School is equal in all other respects to the Law School of the University of Texas, except in respect to the size of the student body, and further assuming that the proposed Negro Law School has a student body which consists of one student; in your opinion, would the Negro Law School offer to that Negro student a legal education equal to that offered to any student at the University of Texas which has a student body of more than 800 students?

A. Certainly not.

Q. With the same hypothetical question put as to the Negro Law School, inserting the word "ten" for the word "one" student, would that change your answer at all?

A. It seems to me still very clearly that the education there wouldn't be in any sense equal.

Q. In your opinion, would it offer to that Negro student a legal education substantially equivalent to that offered to the students at the University of Texas?

A. As far as I can visualize the situation, it would not.

Q. Assuming that the Negro Law School is equal in all respects to that of the University of Texas, and had a sizable number of students, but all restricted to the Negro race, would that school give an education equal to that at the University of Texas, which accepts all students of all groups and all nationalities, other than Negroes?

A. I do not see how it could, for many years, at least.

Q. Will you give your reason for that?

A. You are back to that point about competition. Not only does it give you argument and give you the examination of the issues that you get in the class room, and having a pretty good class, some size, some opportunity for competition, but a great deal of the student's education occurs outside the class room, as we all know. There has been a saying in the teaching profession for some time that students at Harvard Law School got a good deal of their education by arguing on street corners and in restaurants, and bickering back and forth among themselves. The best thing a teacher can do is start that sort of arguing going, and let it go on all day, with intervals out for briefing cases; a good deal of discussion back and forth.

In view of the testimony that has been given about the character of Negro education at the lower levels—

MR. DANIEL: We object to that. That isn't responsive.

THE COURT: I think not.

MR. MARSHALL: Very well. Go right ahead.

A. Unless the education of the Negro group at all lower levels is equal to that of the white group, we can't expect the competition of the Negro Law

School to be as stimulating as the competition in the white law school, which we have assumed to be equivalent in other respects. I should think that one very important function of legal training would be neglected in the Negro school. That is the function of preparing law students for positions of responsibility as lawyers in Government. The experience of three colored lawyers whom I know particularly well—

MR. DANIEL: We object to that.

MR. MARSHALL: I was going to ask him that anyhow.

Q. Doctor Sharp, the University of Chicago, as to race, is the faculty of its law school mixed, or is it separate?

A. It is mixed. We have just called back one of our colored graduates to take a position on our staff as Associate Professor, and Research Professor.

Q. What about the student body?

A. It is mixed. The first time I had had occasion to count the Negroes, I found we had 13 in a student body of about 300.

Q. You mentioned the fact of the purpose of the law school to develop men and women for public service to the country. Well, in your experience at the University of Chicago, can you name any students who happen to be Negroes who have graduated from the Law School, and of your own personal knowledge, gave themselves to public service to the country?

———

A. There are a number of such cases. Three or four come to mind, particularly. Mr. Ming, who has just come back on our staff, has had a career of public service. Mr. Truman Gibson has had a distinguished public service career.

Q. Would you mind giving that?

A. I am coming back. I was just selecting. Judge Hastie is not one of our graduates, is one of the best I know.

Q. Do you know which school he is from, law school?

A. He is from Harvard; a different generation from mine, but I know of his career. Earl Dickerson, one of our graduates, served on the Council in Chicago. Mr. Charles Houston, a year ahead of me at the Harvard Law School, and on the Harvard Law Review with me, is a bills and notes expert. I can say a word about the career of two or three of these men particularly that seem to illustrate the importance of the point. We naturally think teaching is important. I see no reason for losing talent to the teaching profession on account of color. We are glad to have Mr. Ming back with us, and it is an advantage to us and to the school that he was not trained in a separate school. He is an American, working on the problems of the State, public utility problems, in which he has had special experience, on cases of problems relating to the regulation of business by Government, which is an increasingly important problem for lawyers, and it is important, it seems to me, that he should be trained to think as a member of the total community. Particularly, he should be trained to think professionally as a member of the total community.

Mr. Gibson is a striking example. He was Special Assistant to the Secretary of War during the war, and was given a medal for his services, and is a member of the President's distinguished committee on public military training. He is a member of the National community, and it is of utmost importance that he was not trained at a segregated school.

Mr. Houston, another schoolmate at Harvard, is working in the field of labor, Government regulation and industrial regulation, working on problems of seniority in the law.

He is sometimes able to point out the effects and the abuses of the labor organization practice.

Judge Hastie had a very distinguished career in the field of law—

MR. DANIEL: We will agree in their bill of exception they can write all of that out in there. We can agree they can write up everything he would have testified to about it.

MR. MARSHALL: We have just a few more.

THE COURT: Maybe you can conclude it here now.

By MR. MARSHALL:

Q. Will you give Judge Hastie's present position?

A. Governor of the Virgin Islands.

Q. In your experience with these and other students, do you believe that those students, excluding Hastie, whom you do not know personally, from personal contact with him, could any of those men you have named obtained their information that they have used for public service, in a segregated law school?

A. That question of "could" again troubles me. There are distinguished graduates of Howard, which is not strictly a colored law school, but it is largely colored. I wouldn't want to be that sweeping in my statement.

Q. Do you believe you can get equal value with training of other students, in a segregated law school?

A. Other things being equal, I most emphatically do not.

———

Q. In your opinion, is it possible for one student or ten students entering the first year law class in the proposed Negro Law School that you have heard testified about here where there are no upper classmen, second and third year students, to secure equal or substantially equivalent of legal training to that received by first year law students at the University of Texas where there are hundreds of upper classmen?

A. I think it is not possible for them to receive equal training.

Q. Will you give your reason?

A. What has been said about the competition among classmates, the emphasis has been on the competition of classmates so far. What has been said about that applies to the stimulation a man gets from the upper classmen, and the guidance. Sometimes loose guidance is very healthy, worried about one thing and encouraged about another, and the stimulus which comes from having a full complement of classes and full complement of upper classmen is a matter of first rating in any school. It is essential to the existence of what I should call an operating school.

Q. Do you consider a law review as extraneous to a legal education?

A. Certainly not. One of the most important devices, most important instruments of legal education in a modern law school is the law review.

Q. Is it of any value to a first year student?

A. It is, in so far as the competition for that outstanding honor, as it is in most schools, makes itself felt all the way down the years. It sets the tone. The law review men are the people that set the tones.

Q: Do you believe the Order of the Coif and other honors are extraneous to a legal education?

A. No, I do not.

Q. What do you classify them as, in your mind?

A. Actually, I think those awards are next important to the law review. The law review is of first-rate importance, but all awards which recognize attainment help in the process of stimulating friendly competition. Competition and friendly association are not by any means incompatible. In fact, they go together, a part of the business in preparing people to deal with the community as a whole. All of these awards step up competition in what I regard as a healthy manner.

Q. In your opinion, do you believe—first of all, you know about the University of Texas and its accreditation?

A. It is a thoroughly accredited school, a first-rate school in excellent standing, of course.

Q. Do you believe that a Negro student could get an equal education in a law school that started in Houston, Texas, in February of this year, moved to Austin in March of this year—

MR. DANIEL: We object to that part of the statement, because it is not in accordance with the facts of the case.

They are entirely separate schools, Your Honor. There is no move of that school to Austin.

MR. MARSHALL: I will change the question.

THE COURT: I believe I will let you—I believe I had better sustain his objection as to its moving.

MR. MARSHALL: Yes, sir.

Q. Do you believe that a Negro could get a legal education in a law school which had been previously established in Houston, Texas, in February of this year, and was closed the same month, and another law school opened in Austin in March of this year, and the record further showing that that school would be moved to Houston in August of 1948; do you believe that a law school student, whether he be white or colored, could get an adequate education in a school, law school of that type?

A. I don't see how he possibly could.

Q. Well, of what importance is the stability of a law school?

A. Well, it has a human importance which we all recognize. If you settle down to study, you want to stay at least a year, certainly at least a semester. Normally, when you start in, you plan to finish your course in the school that you select, go right through. Occasionally there are occasions for moving, sometimes there are advantages.

Certainly, the normal law student settles down to complete a course, and he can look three or four years ahead, depending on whether it is a three or four year course.

Q. Is the reputation of a law school of any value to the student, its reputation in the legal field?

A. To the student while he is a student?

Q. To the student while he is a student?

A. I think it is; it gives him confidence, pride, interest; it is a good deal of difference to the student if he feels he is in a good school, running well.

Q. Is the reputation of a law school of any value to the student after he graduates?

A. Well, we all know it may be of importance getting a job for a time; as one builds up a practice it may become of less importance, rank of the schools from which they come. Certainly, in the earlier stages of the lawyer's career, it may make a good deal of difference.

Q. You have heard the testimony about the so-called Negro Law School. I will ask you if a school which opened on March 10th in a—the ground floor of a building which had been leased for a period of one year, and in which there were three part-time professors to teach, and a library consisting solely of a hundred or two text reference books, could give a Negro an education equal to that at the University of Texas?

A. May I ask one question there?

THE COURT: Yes.

A. May I ask what you mean by "opening"?

By MR. MARSHALL:

Q. It opened on—that the doors were opened, and there was a person to register other students?

A. That is all you mean?

Q. Yes, that is all.

A. I don't see how it could possibly.

Q. Then, I will ask you the next question. Is it possible to get a legal education equal to that at the University of Texas in a law school consisting of one student?

A. No, I should think not.

Q. In a law school consisting of ten students?

A. I think not.

Q. In a law school consisting of a hundred students?

A. One hundred students, how selected?

Q. One hundred Negro students?

A. No, certainly not.

Q. Well, would that type of school with one, ten or a hundred Negro students give a legal education substantially equivalent to that obtained at the University of Texas?

A. I should think not. I am a little troubled by your one hundred case, if you can imagine such a case, conditions would be a good deal changed, but nothing I can visualize now would give substantial equality in any of the cases you supposed.

Q. Dr. Sharp, assuming a law school established in the basement of a building, ground floor, rather, of a building, and with a library of ten thousand volumes, assuming that they met the requirements of the Association of American Law Schools, and with three part-time professors, and from one to ten students, would that give education substantially equivalent to that at the University of Texas—Negroes only?

A. I should think not.

Q. Dr. Sharp, a law school established in a building with three floors, assuming that the three floors are adequate in space, adequate in space to accommodate ten students, and assuming further that a total budget of a hundred thousand dollars is spent for reconditioning and stacks, et cetera, would that type of law school give an education substantially equivalent to the Negroes there as that given other students at the University of Texas?

A. I think I have lost the trend of the question.

Q. The difference between the two questions is that one we have one floor and the other we have three floors, plus a library of ten thousand books, plus a budget of a hundred thousand dollars.

A. That budget is for repairs?

Q. It is for everything.

A. Salaries?

Q. Including books, salaries, and everything else.

A. I should think not, by any means.

Q. Would your answer be changed if we added that there were four full-time professors there, and all Negro students, in the same situation?

A. Well, if you got four most eminent professors in the United States, about whose names I would have to think a little before I decided who they were, it is perhaps conceivable that this select group of Negroes would get an education that was at any rate comparable to that which the boys got, sizable classes with competition and so forth, at Texas, but I should think even then it unlikely, and I suppose no one school can hope to have the four greatest teachers in the United States, least of all, a new school, and least of all, one established under these conditions.

Q. Even with those circumstances, could you get the total community thinking in a school of that type?

A. I wouldn't think so. It would take extraordinary teachers, indeed.

Q. That is all.

Briggs v. Elliott—Brown v. Board of Education, 347 U.S. 483 (1954)

Harry Briggs and nineteen other parents of Black students in Clarendon County, South Carolina, requested that the county provide school buses for Black students, as the county did for white students. After the parents' requests were ignored, a school principal enlisted the help of the NAACP; the parents then charged that racial segregation in the schools was harming their children and violated their rights under the Fourteenth Amendment's equal protection clause. Thurgood Marshall and a local lawyer representing the parents filed suit in *Briggs v. Elliott* in fall 1950.

The trial featured evidence about experiments by Kenneth and Mamie Clark using dolls to investigate the attitudes of children in segregated schools about race. The Clarks concluded that because the Black schoolchildren preferred white dolls, segregated schools decreased Black children's self-esteem. It was not seriously disputed at trial that conditions in the segregated Black schools were also not equal to those in white schools.[9]

The district court denied the Black parents' request to do away with segregation and instead ordered the school board to make conditions in the Black schools equal to those in the white schools. Judge Julius Waring dissented from this ruling, writing that "segregation is per se inequality."[10]

Briggs v. Elliott was consolidated on appeal with four other class actions involving the same issue: a case from Kansas, *Brown v. Board of Education of Topeka*; one from Virginia, *Davis v. County School Board*; and one from Delaware, *Gebhart v. Belton*. In all these cases except *Gebhart*, the lower courts had refused to order an end to segregation; in the Delaware case, the defendants were appealing a lower court order requiring Black students to be immediately admitted to previously all-white schools. The Supreme Court treated *Brown v. Board of Education of Topeka* as the lead case in the appeal, even though that honor rightfully belonged to *Briggs*—the case that was filed first and whose attorney of record, Marshall, argued the consolidated appeal before the Court.[11]

In a unanimous decision overruling the "separate but equal" doctrine of *Plessy v. Ferguson*, 163 U.S. 537 (1896), Chief Justice Warren announced that segregation violated the equal protection clause of the Fourteenth Amendment:

To separate [Black schoolchildren] from others of similar age and qualifications solely because of their race generates a feeling of inferiority as to their status in the community that may affect their hearts and minds in a way unlikely ever to be undone. . . .

Whatever may have been the extent of psychological knowledge at the time of *Plessy v. Ferguson,* this finding is amply supported by modern authority. . . . Any language in *Plessy v. Ferguson* contrary to this finding is rejected.

We conclude that, in the field of public education, the doctrine of "separate but equal" has no place. Separate educational facilities are inherently unequal.

In the Supreme Court of the United States
Harry Briggs, Jr., et al., Appellants, vs. R. W. Elliott, Chairman, J. D. Carson, et al., Members of Board of Trustees of School District No. 22, Clarendon County, S.C., et al., Appellees.

ORAL ARGUMENT
Washington, D.C., Tuesday, December 9, 1952.
The above-entitled cause came on for oral argument at 3:15 p.m.

—

Appearances: Thurgood Marshall, Esq., on behalf of the Appellants. John W. Davis, Esq., on behalf of the Appellees.

Opening Argument of Thurgood Marshall Esq. on Behalf of Appellants, Harry Briggs, Jr., et al.

MR. MARSHALL: May it please the Court:
⁣ ⁣ ⁣ This case is here on direct appeal from the United States District Court for the Eastern District of South Carolina. The issue raised in this case was clearly raised in the pleadings and clearly raised throughout the first hearing. After the first hearing, on appeal to this Court, it was raised prior to the second hearing. It was raised on motion for judgment, and there can be no question

that from the beginning of this case, the filing of the initial complaint, up until the present time, the appellants have raised and have preserved their attack on the validity of the provision of the South Carolina Constitution and the South Carolina statute.

The specific provision of the South Carolina Code…reads as follows:

It shall be unlawful for pupils of one race to attend the schools provided by boards of trustees for persons of another race.

That is the Code provision.
The constitutional provision…is:

Separate schools shall be provided for children of the white races—

This is the significant language:

…and no child of either race shall ever be permitted to attend a school provided for children of the other race.

Those are the two provisions of the law of the State of South Carolina under attack in this particular case.

At the first hearing, before the trial got under way, counsel for the appellees [*John W. Davis*] in open court read a statement in which he admitted that, although prior to that time they had decided that the physical facilities of the separate schools were equal, they had concluded finally that they were not equal, and they admitted in open court that they did not have equality; and at the suggestion of senior Judge Parker, this was made as an amendment to the answer, and the question as to physical facilities from that stage on was not in dispute.

At that time, counsel for the appellants, however, made the position clear that the attack was not being made on the "separate but equal" basis as to physical facilities, but the position we were taking was that these statutes were unconstitutional in their enforcement because they not only produced these inevitable inequalities in physical facilities, but that evidence would be produced by expert witnesses to show that the governmentally imposed racial segregation in and of itself was also a denial of equality.

I want to point out that our position is not that we are denied equality in these cases. I think there has been a considerable misunderstanding on that point. We are saying that there is a denial of equal protection of the laws, the legal phraseology of the clause in the Fourteenth Amendment, and not just this point as to equality, and I say that because I think most of the cases in the past have gone off on the point of whether or not you have substantial equality. It is a type of provision that, we think, tends to get us into trouble.

So, pursuing that line, we produced expert witnesses, who had surveyed the school situation, to show the full extent of the physical inequalities, and then we produced expert witnesses. Appellees in their brief comment say that they do not think too much of them. I do not think that the district court thought too much of them. But they stand in the record as unchallenged as experts in their field, and I think we have arrived at the stage where the courts do give credence to the testimony of people who are experts in their fields.

On the question that was raised a minute ago in the other case about whether or not there is any relevancy to this classification on a racial basis or not, in the case of the testimony of Dr. Robert Redfield—I am sure the Court will remember his testimony in the *Sweatt* case—the district court was unwilling to carry the case over an extra day. Dr. Redfield was stuck with the usual air travel from one city to another. And by agreement of counsel and with approval of the court, we placed into the record Dr. Redfield's testimony.

If you will remember, Dr. Redfield's testimony was to this effect: that there were no recognizable differences from a racial standpoint between children, and that if there could be such a difference that would be recognizable and connected with education, it would be so insignificant as to be unworthy of anybody's consideration. In substance, he said... that given a similar learning situation, a Negro child and a white child would tend to do about the same thing.

I think I have it here. It is on page 161:

Question: As a result of your studies that you have made, the training that you have had in your specialized field over some twenty years, given a similar learning situation, what, if any difference, is there between the accomplishment of a white and a Negro student, given a similar learning situation?

Answer: I understand, if I may say so, a similar learning situation to include a similar degree of preparation?

Question: Yes.

Answer: Then I would say that my conclusion is that the one does as well as the other on the average.

He has considerable testimony along the lines. But we produced testimony to show what we considered to be the normal attack on a classification statute, that this Court has laid down the rule in many cases set out in our brief, that in the case of the object or persons being classified, it must be shown: one, that there is a difference in the two; two, that the state must show that the difference has a significance with the subject matter being legislated; and the state has made no effort up to this date to show any basis for that classification other than that it would be unwise to do otherwise.

Witnesses testified that segregation deterred the development of the personalities of these children. Two witnesses testified that it deprives them of equal status in the school community, that it destroys their self-respect. Two other witnesses testified that it denies them full opportunity for democratic social development. Another witness said that it stamps him with a badge of inferiority. The summation of that testimony is that the Negro children have road blocks put up in their minds as a result of this segregation, so that the amount of education that they take in is much less than other students take in.

The other significant point is that one witness, Dr. Kenneth Clark, examined the appellants in this very case and found that they were injured as a result of this segregation. The court completely disregarded that.

I do not know what clearer testimony we could produce in an attack on a specific statute as applied to a specific group of appellants.

The only evidence produced by the appellees in this case was one witness who testified as to, in general, the running of the school system and the difference between rural schools and consolidated schools, which had no basis whatsoever on the constitutional question.

Another witness, E. R. Crow, was produced to testify as to the new bond issue that was to go into effect after the hearing in this case, at which time they would build more schools as a result of that money. That testimony was admitted into the record over objection of the appellants. The appellants took the position that anything that was to be talked about in the future was irrelevant to a constitutional issue where a personal and present right was asserted. However, the court overruled the objection. Mr. Crow testified.

Then he was asked as to whether or not it would not be "unwise" to break down segregation in South Carolina. Then Mr. Crow proceeded to testify as an expert. He had six years of experience, I think, as superintendent of schools, and prior to that time he was principal of a high school in Columbia. He testified that it would be unwise. He also testified that he did not know but what the legislature would not appropriate the money.

On cross-examination he was asked as to whether or not he meant by the first statement that if relief was granted as prayed, the appellees might not conform to the relief, and Judge Parker made a very significant statement which appears in the record, that, "If we issue an order in this case, it will be obeyed, and I do not think there is any question about it."

On this second question on examination, when he was asked, who did he use as the basis for his information that this thing would not work in the South, he said he talked to gangs of people, white and colored, and he was giving the sum total of their testimony, or rather their statements to him. And again on cross-examination he was asked to name at least one of the Negroes he talked to, and he could not recall the name of a single Negro he had ever talked to. I think the basis of his testimony on that point should be weighed by that statement on cross-examination.

He also said that there was a difference between what happened in northern states, because they had a larger number of Negroes in the South, and they had a larger problem because the percentage of Negroes was so high. And again on cross-examination, he was asked the specific question:

Well, assuming that in South Carolina the population was 95 percent white and five percent colored, would your answer be any different?

And he said, no, he would make the same answer regardless.

That is the only evidence in the record for the appellees here. They wanted to put on the speech of Professor Odom, and they were refused the right to put the speech in, because, after all, Professor Odom was right across in North Carolina and could have been called as a witness.

So here we have a record that has made no effort whatsoever—no effort whatsoever—to support the legislative determinations of the State of South Carolina. And this Court is being asked to uphold those statutes, the statute and the constitutional provision, because of two reasons. One is that these matters are legislative matters, as to whether or not we are going to have segregation. For example, the majority of the court in the first hearing said, speaking of equality under the Fourteenth Amendment:

> How this shall be done is a matter for the school authorities and not for the court, so long as it is done in good faith and equality of facilities is offered.

Again the court said, in Chief Judge Parker's opinion:

> We think, however, that segregation of the races in the public schools, so long as equality of rights is preserved, is a matter of legislative policy for the several states, with which the Federal courts are powerless to interfere.

So here we have the unique situation of an asserted federal right which has been declared several times by this Court to be personal and present, being set aside on the theory that it is a matter for the state legislature to decide, and it is not for this Court. And that is directly contrary to every opinion of this Court.

In each instance where these matters come up in what, if I may say "sensitive" field, or whatever I am talking about—civil rights, freedom of speech, et cetera—at all times they have this position: The majority of the people wanted the statute; that is how it was passed.

There are always respectable people who can be quoted as in support of a statute. But in each case, this Court has made its own independent determination as to whether that statute is valid. Yet in this case, the Court is urged to give blanket approval that this field of segregation and, if I may say, this field of racial segregation, is purely to be left to the states, the direct opposite of what the Fourteenth Amendment was passed for, the direct opposite of the intent of the Fourteenth Amendment and the framers of it.

On this question of the sensitiveness of this field, and to leave it to the legislature, I know lawyers at times have a hard time finding a case in point.

But in the reply brief, I think that we have a case in point that is persuasive to this Court. It is the case of *Elkison v. Deliesseline*, a decision by Mr. Justice William Johnson, appointed to this Court, if I remember, from South Carolina. The decision was rendered in 1823. And in 1823, Mr. Justice Johnson, in a case involving the State of South Carolina, which provided that where free Negroes came in on a ship into Charleston, they had to put them in jail as long as the ship was there and then put them back on the ship—and it was argued by people arguing for the statute that this was necessary, it was necessary to protect the people of South Carolina, and the majority must have wanted it and it was adopted—Mr. Justice Johnson made an answer to that argument in 1823, which I think is pretty good law as of today. Mr. Justice Johnson said:

> But to all this the plea of necessity is urged; and of the existence of
> that necessity we are told the state alone is to judge. Where is this
> to land us? Is it not asserting the right in each state to throw off the
> Federal Constitution at its will and pleasure? If it can be done as to
> any particular article it may be done as to all; and, like the old con-
> federation, the Union becomes a mere rope of sand.

There is a lot of other language and other opinions, but I think that this is very significant.

———

In this case in the trial we conceived ourselves as conforming to the rule set out in the *McLaurin* and the *Sweatt* cases, where this Court held that the only question to be decided was the question as to whether or not the action of the state in maintaining its segregation was denying to the students the equal protection of the laws.

Of course, those decisions were limited to the graduate and professional schools. But we took the position that the rationale if you please, or the principle, to be stronger, set out in those cases would apply just as well down the line, provided evidence could be introduced which would show the same type of injury.

That is the type of evidence we produced, and we believed that on the basis of that testimony the district court should properly have held that in the area of elementary and high schools the same type of injury was present as would be present in the *McLaurin* or the *Sweatt* case.

However, the district court held just to the contrary and said that there was a significant difference between the two. That is, in the *Sweatt* case it was a matter of inequality, and in the *McLaurin* case, McLaurin was subject to such humiliation, etcetera that nobody should put up with it, whereas in this case, we have positive testimony from Dr. Clark that the humiliation that these children have been going through is the type of injury to the minds that will be permanent as long as they are in segregated schools, not theoretical injury, but actual injury.

We believe that on the basis of that, on that narrow point of *Sweatt* and *McLaurin*—on that I say, sir, that we do not have to get to *Plessy v. Ferguson*; we do not have to get to any other case, if we lean right on these two cases. We believe that there is a broader issue involved in these two cases, and despite the body of the law, *Plessy v. Ferguson*, *Gong Lum v. Rice*, the statement of Chief Justice Hughes in the *Gaines* case, some of the language in the *Cumming* case, even though not applicable as to here—we also believe that there is another body of law, and that is the body of law on the Fifth Amendment cases, on the Japanese exclusion cases, and the Fourth Amendment cases, language that was in *Nixon v. Herndon*, where Mr. Justice Holmes said that the states can do a lot of classifying that nobody can see any reason for but certainly it cannot go contrary to the Fourteenth Amendment; then the language in the *Skinner* case, the language of Mr. Justice Jackson in his concurring opinion in the *Edwards* case.

So on both the Fourteenth Amendment and the Fifteenth Amendment, this Court has repeatedly said that these distinctions on a racial basis or on a basis of ancestry are odious and invidious, and those distinctions, I think, are entitled to just as much weight as *Plessy v. Ferguson* or *Gong Lum v. Rice*.

MR. CHIEF JUSTICE VINSON: Mr. Marshall, in *Plessy v. Ferguson*, in the Harlan dissent—

MR. MARSHALL: Yes, sir.

MR. CHIEF JUSTICE VINSON: Do you attach any significance when he is dealing with illustrations of the absence of education?

MR. MARSHALL: Yes, sir. I do not know, sir. I tried to study his opinions all along. But I think that he was trying to take the position of the narrow issue involved in this case, and not touch on schools, because of the fact that at that time—and this is pure speculation—at that time the public school system was in such bad shape, when people were fighting compulsory attendance laws, they were fighting the money to be put in schools, and it was in a state of flux. But on the other hand, in the majority opinion, the significant thing, the case that they relied on, was the *Roberts* case, which was decided before the Fourteenth Amendment was even passed [*the case is* Sarah C. Roberts v. The City of Boston *(1849): Black parents sought unsuccessfully to have their children admitted to all-white public schools; six years later, the Massachusetts legislature outlawed segregation in public schools in the state*].

MR. JUSTICE FRANKFURTER: But that does not do away with a consideration of the *Roberts* case, does it?

MR. MARSHALL: No, sir, it does not.

MR. JUSTICE FRANKFURTER: The significance of the *Roberts* case is that that should be considered by the Supreme Court at a time when that issue was rampant in the United States.

MR. MARSHALL: Well, sir, I do not know about those days. But I cannot conceive of the *Roberts* case being good for anything except that the legislatures of the states at those times were trying to work out their problems as they best could understand. And it could be that up in Massachusetts at that time they thought that Negroes—some of them were escaping from slavery, and all—but I still say that the considerations for the passage of any legislation before the Civil War and up to 1900, certainly, could not apply at the present time. I think that every race has made progress, but I do not believe that those considerations have any bearing at this time. The question today is—

MR. JUSTICE FRANKFURTER: They do not study these cases. But may I call your attention to what Mr. Justice Holmes said about the Fourteenth Amendment?

> The Fourteenth Amendment itself as an historical product did not destroy history for the state and substitute mechanical departments of law . . .

MR. MARSHALL: I agree, sir.

MR. JUSTICE FRANKFURTER: Then you have to face the fact that this is not a question to be decided by an abstract starting point of natural law, that you cannot have segregation. If we start with that, of course, we will end with that.

———

MR. JUSTICE FRANKFURTER: Do you really think it helps us not to recognize that behind this are certain facts of life, and the question is whether a legislature can address itself to those facts of life in spite of or within the

Fourteenth Amendment, or whether, whatever the facts of life might be, where there is a vast congregation of Negro population as against the states where there is not, whether that is an irrelevant consideration? Can you escape facing those sociological facts, Mr. Marshall?

MR. MARSHALL: No, I cannot escape it. But if I did fail to escape it, I would have to throw completely aside the personal and present rights of those individuals.

MR. JUSTICE FRANKFURTER: No, you would not. It does not follow because you cannot make certain classifications, you cannot make some classifications.

—

MR. MARSHALL: I think that when an attack is made on a statute on the ground that it is an unreasonable classification, and competent, recognized testimony is produced, I think then the least that the state has to do is to produce something to defend their statutes.

MR. JUSTICE FRANKFURTER: I follow you when you talk that way.

MR. MARSHALL: That is part of the argument, sir.

MR. JUSTICE FRANKFURTER: But when you start, as I say, with the conclusion that you cannot have segregation, then there is no problem. If you start with the conclusion of a problem, there is no problem.

MR. MARSHALL: But Mr. Justice Frankfurter, I was trying to make three different points. I said that the first one was peculiarly narrow, under the *McLaurin* and the *Sweatt* decisions. The second point was that on a classification basis, these statutes were bad. The third point was the broader point, that racial distinctions in and of themselves are invidious. I consider it as a three-pronged attack. Any one of the three would be sufficient for reversal.

MR. JUSTICE FRANKFURTER: You may recall that this Court not so many years ago decided that the legislature of Louisiana could restrict the calling of pilots on the Mississippi to the question of who your father was.

MR. MARSHALL: Yes, sir.

MR. JUSTICE FRANKFURTER: And there were those of us who sustained that legislation, not because we thought it was admirable or because we thought it comported with human notions or because we believed in primogeniture, but for different reasons, that it was so imbedded in the conflict of the history of that problem in Louisiana that we thought on the whole that was an allowable justification.

MR. MARSHALL: I say, sir, that I do not think—

MR. JUSTICE FRANKFURTER: I am not taking that beside this case. I am not meaning to intimate any of that, as you well know, on this subject. I am just saying how the subjects are to be dealt with.

MR. MARSHALL: But Mr. Justice Frankfurter, I do not think that segregation in public schools is any more ingrained in the South than segregation in transportation, and this Court upset it in the *Morgan* case [Morgan v. Virginia, *328 U.S. 373 (1946), a case Marshall argued, in which the Court struck down a Virginia law requiring racial segregation on commercial interstate buses as a violation of the commerce clause of the Constitution*]. I do not think it is any more ingrained.

MR. JUSTICE FRANKFURTER: It upset it in the *Morgan* case on the ground that it was none of the business of the state; it was an interstate problem.

MR. MARSHALL: That is a different problem. But a minute ago the very question was raised that we have to deal with realities, and it did upset that. Take the primary case. There is no more ingrained rule than there were in the cases of *McLaurin* and *Sweatt*, the graduate school cases.

MR. JUSTICE FRANKFURTER: I am willing to suggest that this problem is more complicated than the simple recognition of an absolute *non possumus* [*Latin for "we cannot," an expression of inability to act in a matter*].

MR. MARSHALL: I agree that it is not only complicated. I agree that it is a tough problem. But I think that it is a problem that has to be faced.

MR. JUSTICE FRANKFURTER: That is why we are here.

MR. MARSHALL: That is what I appreciate, Your Honor. But I say, sir, that most of my time is spent down in the South, and despite all these predictions as to what might happen, I do not think that anything is going to happen any more except on the graduate and professional level. And this Court can take notice of the reports that have been in papers such as the *New York Times*. But it seems to me on that question, this Court should go back to the case of *Buchanan v. Warley* [245 U.S. 60 (1917), *holding that a Louisville, Kentucky city ordinance prohibiting the sale to Black buyers of real property in majority-white neighborhoods violated the Fourteenth Amendment*], where on the question as to whether or not there was this great problem, this Court in *Buchanan v. Warley* said:

That there exists a serious and difficult problem arising from a feeling of race hostility which the law is powerless to control, and to which it must give a measure of consideration, may be freely admitted. But its solution cannot be promoted by depriving citizens of their constitutional rights and privileges.

In this case, granting that there is a feeling of race hostility in South Carolina if there be such a thing, or granting that there is that problem, we cannot have the individual rights subjected to this consideration of what the groups might do. For example, it was even argued that it will be better for both the Negro and the so-called white group. This record is not quite clear as to who is in the white group, because the superintendent of schools said that he did not know; all he knew was that Negroes were excluded. So I imagine that the other schools take in everybody.

So it seems to me that insofar as this case is concerned, whereas in the Kansas case there was a finding of fact that was favorable to the appellants—in this case the opinion of the court mentions the fact that the findings are embodied in the opinion, and the court in that case decided that the only issue would be these facilities, the curriculum, transportation, etcetera.

In the brief for the appellees in this case and the argument in the lower court, I have yet to hear anyone say that they denied that these children are harmed by reason of this segregation. Nobody denies that, at least up to now. So there is a grant, I should assume, that segregation in and of itself harms these children.

Now, the argument is made that because we are drawn into a broader problem down in South Carolina, because of a situation down there, that this statute should be upheld.

So there we have a direct cleavage from one side to the other side. I do not think any of that is significant. As a matter of fact, I think all of that argument is made without foundation. I do not believe that in the case of the sworn testimony of the witnesses, statements and briefs and quotations from magazine articles will counteract what is actually in the brief.

So what do we have in the record? We have testimony of physical inequality. It is admitted. We have the testimony of experts as to the exact harm which is inherent in segregation wherever it occurs. That I would assume is too broad for the immediate decision, because after all, the only point before this Court is the statute as it was applied in Clarendon County. But if this Court would reverse and the case would be sent back, we are not asking for affirmative relief. That will not put anybody in any school.

The only thing that we ask for is that the state-imposed racial segregation be taken off, and to leave the county school board, the county people, the district people, to work out their own solution of the problem, to assign children on any reasonable basis they want to assign them on.

MR. JUSTICE FRANKFURTER: You mean, if we reverse, it will not entitle every mother to have her child go to a nonsegregated school in Clarendon County?

MR. MARSHALL: No, sir.

MR. JUSTICE FRANKFURTER: What will it do? Would you mind spelling this out? What would happen?

MR. MARSHALL: Yes, sir. The school board, I assume, would find some other method of distributing the children, a recognizable method, by drawing district lines.

MR. JUSTICE FRANKFURTER: What would that mean?

MR. MARSHALL: The usual procedure—

MR. JUSTICE FRANKFURTER: You mean that geographically the colored people all live in one district?

MR. MARSHALL: No, sir, they do not. They are mixed up somewhat.

MR. JUSTICE FRANKFURTER: Then why would not the children be mixed?

MR. MARSHALL: If they are in the district, they would be. But there might possibly be areas—

MR. JUSTICE FRANKFURTER: You mean we would have gerrymandering of school districts?

MR. MARSHALL: Not gerrymandering, sir. The lines could be equal.

MR. JUSTICE FRANKFURTER: I think that nothing would be worse than for this Court—I am expressing my own opinion—nothing would be worse, from my point of view, than for this Court to make an abstract declaration that segregation is bad and then have it evaded by tricks.

MR. MARSHALL: No, sir. As a matter of fact, sir, we have had cases where we have taken care of that. But the point is that it is my assumption that where this is done, it will work out, if I might leave the record, by statute in some states.

MR. JUSTICE FRANKFURTER: It would be more important information in my mind to have you spell out in concrete what would happen if this Court reverses and the case goes back to the district court for the entry of a decree.

MR. MARSHALL: I think, sir, that the decree would be entered which would enjoin the school officials from, one, enforcing the statute; two, from segregating on the basis of race or color. Then I think whatever district lines they draw, if it can be shown that those lines are drawn on the basis of race or color, then I think they would violate the injunction. If the lines are drawn on a natural basis, without regard to race or color, then I think that nobody would have any complaint.

For example, the colored child that is over here in this school would not be able to go to that school. But the only thing that would come down would be the decision that whatever rule you set in, if you set in, it shall not be on race, either actually or by any other way. It would violate the injunction, in my opinion.

MR. JUSTICE FRANKFURTER: There is a thing that I do not understand. Why would not that inevitably involve—unless you have Negro ghettoes, or if you find that language offensive, unless you have concentrations of Negroes, so that only Negro children would go there, and there would be no white children mixed with them, or vice versa—why would it not involve Negro children saying, "I want to go to this school instead of that school"?

MR. MARSHALL: That is the interesting thing in this procedure. They could move over into that district, if necessary. Even if you get stuck in one district, there is always an out, as long as this statute is gone.

There are several ways that can be done. But we have instances, if I might, sir, where they have been able to draw a line and to enclose—this is in the North—to enclose the Negroes, and in New York those lines have on every occasion been declared unreasonably drawn, because it is obvious that they were drawn for that purpose.

MR. JUSTICE FRANKFURTER: Gerrymandering?

MR. MARSHALL: Yes, sir. As a matter of fact, they used the word "gerrymander."

So in South Carolina, if the decree was entered as we have requested, then the school district would have to decide a means other than race, and if it ended up that the Negroes were all in one school, because of race, they would be violating the injunction just as bad as they are by violating what we consider to be the Fourteenth Amendment now.

MR. JUSTICE FRANKFURTER: Now, I think it is important to know, before one starts, where he is going. As to available schools, how would that cut across this problem? If everything was done that you wanted done, would there be physical facilities within such drawing of lines as you would regard as not evasive of the decree?

MR. MARSHALL: Most of the school buildings are now assigned to Negroes, so that the Negro buildings are scattered around in that county. Now, as to whether or not lines could be properly drawn, I say quite frankly, sir, I do not know. But I do know that in most of the southern areas—it might be news to the Court—there are very few areas that are predominantly one race or the other.

MR. JUSTICE FRANKFURTER: Are you going to argue the District of Columbia case?

MR. MARSHALL: No, sir. If you have any questions, I would try, but I cannot bind the other side.

MR. JUSTICE FRANKFURTER: I just wondered, in regard to this question that we are discussing, how what you are indicating or contemplating would work out in the District if tomorrow there were the requirement that there must be mixed groups.

MR. MARSHALL: Most of the schools in the District of Columbia would be integrated. There might possibly be some in the concentrated areas up in the northwest section. There might be. But I doubt it. But I think the question as to what would happen if such decree was entered—I again point out that it is actually a matter that is for the school authorities to decide, and it is not a matter for us, it seems to me, as lawyers, to recommend except where there is racial discrimination or discrimination on one side or the other.

But my emphasis is that all we are asking for is to take off this state-imposed segregation. It is the state-imposed part of it that affects the individual children. And the testimony in many instances is along that line.

> . . . The important thing is to get the principle established and if a decree were entered saying that facilities are declared to be unequal and that the appellants are entitled to an injunction, and then the district court issues the injunction, it would seem to me that it

would go without saying that the local school board had the time to do it. But obviously it could not do it overnight, and it might take six months to do it one place and two months to do it another place.

Again, I say it is not a matter for judicial determination. That would be a matter for legislative determination.

—

MR. JUSTICE JACKSON: Coming back to the question that Justice Black asked you, could I ask you what, if any, effect does your argument have on the Indian policy, the segregation of the Indians? How do you deal with that?

MR. MARSHALL: I think that again that we are in a position of having grown up. Indians are no longer wards of the Government. I do not think that they stand in any special category. And in all of the southern states that I know of, the Indians are in a preferred position so far as Negroes are concerned, and I do not know of any place where they are excluded.

MR. JUSTICE JACKSON: In some respects, in taxes, at least, I wish I could claim to have a little Indian blood.

MR. MARSHALL: But the only time it ever came up was in the—

JUSTICE JACKSON: But on the historical argument, the philosophy of the Fourteenth Amendment which you contended for does not seem to have been applied by the people who adopted the Fourteenth Amendment, at least in the Indian case.

MR. MARSHALL: I think, sir, that if we go back even as far as *Slaughter-House* and come up through *Strauder*, where the Fourteenth Amendment was passed for the specific purpose of raising the newly freed slaves up, etcetera, I do not know.

MR. JUSTICE JACKSON: Do you think that might not apply to the Indians?

MR. MARSHALL: I think it would. But I think that the biggest trouble with the Indians is that they just have not had the judgment or the wherewithal to bring lawsuits.

MR. JUSTICE JACKSON: Maybe you should bring some up.

MR. MARSHALL: I have a full load now, Mr. Justice.

Rebuttal Argument on Behalf of Appellants, Harry Briggs, Jr., et al.

With education, this Court has made segregation and inequality equivalent concepts. They have equal rating, equal footing, and if segregation thus necessarily imports inequality, it makes no great difference whether we say that the Negro is wronged because he is segregated, or that he is wronged because he received unequal treatment. . . .

I would like to say that each lawyer on the other side has made it clear as to what the position of the state was on this, and it would be all right possibly but for the fact that this is so crucial. There is no way you can repay lost school years.

These children in these cases are guaranteed by the states some twelve years of education in varying degrees, and this idea, if I understand it, to leave it to the states until they work it out—and I think that is a most ingenious argument—you leave it to the states, they say, and then they say that the states haven't done anything about it in a hundred years, so for that reason this Court doesn't touch it.

The argument of judicial restraint has no application in this case. There is a relationship between federal and state, but there is no corollary or relationship as to the Fourteenth Amendment.

The duty of enforcing, the duty of following the Fourteenth Amendment, is placed upon the states. The duty of enforcing the Fourteenth Amendment is placed upon this Court. . . . It is our position that whether or not you base this case solely on the intent of Congress or whether you base it on the logical extension of the doctrine as set forth in the *McLaurin* case [*the 1950 case in which the Court ruled that Oklahoma's racial segregation of graduate education violated the Fourteenth Amendment*], on either basis the same conclusion is required, which is that this Court makes it clear to all of these states that in administering their governmental functions, at least those that are vital not to the life of the state alone, not to the country alone, but vital to the world in general, that little pet feelings of race, little pet feelings of custom—I got the feeling on hearing the discussion yesterday that when you put a white child in a school with a whole lot of colored children, the child would fall apart or something. Everybody knows that is not true.

Those same kids in Virginia and South Carolina—and I have seen them do it—they play in the streets together, they play on their farms together, they go down the road together, they separate to go to school, they come out of school and play ball together. They have to be separated in school.

There is some magic to it. You can have them voting together, you can have them not restricted because of law in the houses they live in. You can have them going to the same state university and the same college, but if they go to elementary and high school, the world will fall apart. And it is the exact same argument that has been made to this Court over and over again, and we submit that when they charge us with making a legislative argument, it is in truth they who are making the legislative argument.

They can't take race out of this case. From the day this case was filed until this moment, nobody has in any form or fashion, despite the fact I made it clear in the opening argument that I was relying on it, done anything to distinguish this statute from the Black Codes [*systems of state laws passed after the Civil War that used various methods to control the Black labor force—for example, by making it a criminal offense for Blacks to refuse to accept yearly labor contracts*], which they must admit, because nobody can dispute, say anything anybody wants to say, one way or the other, the Fourteenth Amendment was intended to deprive the states of power to enforce Black Codes or anything else like it.

We charge that they are Black Codes. They obviously are Black Codes if you read them. They haven't denied that they are Black Codes, so if the Court wants to very narrowly decide this case, they can decide it on that point.

So whichever way it is done, the only way that this Court can decide this case in opposition to our position, is that there must be some reason which gives the state the right to make a classification that they can make in regard to nothing else in regard to Negroes, and we submit the only way to arrive at that decision is to find that for some reason Negroes are inferior to all other human beings.

Nobody will stand in the Court and urge that, and in order to arrive at the decision that they want us to arrive at, there would have to be some recognition of a reason why of all of the multitudinous groups of people in this country you have to single out Negroes and give them this separate treatment.

It can't be because of slavery in the past, because there are very few groups in this country that haven't had slavery some place back in history of their groups. It can't be color because there are Negroes as white as the drifted snow, with blue eyes, and they are just as segregated as the colored man.

The only thing can be is an inherent determination that the people who were formerly in slavery, regardless of anything else, shall be kept as near that stage as is possible, and now is the time, we submit, that this Court should make it clear that that is not what our Constitution stands for.

Thank you, sir.

Cooper v. Aaron, 358 U.S. 1 (1958)

As British prime minister William E. Gladstone said in 1868, "justice delayed is justice denied." In a follow-up decision to *Brown v. Board of Education* in 1955, the Supreme Court had ordered states to integrate their schools "with all deliberate speed"—a phrase that soon provided cover for delays. Black schoolchildren who had been promised admission to integrated public schools in the *Brown v. Board of Education* decision waited for those promises to be fulfilled as they neared graduation, still attending segregated schools.

In the aftermath of the *Brown* decisions, in Little Rock, Arkansas, the school board developed a plan to integrate Little Rock schools that was approved by the federal district court. At the same time, the Arkansas governor, Orval Faubus, and legislature began enacting new state laws and constitutional amendments outlawing integration in Arkansas.

On September 4, 1957, the Arkansas National Guard, under Faubus's orders, prevented nine Black students from enrolling at Central High School in Little Rock in accordance with the school board's integration plan. The next day, the federal government obtained an injunction forcing Faubus to withdraw the National Guard; the school, however, continued to serve as the gathering place for a violent mob bent on preserving segregation. President Dwight Eisenhower eventually sent in federal troops to protect the nine students, who began attending classes by the end of September.

In February 1958, however, the Little Rock school board asked the federal district court to be allowed to postpone the integration plan, in view of the "chaos, bedlam, and turmoil" at the high school. Judge Harry J. Lemley of the district court accordingly ordered the nine students to leave the school and the integration plan to be delayed for another two and a half years. The students appealed the decision with the help of Thurgood Marshall and the NAACP.[12]

The intermediate appellate court, the U.S. Court of Appeals for the Eighth Circuit, while ruling in favor of the students that the integration plan should proceed, nonetheless granted an automatic stay, or delay, of its ruling so that the school board could appeal to the U.S. Supreme Court. This delay offered further opportunities for Arkansas's governor and state legislature to attempt legislatively to avoid compliance with federal mandates to end school segregation in the state. Marshall's attempt to have the stay lifted so that the integration plan could proceed right away came on for oral argument in a special term held by the Supreme Court in August, just before the school year was set to begin. Marshall argued that the school board had no valid basis for its appeal to the U.S. Supreme Court except to obtain a further delay, which would constitute yet another violation of the constitutional rights of the Black students whose schooling was being interrupted.

The Supreme Court unanimously ruled that the constitutional rights of the students could not be waived to maintain order. The Court stated that its orders were binding on the governor and legislature of Arkansas, who could not annul these orders with legislation, constitutional amendments, or gubernatorial directives. One observer noted, "If *Brown v. Board of Education* provided the foundation for school integration in the 1950s and 1960s, *Cooper v. Aaron* provided the muscle."[13]

In the Supreme Court of the United States
August Special Term 1958
John Aaron, et al., Petitioners, v. William G. Cooper, et al., Members of the Board of Directors of the Little Rock, Arkansas Independent School District, and Virgil T. Blossom, Superintendent of Schools, Respondents

ORAL ARGUMENT

Proceedings, August 28, 1958

THE CHIEF JUSTICE: The Court is now convened in special term to consider an application by the petitioners for the vacation of the order of the United States Court of Appeals for the Eighth Circuit, staying the issue of its mandate, and for a stay of the order of the United States District Court for the Eastern District of Arkansas of June 21, 1958 in *John Aaron, et al. vs. William G. Cooper, et al.*

Argument on Behalf of Petitioners

MR. MARSHALL: May it please the Court, this afternoon's extraordinary session was necessitated because of the fact of the constitutional rights of the petitioners here, the Negro plaintiffs in the cases below, their right to remain in attendance at a desegregated school in Central High School, Little Rock.

And this was pursuant to court order; and I would like to emphasize that at outset the rights we are seeking protection for are not rights that are in the abstract, but rights that have been determined, not necessarily by the *Brown* decision, but the Court will remember that in this case, the District Court approved a plan of desegregation.

The plaintiffs below appealed to the Court of Appeals of the Eighth Circuit, and it was affirmed, and the court record also shows that in September of last year there were two applications for stay to Judge Davies, sitting specially in the District Court for the Eastern District of Arkansas, and they were both denied.

So the rights we seek are rights that have been recognized by the Federal Courts and, as such, we believe they are in a different category from a normal litigant in an injunction proceeding prior to judgment.

———

And the truth of the matter is these entire proceedings, starting with the filing of the petition of the School Board way back in February, asking for time, the whole purpose of these proceedings is to get time.

The objective of the proceedings is that the Little Rock schools be returned from desegregated to segregated status as of the September school term.... In this case the stay of the issuance of the mandate [*i.e., the court order delaying desegregation of the Little Rock schools*] decided the merits of the case directly contrary to the opinion of the case.

The opinion said that the School Board was not entitled to a suspension of the integration plan. The stay of the mandate said, "You don't have to act on this until after the school term begins."

At that time the school term was to begin on September 2nd.

This Court can take judicial notice that that has been postponed to September 8. But, at any rate, the staying of the mandate would effectively mean that if this Court would wait until October, the school term would be in session, and I believe anybody would agree it is not educational policy to transfer children in the middle of a school term.

So we have this extreme situation in the law of a procedural device of staying a mandate actually ruling on the merits in the case.

That point, plus this additional point, and that is that the Court certainly can take judicial notice of what is going on in the Legislature in Arkansas today.

It is quite obvious that any time spent in delay in this matter would bring about not less litigation but more litigation, and that is why—and I think we are entitled to it—we believe that this Court must not only vacate the stay of the Court of Appeals for the Eighth Circuit, but I think that in the present posture of this litigation, in the very peculiar status that it is in, and the atmosphere that now exists in the State of Arkansas with the Governor, the Legislature and everybody determined to set themselves up against the whole United States, that the only effective relief that this Court can give that will protect the rights of the petitioners here would be to stay the—I mean vacate the stay of issuance of the mandate; too, to stay Judge Lemley's order suspending the previous orders of the District Court and, as was done in the *Lucy* case, for entirely different reasoning, to order that the existing orders of Judge Miller, who originally heard the case, and Judge Davies, who heard it sitting specially assigned, last September, be reinstated and in full force and effect.

The question immediately arises as to whether this Court has authority to do it. Well, as was pointed out in many cases, the all writ statute, for one, gives authority and, indeed, the procedural statute on the staying of the mandate gives credence to our position; and if there is any exact authority that is needed, we take the flat position that the *Lucy* case says specifically that this Court has authority, and need go no further.

I do not believe, as might be argued, that this Court cannot and should not go into the merits of this.

It tends to raise the question in my mind as to what do we mean by the merits.

The merits in this case have already been decided by the stay, and the stay is now being refused by this Court.

—

JUSTICE FRANKFURTER: May I ask you this on something you said just a few minutes ago: Which order of Judge Davies, the original order approving the plan proposed by the School Board, was it, you stated, by Judge Miller?

MR. MARSHALL: Judge Miller.

JUSTICE FRANKFURTER: What the judgment of Judge Davies later repeated, in effect, that, other than the order relating to the intervention of troops, that didn't deal with that problem?

MR. MARSHALL: No, sir, Mr. Justice Frankfurter. What happened was as soon as the Governor threatened to bring out the troops, the School Board went to Judge Davies, and asked for instructions, and he told them to move ahead with the plan.

Subsequent to that time, a day or so later, I do not remember the exact date, I can get it for you though, sir, the Board formally appeared before Judge Davies and asked for the right to postpone the operation of the plan, and Judge Davies ordered them "to proceed forthwith with the plan," and the petition filed by the respondents here [*i.e., the Little Rock school board*] requested the Court to stay the whole business, saying that they considered the first order of Judge Miller to be in effect an injunction, and if not, then the order of Judge Davies, but it was aimed at all three, the petition, as set forth.

——

MR. MARSHALL: With the permission of the Court, I would like to, just in a measure, go into some of the background of this case....

With [one] exception..., the only relief that the School Board has asked from the District Court is postponement.

They have asked for no relief in an affirmative way to help this thing along.

That goes back from the two requests in September of last year and, bear in mind, that the petition in this case which is before you today, was asked for way back in February. It was around February that they gave up.

That is when they asked for this relief, and it sat there for awhile until Chief Judge Gardner assigned Judge Lemley to hear it, and the hearing took place in the early part of June.

So on that basis it seems to us, that the Government points out in its brief and, as we point out in our brief, that there was an affirmative duty on the School Board to get help in this situation, and the only objection at all was that the community was opposed to it.

The other point that they rely on in their memorandum and in their brief is that a stay of this will help, and in the District Court, in the Court of Appeals, and in the response that they filed to our petition, and up to the present day, with the exception of two points, one that Governor Faubus might not be in office two and a half years from now, and that certain statutes of Arkansas now being litigated might be decided within two and a half years, with the reception of those two points, as of this minute the School Board has not given anybody any information of what they propose to do in the two and a half years while these rights are being suspended.

In the question of a stay or the vacation of a stay,... there has got to be a showing of...the irreparable harm on one side as against that on the other side.

The record shows that these children will graduate so, so far as matters now stand, if they are in segregated schools next year their rights are just gone. I mean, that is the end of that.

—

When this case was heard those children in the Central High School, now seven, there were nine—one graduated, Ernest Green graduated, one Minnie-jean Brown was expelled, leaving seven—those seven were in an integrated school system. They had been there for a year.

Under Judge Lemley's order, they are taken out, and that is not only a change of status, it is a physical change of status, and they are taken out as of—it will only be effective, so far as they are concerned, come opening of the school, because school has been in recess.

But that complete change of status must have some extraordinary reason to be sustained.

The normal procedure is to maintain the status quo.... We take the position that the opinion of the Court of Appeals was so clear that the respondents here have nothing that they could successfully bring to this Court.

In many of the rulings of this Court, in chambers, there have been taken into consideration the possibility of whether or not you actually have a justiciable issue, recognizable by this Court; and the petitioners have no such case.

And yet they can toy around with the situation, and effectively deny these rights by using procedural devices, such as a motion to stay.

—

JUSTICE CLARK: What is the basis of your belief that they would not transfer the students in the event the case took its regular course?

MR. MARSHALL: I would say, Mr. Justice Clark, that there is considerable authority among educators that it is not well—it is not good educational practice to transfer students in the middle of a year.

As to one or two days, I imagine that would be all right, but in the middle—

JUSTICE CLARK: Have they advised you to that effect, the School Board?

MR. MARSHALL: No, sir; no, sir. Not at all. But I was basing that solely on good educational practices.

—

As we said in our original petition for certiorari, which this Court can reconsider on its own motion, our original petition for certiorari, when that was filed, this Court said, you will remember that, "We have no doubt that the Court of Appeals will recognize the vital importance of the time element in this litigation, and that it will act upon the application for a stay of the appeal in ample time to permit arrangements to be made for the next school year."

The only thing, I believe, that the way this case stands, there must be a definitive decision—I hate to use the two together—I mean it is bad English, but it is the best way I can do, that there be no doubt in Arkansas that the orders of that District Court down there must be respected, and cannot be suspended, and cannot be interfered with by the legislature or anybody else.

And less than that, I do not think will give these young children the protection that they need, and they most certainly deserve...; and at this time we respectfully suggest that it would be even better for this Court to decide the case on the merits because the stay which is being reviewed, decided it on the merits, and so this Court, in deciding the stay, do not see much chance of doing it, but I do know that technically it could be done without hitting the merits.

You consider the merits...it is because of the present developments out there that I think this Court must consider the whole story.

JUSTICE CLARK: You have not briefed the merits?

MR. MARSHALL: Sir?

JUSTICE CLARK: You have not briefed the merits in your petition?

MR. MARSHALL: In the brief? We did not; no, sir.

JUSTICE CLARK: You would file another brief; is that your idea?

MR. MARSHALL: No, sir; we would be prepared to argue; and, with permission, to submit a brief, and we could do a brief on this case in less than half a day.

We are prepared to argue it now, with the right to submit a brief at a later time; because Judge Matthes' Opinion of the Court of Appeals is so clear.

THE CHIEF JUSTICE: Have you discussed with counsel on the other side the possibility or the propriety of arguing the merits here today?

MR. MARSHALL: I have not, sir.

But I think that as long as this case is undecided on its merits, our plaintiffs, our petitioners in this case will still be under terrific pressure, because of the uncertainty of it, which was recognized by this Court in its denial of our original Petition for Certiorari; and if it were not for the fact that it has been done, I would have hesitated to suggest it. But I think that on several occasions this Court has ordered cases brought up.

I mean, for example, under some precedent, as I understand it—it was kind of late in the morning when we read them—but we understand that this Court could order the School Board to file its petition within one or two days, and be heard promptly before school is opened; or you could consider, as I said, the petition that we have filed.

May it please the Court, finally I would like to wind this up because I don't think that there is too much law that is necessary, because it is certainly not in conflict. . . .

And so I would say, as I said back here, that when you weigh it, I for one can hardly talk about weighing anything against Constitutional rights. I have never been able to find out how to do it.

But here we have Negro children, and the record will show they have done nothing bad except the record will show that one did—the record will show; there is a dispute about it, but it will show, and she was expelled so that is no problem, but that these children must be forced to surrender their constitutional rights is unimportant in this Court today.

The point as set forth in the Court of Appeals decision, and quoting from the *Strutwear Knitting* case [*a 1936 case in which a federal court ruled that the governor of Minnesota could not use National Guard troops to close a factory during a workers' strike*], in the Government's brief which was filed this morning, it points out that it is really a surrender to obstructionist and mob action, and that it is much more destructive of democratic government than it is of some few Negroes' rights.

———

MR. MARSHALL: I think the real problem in this case is as to whether or not the Court wants to go into the merits. I think that is it.

JUSTICE FRANKFURTER: Well, the merits—you use the term "the merits"—it seems to me to be the same merits for determining the propriety of the stay as in asking us to vacate the order which we originally refused to vacate.

———

MR. MARSHALL: I think that is—I am sure that is correct, sir; but, Mr. Justice Frankfurter, I still go back to my other question.

JUSTICE FRANKFURTER: All right.

MR. MARSHALL: That whether you consider the vacation of the stay of the Eighth Circuit or whether you consider a stay of Judge Lemley's order, the merits are so entwined that this is one of the types of cases where it points to the need for it.

JUSTICE FRANKFURTER: What you are saying is that if, as a matter of authorized congressional action, a petition of certiorari can be brought by the School Board, that such a petition would raise claims so frivolous that there is no justification for staying the reversal by the Court of Appeals.

MR. MARSHALL: We take that position, and we have tried to develop it.

. . . The stay in this case was merely given under the procedural statute which says that a stay can be granted for purposes of petitioning to the Supreme Court, but nothing at all on the merits, and I presume the merits weren't considered.

And so that, at this stage of the litigation, is the first time that the merits—I use "merits" merely as to the merits as to whether or not an order is entitled to be stayed—that for the first time the merits of that are being considered.

And we take the position that when you balance these rights of these kids involved, plus what this Court said in the *Brown* case, the public interest, meaning the public interest of the United States over against the School Board's position that there are some people that don't want to let this thing go through, then, certainly, the equities involved lean toward the protection of those constitutional rights, rather than the postponement of them.

And I believe that I have to recognize that that is an issue in this case, and, as expressed by the Court of Appeals, they said there is no problem about it; they just cannot be surrendered, and they mentioned the case I mentioned before, the case that I said before, the *Strutwear Knitting* case, which is famous for the expression about handling bank robbers. You don't close the banks; you put the bank robbers in jail.

And, therefore, it seems to me—and I don't want to prolong the argument—that we are entitled to both.

At the same time, it seems to me that the real justice of the case would not be required by going into either, but that either on our petition originally filed or by some other procedural device, that this Court be given an opportunity to pass on the merits.

And, as I said before, petitioners are perfectly willing to argue the case on the merits, even though we were successful insofar as the opinion of the lower court was concerned.

I think a reading of the three briefs, our brief, the School Board's brief, and the Government's brief, demonstrates that there is really no serious conflict of the law as to the authority of this Court to act. There is a conflict between the School Board as to whether this Court should act; and, on that, we think that the equities on the side of the schoolchildren are such that the only relief that can be granted that will be effective will be for the decision on the merits.

———

[*After opposing counsel made the opening argument on behalf of respondents, Marshall offered the following rebuttal.*]

Rebuttal Argument on Behalf of Petitioners

MR. MARSHALL: Just one or two points, if it please the Court.

THE CHIEF JUSTICE: Go right ahead and take your time.

MR. MARSHALL: There are two points. One was this question of this empty victory. We have had this argument in this case from beginning to end, and I think the Court will remember that the eminent attorney, the late John Davis [*Marshall's opponent in the appeals consolidated as* Brown v. Board of Education], in arguing the *Brown* cases, stood here and argued the story of the dog carrying the bone across the bridge and looking in and dropping the bone, and I submit that that argument has been made to this Court. It has been disposed of in the *Brown* case. It has no bearing here.

On the question, Mr. Justice Black's question about time to resolve these laws, I hope the Court realizes that as the School Board is making that argument, that they must have time to get the courts to pass on the laws that were passed two years ago. The Legislature is now passing a dozen laws or so a day, and I will assume that in a short time they will be back asking for time to have those laws construed, and that, it would seem to me, would result in perpetual delay so far as this is concerned.

The other question that Mr. Butler could not answer and I cannot answer, but I can only answer from the newspapers, is that the three Negro children that did apply to the white schools were declined admission—that was in the newspapers—by Superintendent Blossom, and that he intended to maintain the policy of segregated schools come opening of this school term.

I do not know how to get it in the record. It is a mere newspaper statement, but the last thing I would like to call the Court's attention to, as I construe Mr. Butler's briefs, he seemed to be in complete agreement that the merits of this case have to be gone into. And I wish to restate our position on that particular point.

The balancing of these equities, it is not as easy, as stated. I realize the School Board has a difficult job, but there is no solution. There are just three things that were mentioned in the Court of Appeals' decision. One was that they broke locks off of the lockers, and instead of punishing the people that did it, they replaced the locks, and I hate to mention it in a court of law, but the record shows, and the Court of Appeals opinion shows that the white children, the 20 or 25, a very small group, started the practice of urinating on the radiators, and instead of putting the children out they put the radiators out, and it seems to me that there is no solution to this problem that is recognized as a difficult problem, with the only possible solution, to put the Negro kids out of school.

I do not submit that that is the only solution. The record in this case will bear that out. And so it seems to me that whether or not this Court goes into the merits, certainly these Negro kids and the others that are involved in the class action are entitled to the most affirmative relief possible out of this Court before school opens, even if it is a consideration of the petition of certiorari.

THE CHIEF JUSTICE: Thank you.

BRIEF FOR RESPONDENTS

[*Some citations and footnotes have been omitted for ease of reading. Other omissions are noted in the text with ellipses or an ornament for longer omissions.*]

—

Preliminary Statement

Briefs for petitioners [*the Little Rock, Arkansas, school board and superintendent*] and respondents [*the Black students*] being filed simultaneously we have not seen the "Statement of the Case" in petitioners' brief. We assume that such statement will be accurate and adequate. In any event, the Opinion of the Court of Appeals adequately sets forth the facts. We, however, call this

Court's attention to one paragraph of the Opinion of the Court of Appeals which states as follows:

It is not the province of this Court in this proceeding to advise the Board as to the means of implementing integration in the Little Rock Schools. We are directly concerned only with the legality of the order under review. We do observe, however, that at no time did the Board seek injunctive relief against those who opposed by unlawful acts the lawful integration plan, which action apparently proved successful in the Clinton, Tennessee and Hoxie, Arkansas situations.... The evidence also affords some basis for belief that if more rigid and strict disciplinary methods had been adopted and pursued in dealing with those comparatively few students who were ring leaders in the trouble making, much of the turmoil and strife within Central High School would have been eliminated.

Questions Presented
The questions presented by the Petition for Certiorari are:

(1) Whether a court of equity may postpone the enforcement of the respondents' constitutional rights if the continued enforcement thereof will result in an intolerable situation and great disruption of the educational process to the detriment of the public interest, the schools, and the students including the respondents.

(2) Whether a school district has a duty and obligation, by invoking extraordinary legal processes and otherwise, to quell violence, disorder and organized resistance to desegregation.

Summary of Argument
Neither overt public resistance, nor the possibility of it, constitutes sufficient cause to nullify the orders of the federal court directing petitioners to proceed with their desegregation plan. This Court and other courts have consistently held that the preservation of public peace may not be accomplished by interference with rights created by the Federal Constitution.

Applying this familiar rule, this Court held in the School Segregation Cases, that delay could not be predicated on opposition to desegregation.

The sustension of this principle is all the more imperative where, as here, the forces at work to frustrate the Constitution and the authority of the federal courts were deliberately set in motion by the Governor of a state whose school system is under mandate to achieve conformity with the Constitution. Here one state agency, the School Board, seeks to be relieved of its constitutional obligation by pleading the force majeure brought to bear by another facet of state power. To solve this problem by further delaying the constitutional rights of respondents is unthinkable.

II

Hardship to petitioners is no excuse for abrogating the Rule of Law, but even if it were, petitioners here cannot validly claim it.

Petitioners had at their disposal and still have available to them a legal remedy to prevent interference with the performance of their constitutional duties.

There is no ground for a presumption that the authorities charged with the duty of enforcing the law will refuse or be unable to perform this duty. In fact, the federal government stands ready to perform this duty.

Even if it be claimed that tension will result which will disturb the educational process, this is preferable to the complete breakdown of education which will result from teaching children that courts of law will bow to violence.

Argument

The decision of the Court of Appeals [for the Eighth Circuit] setting aside Judge Lemley's two and one-half years suspension of desegregation was correct and should be sustained. Indeed, the decision is so eminently sound, so clearly in harmony with decisions of this Court and other federal courts, that the questions presented by the Petition for Certiorari could hardly even be characterized as substantial, were it not for two factors:

First, the legal controversy over the obligation of the Little Rock School Board to proceed with the desegregation of Central High School, and other schools it manages, pursuant to the original, and judicially approved, schedule has now become a national test of the vitality of the principles enunciated in *Brown v. Board of Education.*

Second, the principal ground urged for overruling the Court of Appeals' decision is, in essence, that unless petitioners' obligation to proceed with desegregation of the Little Rock schools is suspended, ruffians with or without support from state officials will resume their attempts forcibly to block the execution of valid federal court orders. Acquiescence in any such argument would subvert our entire constitutional framework.

In short, this case involves not only vindication of the constitutional rights declared in *Brown*, but indeed the very survival of the Rule of Law. This case affords this Court the opportunity to restate in unmistakable terms both the urgency of proceeding with desegregation and the supremacy of all constitutional rights over bigots—big and small.

I

Overt public resistance including mob protests is not sufficient cause to nullify federal court orders requiring gradual desegregation of public schools.

The Petition for Certiorari herein filed seeks a reversal of the decision of the Court of Appeals for the Eighth Circuit complaining:

The Circuit Court of Appeals for the Eighth Circuit agreed with the findings of the District Court that the evidence is appalling but that great additional expense, disruption of normal educational procedures, tension and nervous collapse of the school personnel, turmoil, bedlam, and chaos, are not a legal basis for suspension of the plan since this would be an accession to the demands of insurrectionists.

The Court of Appeals defined the issue in the case as: "whether overt public resistance, including mob protest, constitutes sufficient cause to nullify an order of the federal court directing the Board to proceed with its integration plan." There has never been a suggestion that the rule is other than as stated in *Buchanan v. Warley*, 245 U.S. 60,

> It is urged that this proposed segregation will promote the public peace by preventing race conflicts. Desirable as this is, and important as is the preservation of the public peace, this aim cannot be accomplished by laws or ordinances which deny rights created or protected by the Federal Constitution.

This principle has been reiterated in connection with housing in the City of Birmingham which faced threats of bombing because Negroes had purchased in a zone forbidden to their race, *City of Birmingham v. Monk*, 185 F. 2d 859 (5th Cir. 1950), cert. denied 341 U.S. 940; in reversing an order of the United States District Court for the Eastern District of Arkansas which dismissed a writ of habeas corpus submitted by petitioners who had been convicted of murder after a promise of "leading officials" to a lynch mob "that, if the mob would refrain...they would execute those found guilty in the form of law...," *Moore v. Dempsey,* 261 U.S. 86 (1923), 88–89; in holding a governor forbidden to close a factory beset by rioters during a strike, *Strutwear Knitting Co. v. Olson,* 13 F. Supp. 384 (D. Minn. 1936); in rejecting a claim of the government that an American citizen of Japanese ancestry should have been confined because "community hostility towards the evacuees...has not disappeared," *Ex parte Endo,* 323 U.S. 283, 297; and in holding, that notwithstanding a national military emergency, the constitutional rights of steel producers could not be abridged by presidential seizure. *Youngstown Sheet & Tube Co. v. Sawyer,* 343 U.S. 579.

The imperviousness of the Rule of Law to arguments of this sort is, after all, the underlying foundation of equal justice under law. For if criminal defendants, home owners, manufacturers, and others can be routed from their lawful rights by a transient emergency, then we have returned to a state prior to civil society, when there was the Hobbesian state of "a war of all men against all men."

This Court reaffirmed this premise of lawful government in *Brown v. Board of Education,* 349 U.S. 294, 300:

> ... it should go without saying that the vitality of these constitutional principles cannot be allowed to yield simply because of disagreement with them.

The federal judiciary (with the exception of Judge Lemley whom the Court of Appeals reversed herein) has uniformly followed this rule....*

Therefore, the court below acted in consonance with all lawful precedent and the best traditions of constitutional government when it said:

> The issue plainly comes down to the question of whether overt public resistance, including mob protest, constitutes sufficient cause to nullify an order of the federal court directing the Board to proceed with its integration plan. We say the time has not yet come in these United States when an order of a Federal Court must be whittled away, watered down, or shamefully withdrawn in the face of violent and unlawful acts of individual citizens in opposition thereto.

*A like rule was long ago recognized at English common law. ...

II

Any suspension of petitioners' original plan of gradual desegregation would subvert rather than preserve the fundamental objective of public education.

Throughout, petitioners' argument is that education at Central High School has been seriously impaired by lawless acts and the only solution is to revert to segregated education as terms for peace with the lawless elements. This plea is predicated on the argument that unless this is done the total educational system at Central High School will be seriously impaired or destroyed.

In the first *Brown* opinion this Court, however, made the following declaration as to the position of education in our modern day life, 347 U.S. 483, 493:

> Today, education is perhaps the most important function of state and local governments. Compulsory school attendance laws and the great expenditures for education both demonstrate our recognition of the importance of education to our democratic society. It is required in the performance of our most basic public responsibilities, even service in the armed forces. It is the very foundation of good citizenship. Today it is a principal instrument in awakening the child to cultural values, in preparing him for later professional training, and in helping him to adjust normally to his environment.

Applying these principles to this case the Solicitor General effectively disposed of the School Board's contention in his argument before the Court on August 28:

> But when you talk about a deterioration of the educational process in this school, it seems to me that one of the things that all educators, certainly teachers, would recognize, is that part of the educational process is the attitude and conduct of the teachers, the personnel of the school and the children themselves, and part of their responsibility is to get across to these teachers and for the teachers to get across to the children and those that are in the educational process, the responsibility to enforce the laws; that we do live in a country where we seek to maintain law and order for the benefit of all the people, that the Constitution and each of the rights that every

citizen has under it, is precious to every one of us, not just the rights that I like and want for me, or that you like and want for you, but all of them for every man and woman.

And that if you teach these children in Little Rock or any other place in the country that as soon as you get some force and violence, the courts of law in this country are going to bow to it, they have no power to deal with it, they will give way to it, will change everything to accommodate that, I think that you destroy the whole educational process then and there. Transcript of Argument, Aug. 28, 1958, p. 107.

This Court recognized as much in *West Virginia State Board of Education v. Barnette*, 319 U.S. 624, in which Justice Jackson wrote, at p. 637:

The Fourteenth Amendment, as now applied to the States, protects the citizen against the State itself and all of its creatures—Boards of Education not excepted. These have, of course, important, delicate, and highly discretionary functions, but none that they may not perform within the limits of the Bill of Rights. That they are educating the young for citizenship is reason for scrupulous protection of Constitutional freedoms of the individual, if we are not to strangle the free mind at its source and teach youth to discount important principles of our government as mere platitudes.

Indeed, the Supreme Court of Arkansas has embraced the same principle in a case in which it upheld the right of a school board to expel a student who had disobeyed school regulations. While the board was upheld in its enforcement of the particular regulation (concerning the wearing of cosmetics) as reasonable, the language of the court may properly be quoted here: "It will be remembered also that respect for constituted authority, and obedience thereto, is an essential lesson to qualify one for the duties of citizenship, and that the schoolroom is an appropriate place to teach that lesson." *Pugsley v. Sellneyer*, 158 Ark. 247, 253, 250 S. W. 538, 539 (1923).

Petitioners have a duty to accord respondents the equal protection of law and should have sought injunctions against the unlawful interferences with their performance thereof.

Petitioners, in the second of the questions presented in their application for a writ of certiorari, ask whether they have "a duty and obligation, by invoking extraordinary legal processes and otherwise, to quell violence, disorder and organized resistance to desegregation."

Assuming the question is properly before the Court, it cannot be gainsaid that petitioners could have invoked "extraordinary legal processes" to restrain interference with the performance of their duty to accord respondents non-segregated public education.

In addition, petitioners certainly had and have a duty to preserve discipline and order in and about the premises. And where, as here, third parties seek to upset discipline and order in attempts "to deprive (among others) Negro pupils of their constitutional rights, then it would seem proper for [the School Board], so closely related as they were to victims in this case, to bring a restraining suit. They were officials of a great state and an omission by them would, in effect, be a deprivation of rights under the color of law." *Hoxie School Dist. No. 46 of Lawrence Co., Ark. v. Brewer*, 137 F. Supp. 364, 367 (E. D. Ark. 1956), affirmed *Brewer v. Hoxie School Dist. No. 46*, 238 F. 2d 91, 100 (8th Cir., 1956).

Conclusion

To prevent further disorder, petitioners have urged this Court to approve Judge Lemley's order, the purpose of which is not to repress the lawless violence, but to give the sanction of law to the motives which inspired it. The answer can only be: not "while this Court sits."

Wherefore, respondents respectfully urge this Court to affirm the judgment of the Court of Appeals, reinstate the prior order of Judge Davies [*which approved the school board's initial plan to desegregate the schools*] and order its mandate to issue forthwith.

3. The Right Time, the Right Man: 1960–1971

The 1960s were a heady time for Marshall. He and his wife, Cissy, at last had the children he had longed for. In 1960, he took a break from his work with the NAACP to help draft a constitution for Kenya independence at the invitation of Tom Mboya, a leader in the movement for Kenyan independence from Great Britain.[1] In 1961, President John F. Kennedy appointed Marshall to the U.S. Court of Appeals for the Second Circuit, which met in New York.

The richly deserved recognition Marshall received when nominated to the Second Circuit appellate court in 1961 was tempered; to be confirmed by the U.S. Senate, he still had to overcome opposition from his detractors. Southern senators delayed the process, criticizing statements and jokes Marshall had made as displaying racism against whites. Meanwhile Marshall refused President Kennedy's request to call on segregationist senator James Eastland of Mississippi, chair of the Senate Judiciary Committee, and "genuflect." On September 11, 1962, Marshall was finally confirmed by a vote of 54–16 in the full Senate, with the southern Democratic senators voting against him.[2] His subsequent record at the Second Circuit was impeccable: not a single one of the cases for which Judge Marshall wrote the majority opinion was reversed by the Supreme Court on appeal. The Manhattan building in which the Second Circuit meets was renamed the Thurgood Marshall U.S. Courthouse in 2003.

The appellate court judgeship was Marshall's first job offering real financial security. Nevertheless, in 1965, called on by President Lyndon B. Johnson, Marshall consented to give up that lifetime judicial appointment to become the solicitor general—the nation's top lawyer. Marshall served as the first Black solicitor general in U.S. history. In this role, he won fourteen of the nineteen cases that he argued for the government before the U.S. Supreme Court, including the "Mississippi Burning" appeal; excerpts of that argument are included in this chapter. He called his work as solicitor general "the best job I've ever had."[3]

Two years later, LBJ appointed Marshall to the Supreme Court, where he had successfully argued so many important cases. Announcing the nomination, Johnson said, "I believe it is the right thing to do, the right time to do it, the right man, and the right place."[4] Like his earlier nomination to the Second Circuit, Marshall's 1967 nomination to the Supreme Court drew opposition. Senator Eastland of Mississippi asked Marshall directly: "Are you prejudiced against white people in the South?" Before the full Senate could vote, Eastland, along with Senators Sam Ervin and Strom Thurmond of North Carolina and Senator John McLellan of Arkansas, carried out a mini-filibuster to further criticize the nominee. The Senate, however, went on to confirm the first Black associate justice of the Supreme Court by a lopsided vote of 69–11 on August 30, 1967.[5]

The Court that Marshall joined was a liberal one. Beginning in 1953, the Supreme Court of Chief Justice Earl Warren had delivered not just the landmark *Brown v. Board of Education* decision, but also rulings requiring indigent criminal defendants to be allowed court-appointed counsel free of charge (*Gideon v. Wainwright*, 1963) and mandating police to inform suspects of their right to counsel and their right not to incriminate themselves before being interrogated (*Miranda v. Arizona*, 1966). The Warren Court also decided *Griswold v. Connecticut* (1965), ruling that a right of privacy implicit in the Constitution protected the liberty of married couples to purchase and use contraceptives; *Griswold* was the foundation for the 1973 decision protecting women's abortion rights, *Roe v. Wade*.

During his first few years on the Court, Marshall wrote majority opinions in several important cases, including *Amalgamated Food Employees v. Logan Valley Plaza*, 391 U.S. 308 (1968), which protected peaceful union picketing by nonemployees in a private shopping mall under the First Amendment, and *Benton v. Maryland*, 395 U.S. 784 (1969), which gave criminal defendants protection against double jeopardy in state courts. His majority opinion in *Stanley v. Georgia*, 394 U.S. 557 (1969), is included here. In the well-known "Pentagon Papers" case, in which the *New York Times* published secret Defense

Department documents about the progress of the Vietnam War, Marshall wrote a concurrence that is also included in this chapter.

By the end of the 1960s, Chief Justice Earl Warren retired. In his place, President Richard Nixon appointed the conservative Warren Burger, who would serve as chief justice until 1986.

United States v. Cecil Price, et al., 383 U.S. 787 (1966)

United States v. Price is also sometimes called the "Mississippi Burning" case, after the 1988 film *Mississippi Burning*, which was loosely based on the trial of the case. In June 1964, during Freedom Summer, three young civil rights workers—James Chaney, Andrew Goodman, and Michael Schwerner—were murdered in Philadelphia, Mississippi, where they had been jailed following a traffic stop and then released to a lynch mob.

Murder is generally a state crime and not a federal crime. But the state of Mississippi failed to charge anyone with the murders. The federal government stepped in and charged eighteen men, including the chief deputy sheriff of the county, Cecil R. Price, and fellow members of the Ku Klux Klan, with conspiracy under federal Reconstruction-era statutes. The Mississippi district court dismissed one indictment in part and the other indictment in its entirety, and the United States appealed.[6]

The first of the federal government's two indictments charged the men with conspiracy to violate and substantive violations of United States Code Title 18 section 242, which made it a misdemeanor willfully and under color of law to subject any person to the deprivation of any rights secured or protected by the Constitution. The Mississippi court sustained the conspiracy count for all the defendants but sustained the substantive count only against the three official defendants; the substantive count was dismissed as to the fifteen private defendants on the ground that no state action was involved.

The second indictment charged the eighteen men under United States Code Title 18 section 241, which made it a felony to conspire to interfere with a citizen in the free exercise of enjoyment of any right secured or protected by the Constitution or laws of the United States. The Mississippi court dismissed this indictment against all the defendants on the ground that section 241 did not include rights protected by the Fourteenth Amendment.

Marshall as solicitor general argued the case before the Supreme Court on behalf of the United States. The Supreme Court overturned the Mississippi court's rulings, holding that private persons as well as government officials could act "under color of law" for purposes of section 242 and that section 241 did cover Fourteenth Amendment rights.

The trial then proceeded, with an all-white jury. Seven of the men were convicted, including the chief deputy sheriff and a local Ku Klux Klan leader. The Federal Bureau of Investigation noted that "one major conspirator, Edgar Ray Killen, went free after a lone juror couldn't bring herself to convict a Baptist preacher." None served more than six years for their crimes. On June 21, 2005, the forty-first anniversary of the murders, Killen was finally convicted of manslaughter for his part in killing the three young men.[7]

The events call to mind Marshall's words in 1944:

> All of the statutes, both federal and state, which protect the individual rights of Americans are important to Negroes as well as other citizens. Many of these provisions, however, are of peculiar significance to Negroes because of the fact that in many instances these statutes are the only protection to which Negroes can look for redress. It should also be pointed out that many officials of both state and federal governments are reluctant to protect the rights of Negroes. It is often difficult to enforce our rights when they are perfectly clear. It is practically impossible to secure enforcement of any of our rights if there is any doubt whatsoever as to whether or not a particular statute applies to the particular state of facts.
>
> As to law enforcement itself, the rule as to most American citizens is that if there is any way possible to prosecute individuals who have willfully interfered with the rights of other individuals such prosecution is attempted. However, when the complaining party is a Negro, the rule is usually to look for any possible grounds for not prosecuting. It is therefore imperative that Negroes be thoroughly familiar with the rights guaranteed them by law in order that they may be in a position to insist that all of their fundamental rights as American citizens be protected.[8]

In the early days of Republican Ronald Reagan's 1980 campaign for the U.S. presidency, against liberal southerner and incumbent Democratic president Jimmy Carter, Reagan chose to travel to Philadelphia, Mississippi, to give a speech in which he said, "I believe in state's rights....I believe we've distorted the balance of our government today by giving powers that were never intended in the Constitution to that federal establishment." Some observers have viewed this move as a "dog whistle" intended to be heard by voters wary of the legal and social changes worked by the civil rights movement in the South in the space of less than two decades.[9]

United States vs. Cecil Price, et al., Appellees
Appeals from the United States District Court for the Southern District
of Mississippi

ORAL ARGUMENT

Proceedings, November 9, 1965

EARL WARREN:...Mr. Solicitor General.

THURGOOD MARSHALL: Mr. Chief Justice, and may it please the Court.

These cases, as all the world knows, arise out of a brutal incident during the summer of last year in the town of Philadelphia in the County of Neshoba in the State of Mississippi which culminated in the murder of three young civil rights workers: Michael Schwerner, James Chaney and Andrew Goodman.

These federal prosecutions are brought under Sections 241 and 242 of the Criminal Code in which some 18 persons—three of them public officials, are accused of having joined together to deprive the three young victims of their civil rights.

The actual facts cannot be detailed because no trial has taken place and the evidence has not been deduced.

All of that's before the Court today is a bad charge consisting of two indictments. The only question here is whether those indictments, assuming the facts alleged can be proved, state offenses against the United States.

The overall charge is that the 18 defendants conceived and executed a criminal plan directed against the three victims.

It is alleged that the three of the defendants, namely the sheriff of Neshoba County, his deputy, and a local policeman used their official powers to release the victims who were in state custody, turned them over to a lynch mob, which one of the officers had shielded by his presence with the view that they'd be summarily punished without benefit of trial and has alleged in defiance of the Due Process Clause of the Fourteenth Amendment.

The indictment in number 59 is only one charge, [and] charges a conspiracy that was charged to be in violation of Section 241. The whole of that indictment was dismissed as to all defendants.

The first count of indictment in number 60 is the same conspiracy as charged as a violation of the general conspiracy statute, Section 371 of the Criminal Code, as a conspiracy to commit the offense defined in Section 242.

That charge was sustained by the District Court as to all defendants.

The three other counts of indictment—the indictment in number 60 charged all the defendants with substantive violations of Section 242 by executing the criminal plan with respect to each of the three victims.

—

The Government, on both indictments, is [making] the allegation of a conspiracy to willfully subject the victims to the deprivation of "their right, privileges, and immunities secured and protected by the Fourteenth Amendment to the Constitution of the United States, not be summarily punished without due process of law by persons under color of the State of Mississippi."

. . . There is no question that violation to the Fourteenth Amendment alleged, there's no question about it as I see it.

And indeed, the District Judge so found by sustaining the charge of conspiring to violate 242 which he held as to all of them.

The only question in this case I repeat is whether 241 encompasses Fourteenth Amendment rights at all, and that is not a Constitutional question.

At least since the *Screws* case, there can be no doubt whatever about the power of Congress to make it a federal crime for state officers to deprive citizens of their constitutional rights even if the conduct also violates state law; the sole question is one of statutory construction.

Did Congress mean to reach violations of the Fourteenth Amendment in Section 241?

On the face of the statute, it is difficult to see how any such question ever arose.

Indeed, Section 241 punishes interference with exercise or enjoyment of "any right or privilege secured by the Constitution or laws of the United States."

And certainly, the Fourteenth Amendment is a part of that Constitution, and certainly, the Fourteenth Amendment confers "rights or privileges."

Why would Fourteenth and Fifteenth Amendment rights not be embraced by the provision?

One could imagine that doubt had the statute been written before the Fourteenth and Fifteenth Amendments became part of the Constitution, but that's not the fact.

On the contrary, Section 241 was enacted in May of 1870 less than two years after the ratification of the Fourteenth Amendment and only two months after the ratification of the Fifteenth Amendment.

As a matter of fact, Section 241 is a part of the first civil rights law passed after the adoption of the amendments.

The natural assumption is that the new statute was peculiarly concerned with protecting these new constitutional rights.

Is there anything in the conditions of the time that suggested Congress was focusing on rights derived from the relationship of the citizen to the national Government rather than the relationship between the citizen and the state Government?

The time, I repeat, was 1870.

This was a reconstruction measure.

The problem then was of assuring equal rights and protection to the new freedmen who were the victims of racial antagonism; against that background, it seems obvious, that when Congress spoke of constitutional rights had meant to include those derived from the Due Process and Equal Protection Clause of the Fourteenth Amendment, and the right to freedom from racial discrimination, exercise of the right to vote guaranteed in the Fifteenth Amendment.

. . . The Fourteenth Amendment makes no attempt to enumerate the rights it [is] designed to protect; it speaks in general terms, and those are as comprehensive as possible.

Its language is prohibitory, but every prohibition implies the existence of rights and immunities—prominent among which is the immunity from inequality of legal protection either for life, liberty, or property.

Any state action that denies this immunity to a colored man is in conflict with the Constitution.

And in *Ex parte Virginia*, Mr. Justice Strong continued, "One great purpose of these amendments was to raise the colored race," he is speaking of the Thirteenth and Fourteenth Amendments, "was to raise the colored race from that condition of inferiority and servitude in which most of them had previously stood, into perfect equality of civil rights with all other persons within the jurisdiction of the States.

"They were intended to be what they really are—limitations to the power of the States and enlargements of the power of Congress."

I repeat, enlargement of the power of Congress.

"They are to some extent declaratory of rights, and though [they are] in form prohibitions, they imply immunities such as may be protected by congressional legislation."

Now that was the real problem.

... The indictment alleges here more than ordinary murder for personal reasons by a group of individuals, some of whom happened to be state officers.

One, it is alleged that the state law enforcement officers were acting under code of their office.

And two, it is further alleged that they used their official powers to release state prisoners, turn them over to a lynch mob which was shielded by the presence of another state officer, so that they could be summarily punished without benefit of trial.

—

Despite the language and the historical context, which point unmistakably to a congressional intent to protect the Fourteenth and Fifteenth Amendment rights, as rights and privileges, is there some evidence buried in the legislative history that shows a different focus?

There is nothing of the kind.

What became Section 241 was an amendment to the Enforcement Act of 1870 proposed by Senator Pool of North Carolina; he proposed the amendment.

And he made his purpose very clear, and there's nothing in the congressional record to the contrary, on this particular amendment.

The only relevant speech is his own, when he first explained the object of his amendment, we have reproduced the entire speech of Senator Pool in an Appendix to our brief on the merits and it bails out what I have said.

The Senator begins by making it clear that this is a reconstruction measure.

It is entering a plan of new phase and reconstruction that is, he says, "To enforce by appropriate legislation, those great principles upon which the reconstruction policy of Congress was based."

He then tells us more particularly, the conditions he is concerned about. And he says,

"The equality, which by the Thirteenth, Fourteenth, and Fifteenth Amendments has been attempted to be secured for the colored men, has not only subjected them to the operation of the prejudices which had theretofore existed, but it has raised against them still stronger prejudices and stronger feelings in order to fight down the equality by which it is claimed they are to control the legislation of that section of the country.

"They were turned loose among those people, weak, ignorant, and poor.

"Those among the white citizens there who have sought to maintain the rights which you have thrown upon that class of people, have to endure every species of proscription, of opposition, and of vituperation in order to carry out the policy of Congress, in order to lift up and to uphold the rights which you have conferred upon that class.

"It is for that reason not only necessary for the freedmen, but it is necessary for the white people of that section that there should be stringent and effective legislation on the part of Congress in regard to these measures of reconstruction."

Though most of his speech is directed to the Fifteenth Amendment, Senator Pool plainly puts Fourteenth Amendment rights and particularly those derived from the Due Process and Equal Protection Clauses on the same footing.

——

And again later, when he is speaking of the need to...reach unofficial conspiracies, the Senator explicitly refers to the Fourteenth Amendment.

And he says, "But sir, individuals may prevent the exercise of the right of suffrage, individuals may prevent the enjoyment of other rights which are conferred upon the citizen by the Fourteenth Amendment, as well as trespass upon the right conferred by the Fifteenth."

This last statement from Senator Pool's speech, emphasizing his concern with unofficial action, particularly conspiracies like the plan which he explicitly mentions, suggests the only argument against reading Section 241 to reach Fourteenth and Fifteenth Amendment rights.

——

But the true explanation is that neither Senator Pool nor the Congress of 1870 saw any problem with this.

They thought rightly or wrongly, and we believe they were right..., that they could constitutionally reach private conspiracies hostile to the Fourteenth and Fifteenth Amendments.

You cannot read Senator Pool's speech without reaching that conclusion.

—

Stanley v. Georgia, 394 U.S. 557 (1969)

Police with a warrant to search Robert E. Stanley's home for evidence of his alleged bookmaking activities instead found three films that the police concluded were obscene. Stanley was charged with knowingly possessing obscene material in violation of Georgia law and was convicted by a jury. On appeal, he argued that the First Amendment protected his right to private possession of obscene material.

A unanimous Supreme Court agreed. Justice Marshall wrote the Court's opinion, overturning *Roth v. United States*, 354 U.S. 476 (1957), which had redefined the test for determining what constitutes obscene material not protected by the First Amendment. The ruling invalidated all state laws prohibiting the private possession of materials judged to be obscene. Marshall quoted Justice Louis D. Brandeis's dissent in the 1928 case *Olmstead v. United States*: "The makers of our Constitution undertook to secure conditions favorable to the pursuit of happiness.... They conferred, as against the Government, the right to be let alone—the most comprehensive of rights and the right most valued by civilized man."

In the Supreme Court of the United States
Robert Eli Stanley, Appellant, vs. State of Georgia

Decided April 7, 1969
Appeal from the Supreme Court of Georgia

OPINION OF THE COURT

[Some citations and footnotes have been omitted for easier reading. Other omissions are noted in the text with ellipses or an ornament for longer omissions.]

MR. JUSTICE MARSHALL delivered the opinion of the Court.

An investigation of appellant's alleged bookmaking activities led to the issuance of a search warrant for appellant's home. Under authority of this warrant, federal and state agents secured entrance. They found very little evidence of bookmaking activity, but, while looking through a desk drawer in an upstairs bedroom, one of the federal agents, accompanied by a state officer, found three reels of eight-millimeter film. Using a projector and screen found in an upstairs living room, they viewed the films. The state officer concluded that they were obscene and seized them. Since a further examination of the bedroom indicated that appellant occupied it, he was charged with possession of obscene matter and placed under arrest. He was later indicted for "knowingly having possession of...obscene matter" in violation of Georgia law. * Appellant was tried before a jury and convicted. The Supreme Court of Georgia affirmed. *Stanley v. State*, 224 Ga. 259, 161 S.E.2d 309 (1968)....

Appellant raises several challenges to the validity of his conviction.† We find it necessary to consider only one. Appellant argues here, and argued below, that the Georgia obscenity statute, insofar as it punishes mere private possession of obscene matter, violates the First Amendment, as made applicable to the States by the Fourteenth Amendment. For reasons set forth below, we agree that the mere private possession of obscene matter cannot constitutionally be made a crime.

The court below saw no valid constitutional objection to the Georgia statute, even though it extends further than the typical statute forbidding commercial sales of obscene material. It held that "it is not essential to an indictment charging one with possession of obscene matter that it be alleged that such possession was 'with intent to sell, expose or circulate the same.'" *Stanley v. State*, at 261. The State and appellant both agree that the question here before us is whether "a statute imposing criminal sanctions upon the mere [knowing] possession of obscene matter" is constitutional. In this context, Georgia

---

*"Any person who shall knowingly bring or cause to be brought into this State for sale or exhibition, or who shall knowingly sell or offer to sell, or who shall knowingly lend or give away or offer to lend or give away, or who shall knowingly have possession of, or who shall knowingly exhibit or transmit to another, any obscene matter, or who shall knowingly advertise for sale by any form of notice, printed, written, or verbal, any obscene matter, or who shall knowingly manufacture, draw, duplicate or print any obscene matter with intent to sell, expose or circulate the same, shall, if such person has knowledge or reasonably should know of the obscene nature of such matter, be guilty of a felony, and, upon conviction thereof, shall be punished by confinement in the penitentiary for not less than one year nor more than five years: Provided, however, in the event the jury so recommends, such person may be punished as for a misdemeanor. As used herein, a matter is obscene if, considered as a whole, applying contemporary community standards, its predominant appeal is to prurient interest, i.e., a shameful or morbid interest in nudity, sex or excretion." Ga. Code Ann. § 26-6301 (Supp. 1968).

†Appellant does not argue that the films are not obscene. For the purpose of this opinion, we assume that they are obscene under any of the tests advanced by members of this Court....

concedes that the present case appears to be one of "first impression...on this exact point," but contends that, since "obscenity is not within the area of constitutionally protected speech or press," *Roth v. United States*, 354 U.S. 476, 354 U.S. 485 (1957), the States are free, subject to the limits of other provisions of the Constitution, to deal with it any way deemed necessary, just as they may deal with possession of other things thought to be detrimental to the welfare of their citizens. If the State can protect the body of a citizen, may it not, argues Georgia, protect his mind?

It is true that *Roth* does declare, seemingly without qualification, that obscenity is not protected by the First Amendment. That statement has been repeated in various forms in subsequent cases....However, neither *Roth* nor any subsequent decision of this Court dealt with the precise problem involved in the present case. Roth was convicted of mailing obscene circulars and advertising, and an obscene book, in violation of a federal obscenity statute. The defendant in a companion case, *Alberts v. California*, 354 U.S. 476 (1957), was convicted of "lewdly keeping for sale obscene and indecent books, and [of] writing, composing and publishing an obscene advertisement of them...." None of the statements cited by the Court in *Roth* for the proposition that "this Court has always assumed that obscenity is not protected by the freedoms of speech and press" were made in the context of a statute punishing mere private possession of obscene material; the cases cited deal for the most part with use of the mails to distribute objectionable material or with some form of public distribution or dissemination. Moreover, none of this Court's decisions subsequent to *Roth* involved prosecution for private possession of obscene materials. Those cases dealt with the power of the State and Federal Governments to prohibit or regulate certain public actions taken or intended to be taken with respect to obscene matter. Indeed, with one exception, we have been unable to discover any case in which the issue in the present case has been fully considered.

In this context, we do not believe that this case can be decided simply by citing *Roth*. *Roth* and its progeny certainly do mean that the First and Fourteenth Amendments recognize a valid governmental interest in dealing with the problem of obscenity. But the assertion of that interest cannot, in every context, be insulated from all constitutional protections. Neither *Roth* nor any other decision of this Court reaches that far. As the Court said in *Roth* itself, ceaseless vigilance is the watchword to prevent...erosion [of First Amendment rights] by Congress or by the States. The door barring federal and state intrusion into this area cannot be left ajar; it must be kept tightly closed and opened only the slightest crack necessary to prevent encroachment upon more important interests. 354 U.S. at 488.

Roth and the cases following it discerned such an "important interest" in the regulation of commercial distribution of obscene material. That holding cannot foreclose an examination of the constitutional implications of a statute forbidding mere private possession of such material.

It is now well established that the Constitution protects the right to receive information and ideas. "This freedom [of speech and press]...necessarily protects the right to receive...." *Martin v. City of Struthers*, 319 U.S. 141, 143 (1943).... This right to receive information and ideas, regardless of their social worth,... is fundamental to our free society. Moreover, in the context of this case—a prosecution for mere possession of printed or filmed matter in the privacy of a person's own home—that right takes on an added dimension. For also fundamental is the right to be free, except in very limited circumstances, from unwanted governmental intrusions into one's privacy.

The makers of our Constitution undertook to secure conditions favorable to the pursuit of happiness. They recognized the significance of man's spiritual nature, of his feelings and of his intellect. They knew that only a part of the pain, pleasure and satisfactions of life are to be found in material things. They sought to protect Americans in their beliefs, their thoughts, their emotions and their sensations. They conferred, as against the Government, the right to be let alone—the most comprehensive of rights and the right most valued by civilized man. *Olmstead v. United States*, 277 U.S. 438, 277 U.S. 478 (1928) (Brandeis, J., dissenting).

These are the rights that appellant is asserting in the case before us. He is asserting the right to read or observe what he pleases—the right to satisfy his intellectual and emotional needs in the privacy of his own home. He is asserting the right to be free from state inquiry into the contents of his library. Georgia contends that appellant does not have these rights, that there are certain types of materials that the individual may not read or even possess. Georgia justifies this assertion by arguing that the films in the present case are obscene. But we think that mere categorization of these films as "obscene" is insufficient justification for such a drastic invasion of personal liberties guaranteed by the First and Fourteenth Amendments. Whatever may be the justifications for other statutes regulating obscenity, we do not think they reach into the privacy of one's own home. If the First Amendment means anything, it means that a State has no business telling a man, sitting alone in his own house, what books he may read or what films he may watch. Our whole constitutional heritage rebels at the thought of giving government the power to control men's minds.

And yet, in the face of these traditional notions of individual liberty, Georgia asserts the right to protect the individual's mind from the effects of obscenity. We are not certain that this argument amounts to anything more than the assertion that the State has the right to control the moral content of a person's thoughts.* To some, this may be a noble purpose, but it is wholly inconsistent with the philosophy of the First Amendment. As the Court said in *Kingsley International Pictures Corp. v. Regents*, 360 U.S. 684, 688–689 (1959), "this argument misconceives what it is that the Constitution protects. Its guarantee is not confined to the expression of ideas that are conventional or shared by a majority.... And, in the realm of ideas, it protects expression which is eloquent no less than that which is unconvincing."

... Nor is it relevant that obscene materials in general, or the particular films before the Court, are arguably devoid of any ideological content. The line between the transmission of ideas and mere entertainment is much too elusive for this Court to draw, if indeed such a line can be drawn at all.... Whatever

---

*"Communities believe, and act on the belief, that obscenity is immoral, is wrong for the individual, and has no place in a decent society. They believe, too, that adults as well as children are corruptible in morals and character, and that obscenity is a source of corruption that should be eliminated. Obscenity is not suppressed primarily for the protection of others. Much of it is suppressed for the purity of the community and for the salvation and welfare of the 'consumer.' Obscenity, at bottom, is not crime. Obscenity is sin." Henkin, Morals and the Constitution: The Sin of Obscenity, 63 Columbia Law Review 391, 395 (1963).

the power of the state to control public dissemination of ideas inimical to the public morality, it cannot constitutionally premise legislation on the desirability of controlling a person's private thoughts.

Perhaps recognizing this, Georgia asserts that exposure to obscene materials may lead to deviant sexual behavior or crimes of sexual violence. There appears to be little empirical basis for that assertion. But, more important, if the State is only concerned about printed or filmed materials inducing antisocial conduct, we believe that, in the context of private consumption of ideas and information we should adhere to the view that "among free men, the deterrents ordinarily to be applied to prevent crime are education and punishment for violations of the law. . . ." *Whitney v. California*, 274 U.S. 357, 274 U.S. 378 (1927) (Brandeis, J., concurring). . . . Given the present state of knowledge, the State may no more prohibit mere possession of obscene matter on the ground that it may lead to antisocial conduct than it may prohibit possession of chemistry books on the ground that they may lead to the manufacture of homemade spirits.

It is true that, in *Roth*, this Court rejected the necessity of proving that exposure to obscene material would create a clear and present danger of antisocial conduct or would probably induce its recipients to such conduct. But that case dealt with public distribution of obscene materials and such distribution is subject to different objections. For example, there is always the danger that obscene material might fall into the hands of children, . . . or that it might intrude upon the sensibilities or privacy of the general public.*. . . No such dangers are present in this case.

Finally, we are faced with the argument that prohibition of possession of obscene materials is a necessary incident to statutory schemes prohibiting distribution. That argument is based on alleged difficulties of proving an intent to distribute or in producing evidence of actual distribution. We are not convinced that such difficulties exist, but even if they did we do not think that they would justify infringement of the individual's right to read or observe what he pleases. Because that right is so fundamental to our scheme of individual liberty, its restriction may not be justified by the need to ease the administration of otherwise valid criminal laws. . . .

---

*The Model Penal Code provisions dealing with obscene materials are limited to cases of commercial dissemination. Model Penal Code § 251.4 (Prop. Official Draft 1962). . . .

We hold that the First and Fourteenth Amendments prohibit making mere private possession of obscene material a crime.* *Roth* and the cases following that decision are not impaired by today's holding. As we have said, the States retain broad power to regulate obscenity; that power simply does not extend to mere possession by the individual in the privacy of his own home. Accordingly, the judgment of the court below is reversed and the case is remanded for proceedings not inconsistent with this opinion.

It is so ordered.

---

* What we have said in no way infringes upon the power of the State or Federal Government to make possession of other items, such as narcotics, firearms, or stolen goods, a crime. Our holding in the present case turns upon the Georgia statute's infringement of fundamental liberties protected by the First and Fourteenth Amendments. No First Amendment rights are involved in most statutes making mere possession criminal.

Nor do we mean to express any opinion on statutes making criminal possession of other types of printed, filmed, or recorded materials. See, e.g., 18 U.S.C. § 793(d), which makes criminal the otherwise lawful possession of materials which "the possessor has reason to believe could be used to the injury of the United States or to the advantage of any foreign nation. . . ." In such cases, compelling reasons may exist for overriding the right of the individual to possess those materials.

New York Times Co. v. United States, 403 U.S. 713 (1971)

In 1971, Daniel Ellsberg, a U.S. military analyst, leaked to a *New York Times* reporter a top-secret study conducted by the Department of Defense about U.S. involvement in the Vietnam War. The newspaper published part of the leaked information in a front-page story on Sunday, June 13, 1971. President Richard Nixon ordered a halt to further publication of the secret documents, known as the "Pentagon Papers," on national security grounds.

The *New York Times* and the *Washington Post* challenged the president's order on the ground that the United States had not met the heavy burden required for prior restraint of expression to be valid under the First Amendment to the Constitution. The New York federal district court refused the government's request for an injunction prohibiting the publication of the Pentagon Papers, but after the government appealed that decision, the U.S. Court of Appeals for the Second Circuit granted the injunction. Once the *Washington Post* also started publishing articles based on the Pentagon Papers, the federal district court in Washington, D.C., and the intermediate appellate court there, the Court of Appeals for the D.C. Circuit, both refused to grant the government's request for an injunction. To resolve this conflict between the circuit courts, the Supreme Court stepped in.[10]

In a per curiam opinion ("for the court," with no named author), the Supreme Court ruled that Nixon's order was barred by the First Amendment. Justice Marshall filed the concurrence included here to state separately his agreement with the Court's ruling.

Publication of the Pentagon Papers further eroded support among the American public for the Vietnam War, hastening the end of U.S. involvement.

In the Supreme Court of the United States
New York Times Company, Petitioner, vs. United States
United States, Petitioner, vs. The Washington Post Company, et al.

Decided June 30, 1971
Certiorari to the United States Court of Appeals for the Second Circuit

CONCURRENCE

[*Some citations and footnotes have been omitted for easier reading. Other omissions are noted in the text with ellipses or an ornament for longer omissions.*]

MR. JUSTICE MARSHALL, concurring.

The Government contends that the only issue in these cases is whether, in a suit by the United States, "the First Amendment bars a court from prohibiting a newspaper from publishing material whose disclosure would pose a 'grave and immediate danger to the security of the United States.'" With all due respect, I believe the ultimate issue in these cases is even more basic than the one posed by the Solicitor General. The issue is whether this Court or the Congress has the power to make law.

In these cases, there is no problem concerning the President's power to classify information as "secret" or "top secret." Congress has specifically recognized Presidential authority, which has been formally exercised in Exec. Order 10501 (1953), to classify documents and information.... Nor is there any issue here regarding the President's power as Chief Executive and Commander in Chief to protect national security by disciplining employees who disclose information and by taking precautions to prevent leaks.

The problem here is whether, in these particular cases, the Executive Branch has authority to invoke the equity jurisdiction of the courts to protect what it believes to be the national interest.... The Government argues that, in addition to the inherent power of any government to protect itself, the President's power to conduct foreign affairs and his position as Commander in Chief give him authority to impose censorship on the press to protect his ability to deal effectively with foreign nations and to conduct the military affairs of the country. Of course, it is beyond cavil that the President has broad powers by virtue of his primary responsibility for the conduct of our foreign affairs and his position as Commander in Chief.... And, in some situations, it may be that, under whatever inherent powers the Government may have, as well as the implicit authority derived from the President's mandate to conduct foreign affairs and to act as Commander in Chief, there is a basis for the invocation of the equity jurisdiction of this Court as an aid to prevent the publication of material damaging to "national security," however that term may be defined.

It would, however, be utterly inconsistent with the concept of separation of powers for this Court to use its power of contempt to prevent behavior that Congress has specifically declined to prohibit. There would be a similar damage to the basic concept of these co-equal branches of Government if, when the Executive Branch has adequate authority granted by Congress to protect "national security," it can choose, instead, to invoke the contempt power of a court to enjoin the threatened conduct. The Constitution provides that Congress shall make laws, the President execute laws, and courts interpret laws.... It did not provide for government by injunction in which the courts and the Executive Branch can "make law" without regard to the action of Congress. It may be more convenient for the Executive Branch if it need only convince a judge to prohibit conduct, rather than ask the Congress to pass a law, and it may be more convenient to enforce a contempt order than to seek a criminal conviction in a jury trial. Moreover, it may be considered politically wise to get a court to share the responsibility for arresting those who the Executive Branch has probable cause to believe are violating the law. But convenience and political considerations of the moment do not justify a basic departure from the principles of our system of government.

In these cases, we are not faced with a situation where Congress has failed to provide the Executive with broad power to protect the Nation from disclosure of damaging state secrets. Congress has, on several occasions, given extensive consideration to the problem of protecting the military and strategic secrets of the United States. This consideration has resulted in the enactment of statutes making it a crime to receive, disclose, communicate, withhold, and publish certain documents, photographs, instruments, appliances, and information. The bulk of these statutes is found in chapter 37 of U.S.C. Title 18, entitled Espionage and Censorship. In that chapter, Congress has provided penalties ranging from a $10,000 fine to death for violating the various statutes.

Thus, it would seem that in order for this Court to issue an injunction it would require a showing that such an injunction would enhance the already existing power of the Government to act.... It is a traditional axiom of equity that a court of equity will not do a useless thing, just as it is a traditional axiom that equity will not enjoin the commission of a crime.... Here, there has been no attempt to make such a showing. The Solicitor General does not even mention in his brief whether the Government considers that there is probable cause to believe a crime has been committed, or whether there is a conspiracy to commit future crimes.

If the Government had attempted to show that there was no effective remedy under traditional criminal law, it would have had to show that there is no arguably applicable statute. Of course, at this stage, this Court could not and cannot determine whether there has been a violation of a particular statute or decide the constitutionality of any statute. Whether a good faith prosecution could have been instituted under any statute could, however, be determined.

At least one of the many statutes in this area seems relevant to these cases. Congress has provided in 18 U.S.C. § 793(e) that whoever,

> having unauthorized possession of, access to, or control over any document, writing, code book, signal book...or note relating to the national defense, or information relating to the national defense which information the possessor has reason to believe could be used to the injury of the United States or to the advantage of any foreign nation, willfully communicates, delivers, transmits...the same to any person not entitled to receive it, or willfully retains the same and fails to deliver it to the officer or employee of the United States entitled to receive it...shall be fined not more than $10,000 or imprisoned not more than ten years, or both.

Congress has also made it a crime to conspire to commit any of the offenses listed in 18 U.S.C. § 793(e).

It is true that Judge Gurfein [*district court judge Murray Irwin Gurfein, who made the initial ruling allowing the Pentagon Papers' publication*] found that Congress had not made it a crime to publish the items and material specified in § 793(e). He found that the words "communicates, delivers, transmits ..." did not refer to publication of newspaper stories. And that view has some support in the legislative history, and conforms with the past practice of using the statute only to prosecute those charged with ordinary espionage.... Judge

Gurfein's view of the statute is not, however, the only plausible construction that could be given. See my Brother White's concurring opinion.

Even if it is determined that the Government could not in good faith bring criminal prosecutions against the *New York Times* and the *Washington Post*, it is clear that Congress has specifically rejected passing legislation that would have clearly given the President the power he seeks here and made the current activity of the newspapers unlawful. When Congress specifically declines to make conduct unlawful, it is not for this Court to redecide those issues—to overrule Congress....

On at least two occasions, Congress has refused to enact legislation that would have made the conduct engaged in here unlawful and given the President the power that he seeks in this case. In 1917, during the debate over the original Espionage Act, still the basic provisions of § 793, Congress rejected a proposal to give the President in time of war or threat of war authority to directly prohibit by proclamation the publication of information relating to national defense that might be useful to the enemy. The proposal provided that:

"During any national emergency resulting from a war to which the United States is a party, or from threat of such a war, the President may, by proclamation, declare the existence of such emergency and, by proclamation, prohibit the publishing or communicating of, or the attempting to publish or communicate any information relating to the national defense which, in his judgment, is of such character that it is or might be useful to the enemy. Whoever violates any such prohibition shall be punished by a fine of not more than $10,000 or by imprisonment for not more than 10 years, or both: Provided, That nothing in this section shall be construed to limit or restrict any discussion, comment, or criticism of the acts or policies of the Government or its representatives or the publication of the same." 55 Cong.Rec. 1763.

Congress rejected this proposal after war against Germany had been declared, even though many believed that there was a grave national emergency and that the threat of security leaks and espionage was serious. The Executive Branch has not gone to Congress and requested that the decision to provide such power be reconsidered. Instead, the Executive Branch comes to this Court and asks that it be granted the power Congress refused to give.

In 1957, the United States Commission on Government Security found that "airplane journals, scientific periodicals, and even the daily newspaper have featured articles containing information and other data which should have been deleted in whole or in part for security reasons."

In response to this problem, the Commission proposed that "Congress enact legislation making it a crime for any person willfully to disclose without proper authorization, for any purpose whatever, information classified 'secret' or 'top secret,' knowing, or having reasonable grounds to believe, such information to have been so classified." Report of Commission on Government Security 619–620 (1957). After substantial floor discussion on the proposal, it was rejected. If the proposal that Sen. Cotton championed on the floor had been enacted, the publication of the documents involved here would certainly have been a crime. Congress refused, however, to make it a crime. The Government is here asking this Court to remake that decision. This Court has no such power.

Either the Government has the power under statutory grant to use traditional criminal law to protect the country or, if there is no basis for arguing that Congress has made the activity a crime, it is plain that Congress has specifically refused to grant the authority the Government seeks from this Court. In either case, this Court does not have authority to grant the requested relief. It is not for this Court to fling itself into every breach perceived by some Government official, nor is it for this Court to take on itself the burden of enacting law, especially a law that Congress has refused to pass.

I believe that the judgment of the United States Court of Appeals for the District of Columbia Circuit should be affirmed and the judgment of the United States Court of Appeals for the Second Circuit should be reversed insofar as it remands the case for further hearings.

4. "The Humanity of Our Fellow Beings": 1971–1977

Justice Thurgood Marshall was in every case opposed to the death penalty and voted against imposing capital punishment throughout his term on the Court. He had defended many young Black men charged with capital crimes in his years as an attorney with the NAACP, which has long had a capital punishment project. Historically used in "legal lynchings"—when officials would arrange hasty trials and executions of prisoners, usually Black men, to appease lynch mobs—capital punishment continues to be disproportionately imposed on Americans who are Black, Indigenous, or other people of color.[1]

Marshall had been shaken in 1934 when he intervened on behalf of a man who police were initially convinced was guilty of a brutal assault; charged with a capital crime, Marshall's client turned out to be completely innocent, the wrong man entirely.[2] The execution of a client in an early capital case that Marshall lost in Maryland in 1935 also haunted him.[3]

Marshall's experience had taught him how the police sometimes operated, how confessions were sometimes obtained, how witnesses could be motivated by racism. A wrong decision was not correctable. "The difficulty is," he said, "if you make a mistake, you put a man in jail wrongfully, you can let him out. But death is rather permanent. And what do you do if you execute a man illegally, unconstitutionally, and find that out later? What do you say? 'Oops'?"[4]

Marshall's abhorrence of the death penalty led him to file a concurrence in *Furman v. Georgia*, a case in which the Court invalidated Georgia's death penalty statute. In hopes that the case stood for the proposition that the death penalty is always cruel and unusual punishment barred by the Eighth Amendment to the Constitution, Marshall wrote,

In striking down capital punishment, this Court does not malign our system of government. On the contrary, it pays homage to it. Only in a free society could right triumph in difficult times, and could civilization record its magnificent advancement. In recognizing the humanity of our fellow beings, we pay ourselves the highest tribute. We achieve "a major milestone in the long road up from barbarism."

The ruling in the case succeeded in halting executions in the United States. But the moratorium was temporary. Most justices on the Court did not believe that the death penalty was always unconstitutional; they just objected to certain features of the Georgia statute that they struck down in *Furman*. Marshall was devastated when only four years later, in *Gregg v. Georgia*, a majority of the Court approved Georgia's death penalty statute as it had been amended since *Furman*.

The decision was announced on Marshall's birthday, a Friday. After reading out his dissent, the justice went home deeply troubled; he suffered a heart attack that weekend.[5] Executions resumed in 1977, when Gary Gilmore was fatally shot by a firing squad in the state of Utah.

Furman v. Georgia, 408 U.S. 238 (1972)

The three men in these cases had been sentenced to death after being convicted of capital crimes. One man was sentenced in Georgia for murder, another in Georgia for rape, and a third in Texas for rape. The sole question on appeal was whether imposing the death penalty in these cases constituted cruel and unusual punishment in violation of the Eighth Amendment.

In a close vote of 5–4, the Supreme Court held that carrying out the death penalty in these cases would be unconstitutional, but the justices in the majority could not agree on their reasons. The ruling was announced in a brief per curiam ("by the court") opinion that did not state the rationale behind the decision. In the concurrence included here, Justice Marshall set out a history of the ban on cruel and unusual punishments and the reasons behind his belief that imposition of the death penalty is always unconstitutional.

In the Supreme Court of the United States

William Henry Furman, Petitioner, vs. State of Georgia; Lucious Jackson, Petitioner, vs. State of Georgia; Elmer Branch, Petitioner, vs. State of Georgia

Decided June 29, 1972

CONCURRENCE

[*Some citations and footnotes have been omitted for easier reading. Other omissions are noted in the text with ellipses or an ornament for longer omissions.*]

MR. JUSTICE MARSHALL, concurring.

These three cases present the question whether the death penalty is a cruel and unusual punishment prohibited by the Eighth Amendment to the United States Constitution.

In No. 69-5003, Furman was convicted of murder for shooting the father of five children when he discovered that Furman had broken into his home early one morning. Nos. 69-5030 and 69-5031 involve state convictions for forcible rape. Jackson was found guilty of rape during the course of a robbery in the victim's home. The rape was accomplished as he held the pointed ends of scissors at the victim's throat. Branch also was convicted of a rape committed in the victim's home. No weapon was utilized, but physical force and threats of physical force were employed.

The criminal acts with which we are confronted are ugly, vicious, reprehensible acts. Their sheer brutality cannot and should not be minimized. But we are not called upon to condone the penalized conduct; we are asked only to examine the penalty imposed on each of the petitioners and to determine whether or not it violates the Eighth Amendment. The question then is not whether we condone rape or murder, for surely we do not; it is whether capital punishment is "a punishment no longer consistent with our own self-respect" and, therefore, violative of the Eighth Amendment.

The elasticity of the constitutional provision under consideration presents dangers of too little or too much self-restraint. Hence, we must proceed with caution to answer the question presented. By first examining the historical derivation of the Eighth Amendment and the construction given it in the past by this Court, and then exploring the history and attributes of capital punishment in this country, we can answer the question presented with objectivity and a proper measure of self-restraint.

Candor is critical to such an inquiry. All relevant material must be marshaled and sorted and forthrightly examined. We must not only be precise as to the standards of judgment that we are utilizing, but exacting in examining the relevant material in light of those standards.

Candor compels me to confess that I am not oblivious to the fact that this is truly a matter of life and death. Not only does it involve the lives of these three petitioners, but those of the almost 600 other condemned men and women in this country currently awaiting execution. While this fact cannot affect our ultimate decision, it necessitates that the decision be free from any possibility of error.

I.

The Eighth Amendment's ban against cruel and unusual punishments derives from English law. In 1583, John Whitgift, Archbishop of Canterbury, turned the High Commission into a permanent ecclesiastical court, and the Commission began to use torture to extract confessions from persons suspected of various offenses. Sir Robert Beale protested that cruel and barbarous torture violated Magna Carta, but his protests were made in vain.*

Cruel punishments were not confined to those accused of crimes, but were notoriously applied with even greater relish to those who were convicted. Blackstone described in ghastly detail the myriad of inhumane forms of punishment imposed on persons found guilty of any of a large number of offenses. Death, of course, was the usual result.†

The treason trials of 1685—the "Bloody Assizes"—which followed an abortive rebellion by the Duke of Monmouth, marked the culmination of the parade of horrors, and most historians believe that it was this event that finally spurred the adoption of the English Bill of Rights containing the progenitor of our prohibition against cruel and unusual punishments. The conduct of Lord Chief Justice Jeffreys at those trials has been described as an "insane lust for cruelty" which was "stimulated by orders from the King" (James II). The assizes received wide publicity from Puritan pamphleteers, and doubtless had some influence on the adoption of a cruel and unusual punishments clause. But the legislative history of the English Bill of Rights of 1689 indicates that the assizes may not have been as critical to the adoption of the clause as is widely thought. After William and Mary of Orange crossed the channel to invade England, James II fled. Parliament was summoned into session, and a committee was appointed to draft general statements containing "such things as are absolutely necessary to be considered for the better securing of our religion, laws and liberties." An initial draft of the Bill of Rights prohibited "illegal" punishments, but a later draft referred to the infliction by James II of "illegal and cruel" punishments, and declared "cruel and unusual" punishments to be prohibited. The use of the word "unusual" in the final draft appears to be inadvertent.

---

*. . . Beale's views were conveyed from England to America, and were first written into American law by the Reverend Nathaniel Ward, who wrote the Body of Liberties for the Massachusetts Bay Colony. Clause 46 of that work read: "For bodilie punishments we allow amongst us none that are inhumane, Barbarous or cruel." 1 B. Schwartz, The Bill of Rights: A Documentary History 71, 77 (1971).

†Not content with capital punishment as a means of retribution for crimes, the English also provided for attainder ("dead in law") as the immediate and inseparable concomitant of the death sentence. The consequences of attainder were forfeiture of real and personal estates and corruption of blood. An attainted person could not inherit land or other hereditaments, nor retain those he possessed, nor transmit them by descent to any heir. Descents were also obstructed whenever posterity derived a title through one who was attainted. 4 W. Blackstone, Commentaries, 380–381.

This legislative history has led at least one legal historian to conclude "that the cruel and unusual punishments clause of the Bill of Rights of 1689 was, first, an objection to the imposition of punishments that were unauthorized by statute and outside the jurisdiction of the sentencing court, and second, a reiteration of the English policy against disproportionate penalties,"* and not primarily a reaction to the torture of the High Commission, harsh sentences, or the assizes.

Whether the English Bill of Rights prohibition against cruel and unusual punishments is properly read as a response to excessive or illegal punishments, as a reaction to barbaric and objectionable modes of punishment, or as both, there is no doubt whatever that, in borrowing the language and in including it in the Eighth Amendment, our Founding Fathers intended to outlaw torture and other cruel punishments.†

The precise language used in the Eighth Amendment first appeared in America on June 12, 1776, in Virginia's "Declaration of Rights," § 9 of which read: "That excessive bail ought not to be required, nor excessive fines imposed, nor cruel and unusual punishments inflicted." This language was drawn verbatim from the English Bill of Rights of 1689. Other States adopted similar clauses, and there is evidence in the debates of the various state conventions that were called upon to ratify the Constitution of great concern for the omission of any prohibition against torture or other cruel punishments.

---

*In reaching this conclusion, Professor Granucci ["Nor Cruel and Unusual Punishments Inflicted": The Original Meaning, 57 Calif.L.Rev. 839, 848 (1969)] relies primarily on the trial of Titus Oates as the impetus behind the adoption of the clause. Oates was a minister of the Church of England who proclaimed the existence of a plot to assassinate King Charles II. He was tried for perjury, convicted, and sentenced to a fine of 2,000 marks, life imprisonment, whippings, pillorying four times a year, and defrocking. Oates petitioned both the House of Commons and the House of Lords for release from judgment. The House of Lords rejected his petition, but a minority of its members concluded that the King's Bench had no jurisdiction to compel defrocking, and that the other punishments were barbarous, inhumane, unchristian, and unauthorized by law. The House of Commons agreed with the dissenting Lords.

The author also relies on the dictionary definition of "cruel," which meant "severe" or "hard" in the 17th century, to support his conclusion.

†Most historians reach this conclusion by reading the history of the Cruel and Unusual Punishments Clause as indicating that it was a reaction to inhumane punishments. Professor Granucci reaches the same conclusion by finding that the draftsmen of the Constitution misread the British history and erroneously relied on Blackstone.... It is clear, however, that, prior to the adoption of the Amendment, there was some feeling that a safeguard against cruelty was needed, and that this feeling had support in past practices....

The Virginia Convention offers some clues as to what the Founding Fathers had in mind in prohibiting cruel and unusual punishments. At one point, George Mason advocated the adoption of a Bill of Rights, and Patrick Henry concurred, stating:

> By this Constitution, some of the best barriers of human rights are thrown away. Is there not an additional reason to have a bill of rights?.... Congress, from their general powers, may fully go into business of human legislation. They may legislate, in criminal cases, from treason to the lowest offence—petty larceny. They may define crimes and prescribe punishments. In the definition of crimes, I trust they will be directed by what wise representatives ought to be governed by. But when we come to punishments, no latitude ought to be left, nor dependence put on the virtue of representatives. What says our bill of rights—"that excessive bail ought not to be required, nor excessive fines imposed, nor cruel and unusual punishments inflicted." Are you not, therefore, now calling on those gentlemen who are to compose Congress, to prescribe trials and define punishments without this control? Will they find sentiments there similar to this bill of rights? You let them loose; you do more—you depart from the genius of your country....
>
> In this business of legislation, your members of Congress will loose the restriction of not imposing excessive fines, demanding excessive bail, and inflicting cruel and unusual punishments. These are prohibited by your declaration of rights. What has distinguished our ancestors—that they would not admit of tortures, or cruel and barbarous punishment. But Congress may introduce the practice of the civil law, in preference to that of the common law. They may introduce the practice of France, Spain, and Germany—of torturing, to extort a confession of the crime. They will say that they might as well draw examples from those countries as from Great Britain, and they will tell you that there is such a necessity of strengthening the arm of government, that they must have a criminal equity, and extort confession by torture, in order to punish with still more relentless severity. We are then lost and undone.

Henry's statement indicates that he wished to insure that "relentless severity" would be prohibited by the Constitution. Other expressions with respect to the proposed Eighth Amendment by Members of the First Congress indicate that they shared Henry's view of the need for and purpose of the Cruel and Unusual Punishments Clause.

Thus, the history of the clause clearly establishes that it was intended to prohibit cruel punishments. We must now turn to the case law to discover the manner in which courts have given meaning to the term "cruel."

II.

This Court did not squarely face the task of interpreting the cruel and unusual punishments language for the first time until *Wilkerson v. Utah*, 9 U.S. 130 (1879), although the language received a cursory examination in several prior cases.... In Wilkerson, the Court unanimously upheld a sentence of public execution by shooting imposed pursuant to a conviction for premeditated murder. In his opinion for the Court, Mr. Justice Clifford wrote:

> Difficulty would attend the effort to define with exactness the extent of the constitutional provision which provides that cruel and unusual punishments shall not be inflicted; but it is safe to affirm that punishments of torture,...and all others in the same line of unnecessary cruelty, are forbidden by that amendment to the Constitution. 99 U.S. 135–136.

Thus, the Court found that unnecessary cruelty was no more permissible than torture. To determine whether the punishment under attack was unnecessarily cruel, the Court examined the history of the Utah Territory and the then-current writings on capital punishment, and compared this Nation's practices with those of other countries. It is apparent that the Court felt it could not dispose of the question simply by referring to traditional practices; instead, it felt bound to examine developing thought.

Eleven years passed before the Court again faced a challenge to a specific punishment under the Eighth Amendment. In the case of *In re Kemmler*, 136 U.S. 436 (1890), Chief Justice Fuller wrote an opinion for a unanimous Court upholding electrocution as a permissible mode of punishment. While the Court ostensibly held that the Eighth Amendment did not apply to the States, it is very apparent that the nature of the punishment involved was examined under the Due Process Clause of the Fourteenth Amendment. The Court held that the punishment was not objectionable. Today, *Kemmler* stands primarily for the proposition that a punishment is not necessarily unconstitutional simply because it is unusual, so long as the legislature has a humane purpose in selecting it.*

Two years later, in *O'Neil v. Vermont*, 144 U.S. 323 (1892), the Court reaffirmed that the Eighth Amendment was not applicable to the States. O'Neil was found guilty on 307 counts of selling liquor in violation of Vermont law. A fine of $6,140 ($20 for each offense) and the costs of prosecution ($497.96) were imposed. O'Neil was committed to prison until the fine and the costs were paid, and the court provided that, if they were not paid before a specified date, O'Neil was to be confined in the house of corrections for 19,914 days (approximately 54 years) at hard labor. Three Justices—Field, Harlan, and Brewer—dissented. They maintained not only that the Cruel and Unusual Punishments Clause was applicable to the States, but that, in O'Neil's case, it had been violated. Mr. Justice Field wrote:

> That designation [cruel and unusual], it is true, is usually applied to punishments which inflict torture, such as the rack, the thumbscrew, the iron boot, the stretching of limbs and the like, which are attended with acute pain and suffering.... The inhibition is directed not only against punishments of the character mentioned, but against all punishments which, by their excessive length or severity, are greatly disproportioned to the offences charged. The whole inhibition is against that which is excessive.... 144 U.S. 339–340.

In *Howard v. Fleming*, 191 U.S. 126 (1903), the Court, in essence, followed the approach advocated by the dissenters in *O'Neil*. In rejecting the claim that 10-year sentences for conspiracy to defraud were cruel and unusual, the Court (per Mr. Justice Brewer) considered the nature of the crime, the purpose of the law, and the length of the sentence imposed.

The Court used the same approach seven years later in the landmark case of *Weems v. United States*, 217 U.S. 349 (1910). Weems, an officer of the

---

*The New York Court of Appeals had recognized the unusual nature of the execution, but attributed it to a legislative desire to minimize the pain of persons executed.

Bureau of Coast Guard and Transportation of the United States Government of the Philippine Islands, was convicted of falsifying a "public and official document." He was sentenced to 15 years' incarceration at hard labor with chains on his ankles, to an unusual loss of his civil rights, and to perpetual surveillance. Called upon to determine whether this was a cruel and unusual punishment, the Court found that it was.* The Court emphasized that the Constitution was not an "ephemeral" enactment, or one "designed to meet passing occasions." Recognizing that "time works changes, and brings into existence new conditions and purposes," the Court commented that, "in the application of a constitution... our contemplation cannot be only of what has been, but of what may be."

In striking down the penalty imposed on Weems, the Court examined the punishment in relation to the offense, compared the punishment to those inflicted for other crimes and to those imposed in other jurisdictions, and concluded that the punishment was excessive. Justices White and Holmes dissented, and argued that the cruel and unusual prohibition was meant to prohibit only those things that were objectionable at the time the Constitution was adopted.

Weems is a landmark case because it represents the first time that the Court invalidated a penalty prescribed by a legislature for a particular offense. The Court made it plain beyond any reasonable doubt that excessive punishments were as objectionable as those that were inherently cruel. Thus, it is apparent that the dissenters' position in *O'Neil* had become the opinion of the Court in *Weems*.

Weems was followed by two cases that added little to our knowledge of the scope of the cruel and unusual language, *Badders v. United States*, 240 U.S. 391 (1916), and *United States ex rel. Milwaukee Social Democratic Publishing Co. v. Burleson*, 255 U.S. 407 (1921). Then came another landmark case, *Louisiana ex rel. Francis v. Resweber*, 329 U.S. 459 (1947).

Francis had been convicted of murder and sentenced to be electrocuted. The first time the current passed through him, there was a mechanical failure, and he did not die. Thereafter, Francis sought to prevent a second electrocution on the ground that it would be a cruel and unusual punishment. Eight

---

*The prohibition against cruel and unusual punishments relevant to *Weems* was that found in the Philippine Bill of Rights. It was, however, borrowed from the Eighth Amendment to the United States Constitution, and had the same meaning....

members of the Court assumed the applicability of the Eighth Amendment to the States. The Court was virtually unanimous in agreeing that "the traditional humanity of modern Anglo-American law forbids the infliction of unnecessary pain," but split 5–4 on whether Francis would, under the circumstances, be forced to undergo any excessive pain. Five members of the Court treated the case like *In re Kemmler*, and held that the legislature adopted electrocution for a humane purpose, and that its will should not be thwarted because, in its desire to reduce pain and suffering in most cases, it may have inadvertently increased suffering in one particular case.

The four dissenters felt that the case should be remanded for further facts.

As in *Weems*, the Court was concerned with excessive punishments. *Resweber* is perhaps most significant because the analysis of cruel and unusual punishment questions first advocated by the dissenters in *O'Neil* was at last firmly entrenched in the minds of an entire Court.

Trop v. Dulles, 356 U.S. 86 (1958), marked the next major cruel and unusual punishment case in this Court. Trop, a native-born American, was declared to have lost his citizenship by reason of a conviction by court-martial for wartime desertion. Writing for himself and Justices Black, Douglas, and Whittaker, Chief Justice Warren concluded that loss of citizenship amounted to a cruel and unusual punishment that violated the Eighth Amendment.

Emphasizing the flexibility inherent in the words "cruel and unusual," the Chief Justice wrote that "the Amendment must draw its meaning from the evolving standards of decency that mark the progress of a maturing society." His approach to the problem was that utilized by the Court in *Weems*: he scrutinized the severity of the penalty in relation to the offense, examined the practices of other civilized nations of the world, and concluded that involuntary statelessness was an excessive and, therefore, an unconstitutional punishment. Justice Frankfurter, dissenting, urged that expatriation was not punishment, and that even if it were, it was not excessive. While he criticized the conclusion arrived at by the Chief Justice, his approach to the Eighth Amendment question was identical.

Whereas, in *Trop*, a majority of the Court failed to agree on whether loss of citizenship was a cruel and unusual punishment, four years later, a majority did agree in *Robinson v. California*, 370 U.S. 660 (1962), that a sentence of 90 days' imprisonment for violation of a California statute making it a crime to "be addicted to the use of narcotics" was cruel and unusual. Mr. Justice

Stewart, writing the opinion of the Court, reiterated what the Court had said in *Weems* and what Chief Justice Warren wrote in *Trop*—that the cruel and unusual punishment clause was not a static concept, but one that must be continually reexamined "in the light of contemporary human knowledge." The fact that the penalty under attack was only 90 days evidences the Court's willingness to carefully examine the possible excessiveness of punishment in a given case even where what is involved is a penalty that is familiar and widely accepted.

We distinguished *Robinson* in *Powell v. Texas*, 392 U.S. 514 (1968), where we sustained a conviction for drunkenness in a public place and a fine of $20. Four Justices dissented on the ground that *Robinson* was controlling. The analysis in both cases was the same; only the conclusion as to whether or not the punishment was excessive differed. *Powell* marked the last time prior to today's decision that the Court has had occasion to construe the meaning of the term "cruel and unusual" punishment.

Several principles emerge from these prior cases and serve as a beacon to an enlightened decision in the instant cases.

III.

Perhaps the most important principle in analyzing "cruel and unusual" punishment questions is one that is reiterated again and again in the prior opinions of the Court: i.e., the cruel and unusual language "must draw its meaning from the evolving standards of decency that mark the progress of a maturing society." Thus, a penalty that was permissible at one time in our Nation's history is not necessarily permissible today.

The fact, therefore, that the Court, or individual Justices, may have in the past expressed an opinion that the death penalty is constitutional is not now binding on us. A fair reading of *Wilkerson v. Utah*, *In re Kemmler*, and *Louisiana ex rel. Francis v. Resweber* would certainly indicate an acceptance *sub silentio* ["in silence"] of capital punishment as constitutionally permissible. Several Justices have also expressed their individual opinions that the death penalty is constitutional. Yet, some of these same Justices and others have at times expressed concern over capital punishment.*

*See, e.g., *Louisiana ex rel. Francis v. Resweber*, 329 U.S. at 329 U.S. 474 (Burton, J., dissenting); *Trop v. Dulles*, at 356 U.S. 99 (Warren, C.J.); *Rudolph v. Alabama*, 375 U.S. 889 (1963) (Goldberg, J., dissenting from denial of certiorari); F. Frankfurter, *Of Law and Men* 81 (1956). *(cont'd)*

There is no holding directly in point, and the very nature of the Eighth Amendment would dictate that, unless a very recent decision existed, stare decisis would bow to changing values, and the question of the constitutionality of capital punishment at a given moment in history would remain open.

Faced with an open question, we must establish our standards for decision. The decisions discussed in the previous section imply that a punishment may be deemed cruel and unusual for any one of four distinct reasons.

First, there are certain punishments that inherently involve so much physical pain and suffering that civilized people cannot tolerate them—e.g., use of the rack, the thumbscrew, or other modes of torture.... Regardless of public sentiment with respect to imposition of one of these punishments in a particular case or at any one moment in history, the Constitution prohibits it. These are punishments that have been barred since the adoption of the Bill of Rights.

Second, there are punishments that are unusual, signifying that they were previously unknown as penalties for a given offense.... If these punishments are intended to serve a humane purpose, they may be constitutionally permissible.... Prior decisions leave open the question of just how much the word "unusual" adds to the word "cruel." I have previously indicated that use of the word "unusual" in the English Bill of Rights of 1689 was inadvertent, and there is nothing in the history of the Eighth Amendment to give flesh to its intended meaning. In light of the meager history that does exist, one would suppose that an innovative punishment would probably be constitutional if no more cruel than that

---

There is no violation of the principle of stare decisis in a decision that capital punishment now violates the Eighth Amendment. The last case that implied that capital punishment was still permissible was *Trop v. Dulles*, at 356 U.S. 99. Not only was the implication purely dictum, but it was also made in the context of a flexible analysis that recognized that, as public opinion changed, the validity of the penalty would have to be reexamined. *Trop v. Dulles* is nearly 15 years old now, and 15 years change many minds about many things. Mr. Justice Powell suggests, however, that our recent decisions in *Witherspoon v. Illinois*, 391 U.S. 510 (1968), and *McGautha v. California*, 402 U.S. 183 (1971), imply that capital punishment is constitutionally permissible because, if they are viewed any other way, they amount to little more than an academic exercise. In my view, this distorts the "rule of four" by which this Court decides which cases and which issues it will consider, and in what order.... There are many reasons why four members of the Court might have wanted to consider the issues presented in those cases before considering the difficult question that is now before us. While I do not intend to catalogue these reasons here, it should suffice to note that I do not believe that those decisions can, in any way, fairly be used to support any inference whatever that the instant cases have already been disposed of *sub silentio* ["in silence"].

punishment which it superseded. We need not decide this question here, however, for capital punishment is certainly not a recent phenomenon.

Third, a penalty may be cruel and unusual because it is excessive and serves no valid legislative purpose.... The decisions previously discussed are replete with assertions that one of the primary functions of the cruel and unusual punishments clause is to prevent excessive or unnecessary penalties...; these punishments are unconstitutional even though popular sentiment may favor them. Both the Chief Justice and Mr. Justice Powell seek to ignore or to minimize this aspect of the Court's prior decisions. But, since Mr. Justice Field first suggested that "the whole inhibition [of the prohibition against cruel and unusual punishments] is against that which is excessive," *O'Neil v. Vermont,* 144 U.S. at 144 U.S. 340, this Court has steadfastly maintained that a penalty is unconstitutional whenever it is unnecessarily harsh or cruel. This is what the Founders of this country intended; this is what their fellow citizens believed the Eighth Amendment provided; and this was the basis for our decision in *Robinson v. California,* for the plurality opinion by Mr. Chief Justice Warren in *Trop v. Dulles,* and for the Court's decision in *Weems v. United States....* It should also be noted that the "cruel and unusual" language of the Eighth Amendment immediately follows language that prohibits excessive bail and excessive fines. The entire thrust of the Eighth Amendment is, in short, against "that which is excessive."

Fourth, where a punishment is not excessive and serves a valid legislative purpose, it still may be invalid if popular sentiment abhors it. For example, if the evidence clearly demonstrated that capital punishment served valid legislative purposes, such punishment would, nevertheless, be unconstitutional if citizens found it to be morally unacceptable. A general abhorrence on the part of the public would, in effect, equate a modern punishment with those barred since the adoption of the Eighth Amendment. There are no prior cases in this Court striking down a penalty on this ground, but the very notion of changing values requires that we recognize its existence.

It is immediately obvious, then, that since capital punishment is not a recent phenomenon, if it violates the Constitution, it does so because it is excessive or unnecessary, or because it is abhorrent to currently existing moral values.

We must proceed to the history of capital punishment in the United States.

IV

Capital punishment has been used to penalize various forms of conduct by members of society since the beginnings of civilization. Its precise origins are difficult to perceive, but there is some evidence that its roots lie in violent retaliation by members of a tribe or group, or by the tribe or group itself, against persons committing hostile acts toward group members. Thus, infliction of death as a penalty for objectionable conduct appears to have its beginnings in private vengeance.

As individuals gradually ceded their personal prerogatives to a sovereign power, the sovereign accepted the authority to punish wrongdoing as part of its "divine right" to rule. Individual vengeance gave way to the vengeance of the state, and capital punishment became a public function. Capital punishment worked its way into the laws of various countries,* and was inflicted in a variety of macabre and horrific ways.

It was during the reign of Henry II (1154–1189) that English law first recognized that crime was more than a personal affair between the victim and the perpetrator.†

—

By 1500, English law recognized eight major capital crimes: treason, petty treason (killing of husband by his wife), murder, larceny, robbery, burglary, rape, and arson. Tudor and Stuart kings added many more crimes to the list of those punishable by death, and, by 1688, there were nearly 50. George II (1727–1760) added nearly 36 more, and George III (1760–1820) increased the number by 60.

By shortly after 1800, capital offenses numbered more than 200, and not only included crimes against person and property, but even some against the public peace. While England may, in retrospect, look particularly brutal, Blackstone points out that England was fairly civilized when compared to the rest of Europe.

Capital punishment was not as common a penalty in the American Colonies. "The Capitall Lawes of New England," dating from 1636, were

*The Code of Hammurabi is one of the first known laws to have recognized the concept of an "eye for an eye," and consequently to have accepted death as an appropriate punishment for homicide. E. Block, *And May God Have Mercy* ... 13–14 (1962).

†... Prior to this time, the laws of Alfred (871–901) provided that one who willfully slayed another should die, at least under certain circumstances.... But punishment was apparently left largely to private enforcement.

drawn by the Massachusetts Bay Colony, and are the first written expression of capital offenses known to exist in this country. These laws make the following crimes capital offenses: idolatry, witchcraft, blasphemy, murder, assault in sudden anger, sodomy, buggery, adultery, statutory rape, rape, manstealing, perjury in a capital trial, and rebellion. Each crime is accompanied by a reference to the Old Testament to indicate its source. It is not known with any certainty exactly when, or even if, these laws were enacted as drafted; and, if so, just how vigorously these laws were enforced. We do know that the other Colonies had a variety of laws that spanned the spectrum of severity.

By the 18th century, the list of crimes became much less theocratic and much more secular. In the average colony, there were 12 capital crimes. This was far fewer than existed in England, and part of the reason was that there was a scarcity of labor in the Colonies. Still, there were many executions, because "with county jails inadequate and insecure, the criminal population seemed best controlled by death, mutilation, and fines."

Even in the 17th century, there was some opposition to capital punishment in some of the colonies. In his "Great Act" of 1682, William Penn prescribed death only for premeditated murder and treason, although his reform was not long-lived.*

In 1776 the Philadelphia Society for Relieving Distressed Prisoners organized, and it was followed 11 years later by the Philadelphia Society for Alleviating the Miseries of Public Prisons. These groups pressured for reform of all penal laws, including capital offenses. Dr. Benjamin Rush soon drafted America's first reasoned argument against capital punishment, entitled *An Enquiry into the Effects of Public Punishments upon Criminals and upon Society.* In 1793, William Bradford, the Attorney General of Pennsylvania and later Attorney General of the United States, conducted "An Enquiry How Far the Punishment of Death is Necessary in Pennsylvania." He concluded that it was doubtful whether capital punishment was at all necessary, and that, until

---

*For an unknown reason, Pennsylvania adopted the harsher penal code of England upon William Penn's death in 1718. There was no evidence, however, of an increase in crime between 1682 and 1718.... In 1794, Pennsylvania eliminated capital punishment except for "murder of the first degree," which included all "willful, deliberate or premeditated" killings. The death penalty was mandatory for this crime. Pa. Stat. 1794, c. 1777. Virginia followed Pennsylvania's lead and enacted similar legislation. Other States followed suit.

more information could be obtained, it should be immediately eliminated for all offenses except high treason and murder.*

The "Enquiries" of Rush and Bradford and the Pennsylvania movement toward abolition of the death penalty had little immediate impact on the practices of other States. But in the early 1800's, Governors George and DeWitt Clinton and Daniel Tompkins unsuccessfully urged the New York Legislature to modify or end capital punishment. During this same period, Edward Livingston, an American lawyer who later became Secretary of State and Minister to France under President Andrew Jackson, was appointed by the Louisiana Legislature to draft a new penal code. At the center of his proposal was "the total abolition of capital punishment." His *Introductory Report to the System of Penal Law Prepared for the State of Louisiana* contained a systematic rebuttal of all arguments favoring capital punishment. Drafted in 1824, it was not published until 1833. This work was a tremendous impetus to the abolition movement for the next half century.

During the 1830's, there was a rising tide of sentiment against capital punishment. In 1834, Pennsylvania abolished public executions, and, two years later, *The Report on Capital Punishment Made to the Maine Legislature* was published. It led to a law that prohibited the executive from issuing a warrant for execution within one year after a criminal was sentenced by the courts. The totally discretionary character of the law was at odds with almost all prior practices. The "Maine Law" resulted in little enforcement of the death penalty, which was not surprising, since the legislature's idea in passing the law was that the affirmative burden placed on the governor to issue a warrant one full year or more after a trial would be an effective deterrent to exercise of his power. The law spread throughout New England, and led to Michigan's being the first State to abolish capital punishment in 1846.†

Anti-capital-punishment feeling grew in the 1840's as the literature of the period pointed out the agony of the condemned man and expressed the philosophy that repentance atoned for the worst crimes, and that true repentance derived not from fear, but from harmony with nature.

*His advice was in large measure followed. . . .

†. . . Capital punishment was abolished for all crimes but treason. The law was enacted in 1846, but did not go into effect until 1847.

By 1850, societies for abolition existed in Massachusetts, New York, Pennsylvania, Tennessee, Ohio, Alabama, Louisiana, Indiana, and Iowa. New York, Massachusetts, and Pennsylvania constantly had abolition bills before their legislatures. In 1852, Rhode Island followed in the footsteps of Michigan and partially abolished capital punishment. Wisconsin totally abolished the death penalty the following year. Those States that did not abolish the death penalty greatly reduced its scope, and "few states outside the South had more than one or two...capital offenses" in addition to treason and murder.

But the Civil War halted much of the abolition furor. One historian [Davis] has said that, "after the Civil War, men's finer sensibilities, which had once been revolted by the execution of a fellow being, seemed hardened and blunted." Some of the attention previously given to abolition was diverted to prison reform. An abolitionist movement still existed, however. Maine abolished the death penalty in 1876, restored it in 1883, and abolished it again in 1887; Iowa abolished capital punishment from 1872–1878; Colorado began an erratic period of de facto abolition and revival in 1872; and Kansas also abolished it de facto in 1872, and by law in 1907.*

One great success of the abolitionist movement in the period from 1830–1900 was almost complete elimination of mandatory capital punishment. Before the legislatures formally gave juries discretion to refrain from imposing the death penalty, the phenomenon of "jury nullification," in which juries refused to convict in cases in which they believed that death was an inappropriate penalty, was experienced. Tennessee was the first State to give juries discretion, Tenn. Laws 1837–1838, c. 29, but other States quickly followed suit. Then, Rep. Curtis of New York introduced a federal bill that ultimately became law in 1897 which reduced the number of federal capital offenses from 60 to 3 (treason, murder, and rape) and gave the jury sentencing discretion in murder and rape cases.†

By 1917, 12 States had become abolitionist jurisdictions. But, under the nervous tension of World War I, four of these States reinstituted capital punishment and promising movements in other State came grinding to a halt.

---

*Kansas restored it in 1935....

†... More than 90% of the executions since 1930 in this country have been for offenses with a discretionary death penalty. Bedau, The Courts, the Constitution, and Capital Punishment, 1968 Utah L.Rev. 201, 204.

During the period following the First World War, the abolitionist movement never regained its momentum.

It is not easy to ascertain why the movement lost its vigor. Certainly, much attention was diverted from penal reform during the economic crisis of the Depression and the exhausting years of struggle during World War II. Also, executions, which had once been frequent public spectacles, became infrequent private affairs. The manner of inflicting death changed, and the horrors of the punishment were, therefore, somewhat diminished in the minds of the general public.

In recent years, there has been renewed interest in modifying capital punishment. New York has moved toward abolition,* as have several other States.† In 1967, a bill was introduced in the Senate to abolish capital punishment for all federal crimes, but it died in committee.

At the present time, 41 States, the District of Columbia, and other federal jurisdictions authorize the death penalty for at least one crime. It would be fruitless to attempt here to categorize the approach to capital punishment taken by the various States. It is sufficient to note that murder is the crime most often punished by death, followed by kidnaping and treason. Rape is a capital offense in 16 States and the federal system.

The foregoing history demonstrates that capital punishment was carried from Europe to America but, once here, was tempered considerably. At times in our history, strong abolitionist movements have existed. But they have never been completely successful, as no more than one-quarter of the States of the Union have, at any one time, abolished the death penalty. They have had partial success, however, especially in reducing the number of capital crimes, replacing mandatory death sentences with jury discretion, and developing more humane methods of conducting executions.

This is where our historical foray leads. The question now to be faced is whether American society has reached a point where abolition is not dependent

*New York authorizes the death penalty only for murder of a police officer or for murder by a life term prisoner. N.Y. Penal Code § 125.30 (1967).

†. . . Nine States do not authorize capital punishment under any circumstances: Alaska, Hawaii, Iowa, Maine, Michigan, Minnesota, Oregon, West Virginia, and Wisconsin. Puerto Rico and the Virgin Islands also have no provision for capital punishment.... Those States that severely restrict the imposition of the death penalty are: New Mexico...; New York...; North Dakota...; Rhode Island...; Vermont.... California is the only State in which the judiciary has declared capital punishment to be invalid. . . .

on a successful grass roots movement in particular jurisdictions, but is demanded by the Eighth Amendment. To answer this question, we must first examine whether or not the death penalty is today tantamount to excessive punishment.

V

In order to assess whether or not death is an excessive or unnecessary penalty, it is necessary to consider the reasons why a legislature might select it as punishment for one or more offenses, and examine whether less severe penalties would satisfy the legitimate legislative wants as well as capital punishment. If they would, then the death penalty is unnecessary cruelty, and, therefore, unconstitutional.

There are six purposes conceivably served by capital punishment: retribution, deterrence, prevention of repetitive criminal acts, encouragement of guilty pleas and confessions, eugenics, and economy. These are considered seriatim below.

A.

The concept of retribution is one of the most misunderstood in all of our criminal jurisprudence. The principal source of confusion derives from the fact that, in dealing with the concept, most people confuse the question "why do men in fact punish?" with the question "what justifies men in punishing?" Men may punish for any number of reasons, but the one reason that punishment is morally good or morally justifiable is that someone has broken the law. Thus, it can correctly be said that breaking the law is the sine qua non of punishment, or, in other words, that we only tolerate punishment as it is imposed on one who deviates from the norm established by the criminal law.

The fact that the State may seek retribution against those who have broken its laws does not mean that retribution may then become the State's sole end in punishing. Our jurisprudence has always accepted deterrence in general, deterrence of individual recidivism, isolation of dangerous persons, and rehabilitation as proper goals of punishment.... Retaliation, vengeance, and retribution have been roundly condemned as intolerable aspirations for a government in a free society.

Punishment as retribution has been condemned by scholars for centuries, and the Eighth Amendment itself was adopted to prevent punishment from becoming synonymous with vengeance.

In *Weems v. United States*, 217 U.S. 381, the Court, in the course of holding that Weems' punishment violated the Eighth Amendment, contrasted it with penalties provided for other offenses, and concluded:

> This contrast shows more than different exercises of legislative judgment. It is greater than that. It condemns the sentence in this case as cruel and unusual. It exhibits a difference between unrestrained power and that which is exercised under the spirit of constitutional limitations formed to establish justice. The State thereby suffers nothing, and loses no power. *The purpose of punishment is fulfilled, crime is repressed by penalties of just, not tormenting, severity, its repetition is prevented, and hope is given for the reformation of the criminal.* (Emphasis added.)

It is plain that the view of the *Weems* Court was that punishment for the sake of retribution was not permissible under the Eighth Amendment. This is the only view that the Court could have taken if the "cruel and unusual" language were to be given any meaning. Retribution surely underlies the imposition of some punishment on one who commits a criminal act. But the fact that some punishment may be imposed does not mean that any punishment is permissible. If retribution alone could serve as a justification for any particular penalty, then all penalties selected by the legislature would, by definition, be acceptable means for designating society's moral approbation of a particular act. The "cruel and unusual" language would thus be read out of the Constitution, and the fears of Patrick Henry and the other Founding Fathers would become realities. To preserve the integrity of the Eighth Amendment, the Court has consistently denigrated retribution as a permissible goal of punishment.* It is undoubtedly correct that there is a demand for vengeance on the part of many persons in a community against one who is convicted of a particularly offensive act. At times,

---

*. . . In *Powell v. Texas*, 392 U.S. at 392 U.S. 530 (1968), we said:

"This Court has never held that anything in the Constitution requires that penal sanctions be designed solely to achieve therapeutic or rehabilitative effects. . . ."

This is, of course, correct, since deterrence and isolation are clearly recognized as proper.... There is absolutely nothing in the language, the rationale, or the holding of *Powell v. Texas,* that implies that retribution for its own sake is a proper legislative aim in punishing.

a cry is heard that morality requires vengeance to evidence society's abhorrence of the act. But the Eighth Amendment is our insulation from our baser selves. The "cruel and unusual" language limits the avenues through which vengeance can be channeled. Were this not so, the language would be empty, and a return to the rack and other tortures would be possible in a given case.

Mr. Justice Story wrote [*in 1891*] that the Eighth Amendment's limitation on punishment "would seem to be wholly unnecessary in a free government, since it is scarcely possible that any department of such a government should authorize or justify such atrocious conduct."

I would reach an opposite conclusion—that only in a free society would men recognize their inherent weaknesses and seek to compensate for them by means of a Constitution.

The history of the Eighth Amendment supports only the conclusion that retribution for its own sake is improper.

B.

The most hotly contested issue regarding capital punishment is whether it is better than life imprisonment as a deterrent to crime.

While the contrary position has been argued, it is my firm opinion that the death penalty is a more severe sanction than life imprisonment. Admittedly, there are some persons who would rather die than languish in prison for a lifetime. But, whether or not they should be able to choose death as an alternative is a far different question from that presented here—i.e., whether the State can impose death as a punishment. Death is irrevocable; life imprisonment is not. Death, of course, makes rehabilitation impossible; life imprisonment does not. In short, death has always been viewed as the ultimate sanction, and it seems perfectly reasonable to continue to view it as such.*

It must be kept in mind, then, that the question to be considered is not simply whether capital punishment is a deterrent, but whether it is a better deterrent than life imprisonment.

---

*. . . The assertion that life imprisonment may somehow be more cruel than death is usually rejected as frivolous. Hence, I confess to surprise at finding the assertion being made in various ways in today's opinions. If there were any merit to the contention, it would do much to undercut even the retributive motive for imposing capital punishment. In any event, there is no better response to such an assertion than that of former Pennsylvania Supreme Court Justice Musmanno in his dissent in *Commonwealth v. Elliott*, at 79–80, 89 A.2d at 787:   (*cont'd*)

There is no more complex problem than determining the deterrent efficacy of the death penalty.

"Capital punishment has obviously failed as a deterrent when a murder is committed. We can number its failures. But we cannot number its successes. No one can ever know how many people have refrained from murder because of the fear of being hanged."*

This is the nub of the problem, and it is exacerbated by the paucity of useful data. The United States is more fortunate than most countries, however, in that it has what are generally considered to be the world's most reliable statistics.†

The two strongest arguments in favor of capital punishment as a deterrent are both logical hypotheses devoid of evidentiary support, but persuasive nonetheless. The first proposition was best stated by Sir James Stephen in 1864:

> No other punishment deters men so effectually from committing crimes as the punishment of death. This is one of those propositions which it is difficult to prove simply because they are, in themselves, more obvious than any proof can make them. It is possible to display ingenuity in arguing against it, but that is all. The whole experience of mankind is in the other direction. The threat of instant death is the one to which resort has always been made when there was an absolute necessity for producing some result.... No one goes to certain inevitable death except by compulsion. Put the matter the other way. Was

---

One of the judges of the lower court indicated from the bench that a sentence of life imprisonment is not to be regarded as a lesser penalty than that of death. I challenge that statement categorically. It can be stated as a universal truth stretching from nadir to zenith that, regardless of circumstances, no one wants to die. Some person may, in an instant of spiritual or physical agony express a desire for death as an anodyne from intolerable pain, but that desire is never full-hearted, because there is always the reserve of realization that the silken cord of life is not broken by a mere wishing. There is no person in the actual extremity of dropping from the precipice of life who does not desperately reach for a crag of time to which to cling even for a moment against the awful eternity of silence below. With all its "slings and arrows of outrageous fortune," life is yet sweet and death is always cruel.

* Royal Commission [*Report of Royal Commission on Capital Punishment*, 1949–1953, Cmd. 8932, 52–53, pp. 17–18 (1953)].

†... The great advantage that this country has is that it can compare abolitionist and retentionist States with geographic, economic, and cultural similarities.

there ever yet a criminal who, when sentenced to death and brought out to die, would refuse the offer of a commutation of his sentence for the severest secondary punishment? Surely not. Why is this? It can only be because "All that a man has will he give for his life." In any secondary punishment, however terrible, there is hope; but death is death; its terrors cannot be described more forcibly.

This hypothesis relates to the use of capital punishment as a deterrent for any crime. The second proposition is that, [if]"life imprisonment is the maximum penalty for a crime such as murder, an offender who is serving a life sentence cannot then be deterred from murdering a fellow inmate or a prison officer."*

This hypothesis advocates a limited deterrent effect under particular circumstances.

Abolitionists attempt to disprove these hypotheses by amassing statistical evidence to demonstrate that there is no correlation between criminal activity and the existence or nonexistence of a capital sanction. Almost all of the evidence involves the crime of murder, since murder is punishable by death in more jurisdictions than are other offenses, and almost 90% of all executions since 1930 have been pursuant to murder convictions.

Thorsten Sellin, one of the leading authorities on capital punishment, has urged that, if the death penalty deters prospective murderers, the following hypotheses should be true:

(a) Murders should be less frequent in states that have the death penalty than in those that have abolished it, other factors being equal. Comparisons of this nature must be made among states that are as alike as possible in all other respects—character of population, social and economic condition, etc.—in order not to introduce factors known to influence murder rates in a serious manner but present in only one of these states.

(b) Murders should increase when the death penalty is abolished, and should decline when it is restored.

*United Nations, [Department of Economic and Social Affairs, *Capital Punishment*, Pt. II, 82–85, pp. 101–102 (1968)].

(c) The deterrent effect should be greatest, and should therefore affect murder rates most powerfully, in those communities where the crime occurred and its consequences are most strongly brought home to the population.

(d) Law enforcement officers would be safer from murderous attacks in states that have the death penalty than in those without it.

Sellin's evidence indicates that not one of these propositions is true. This evidence has its problems, however. One is that there are no accurate figures for capital murders; there are only figures on homicides, and they, of course, include noncapital killings.* A second problem is that certain murders undoubtedly are misinterpreted as accidental deaths or suicides, and there is no way of estimating the number of such undetected crimes. A third problem is that not all homicides are reported. Despite these difficulties, most authorities have assumed that the proportion of capital murders in a State's or nation's homicide statistics remains reasonably constant, and that the homicide statistics are therefore useful.

Sellin's statistics demonstrate that there is no correlation between the murder rate and the presence or absence of the capital sanction. He compares States that have similar characteristics and finds that, irrespective of their position on capital punishment, they have similar murder rates. In the New England States, for example, there is no correlation between executions† and homicide rates. The same is true for Midwestern States, and for all others studied. Both the United Nations and Great Britain have acknowledged the validity of Sellin's statistics.

Sellin also concludes that abolition and/or reintroduction of the death penalty had no effect on the homicide rates of the various States involved. This conclusion is borne out by others who have made similar inquiries and by the experience of other countries. Despite problems with the statistics,‡

*Such crimes might include lesser forms of homicide or homicide by a child or a lunatic. . . .

†Executions were chosen for purposes of comparison because whatever impact capital punishment had would surely be most forcefully felt where punishment was actually imposed.

‡ One problem is that the statistics for the 19th century are especially suspect; another is that de jure abolition may have been preceded by de facto abolition which would have distorted the figures. It should also be noted that the figures for several States reflect homicide convictions, rather than homicide rates.

Sellin's evidence has been relied upon in international studies of capital punishment.

Statistics also show that the deterrent effect of capital punishment is no greater in those communities where executions take place than in other communities. In fact, there is some evidence that imposition of capital punishment may actually encourage crime, rather than deter it.* And, while police and law enforcement officers are the strongest advocates of capital punishment, the evidence is overwhelming that police are no safer in communities that retain the sanction than in those that have abolished it.

There is also a substantial body of data showing that the existence of the death penalty has virtually no effect on the homicide rate in prisons.† Most of the persons sentenced to death are murderers, and murderers tend to be model prisoners.‡

In sum, the only support for the theory that capital punishment is an effective deterrent is found in the hypotheses with which we began and the occasional stories about a specific individual being deterred from doing a contemplated criminal act. These claims of specific deterrence are often spurious, however, and may be more than counterbalanced by the tendency of capital punishment to incite certain crimes.

The United Nations Committee that studied capital punishment found that "it is generally agreed between the retentionists and abolitionists, whatever their opinions about the validity of comparative studies of deterrence, that the data which now exist show no correlation between the existence of capital punishment and lower rates of capital crime."§

Despite the fact that abolitionists have not proved non-deterrence beyond a reasonable doubt, they have succeeded in showing by clear and convincing evidence that capital punishment is not necessary as a deterrent to crime in our

*... Capital punishment may provide an outlet for suicidal impulses or a means of achieving notoriety, for example.

†... The argument can be made that the reason for the good record of murderers is that those who are likely to be recidivists are executed. There is, however, no evidence to show that, in choosing between life and death sentences, juries select the lesser penalties for those persons they believe are unlikely to commit future crimes.

‡... This is supported also by overwhelming statistics showing an extremely low rate of recidivism for convicted murderers who are released from prison. . . .

§ United Nations, [Department of Economic and Social Affairs, *Capital Punishment*, Pt. II, 82–85, pp. 101–102 (1968)].

society. This is all that they must do. We would shirk our judicial responsibilities if we failed to accept the presently existing statistics and demanded more proof. It may be that we now possess all the proof that anyone could ever hope to assemble on the subject. But, even if further proof were to be forthcoming, I believe there is more than enough evidence presently available for a decision in this case.

In 1793, William Bradford studied the utility of the death penalty in Pennsylvania and found that it probably had no deterrent effect, but that more evidence was needed. Edward Livingston reached a similar conclusion with respect to deterrence in 1833 upon completion of his study for Louisiana. Virtually every study that has since been undertaken has reached the same result.*

In light of the massive amount of evidence before us, I see no alternative but to conclude that capital punishment cannot be justified on the basis of its deterrent effect.†

C.

Much of what must be said about the death penalty as a device to prevent recidivism is obvious—if a murderer is executed, he cannot possibly commit another offense. The fact is, however, that murderers are extremely unlikely to commit other crimes, either in prison or upon their release. For the most part, they are first offenders, and, when released from prison, they are known to become model citizens. Furthermore, most persons who commit capital crimes are not executed. With respect to those who are sentenced to die, it is critical

---

* . . . One would assume that if deterrence were enhanced by capital punishment, the increased deterrence would be most effective with respect to the premeditating murderer or the hired killer who plots his crime before committing it. But such people rarely expect to be caught, and usually assume that, if they are caught, they will either be acquitted or sentenced to prison. This is a fairly dependable assumption, since a reliable estimate is that one person is executed for every 100 capital murders known to the police.... For capital punishment to deter anybody, it must be a certain result of a criminal act,... and it is not. It must also follow swiftly upon completion of the offense, and it cannot in our complicated due process system of justice.... It is ironic that those persons whom we would like to deter the most have the least to fear from the death penalty, and recognize that fact....

† In reaching this conclusion, I maintain agreement with that portion of Stephen's hypothesis that suggests that convicted criminals fear death more than they fear life imprisonment. As I stated earlier, the death penalty is a more severe sanction. The error in the hypothesis lies in its assumption that, because men fear death more than imprisonment after they are convicted, they necessarily must weigh potential penalties prior to committing criminal acts, and that they will conform their behavior so as to insure that, if caught, they will receive the lesser penalty. It is extremely unlikely that much thought is given to penalties before the act is committed, and, even if it were, the preceding footnote explains why such thought would not lead to deterrence.

to note that the jury is never asked to determine whether they are likely to be recidivists. In light of these facts, if capital punishment were justified purely on the basis of preventing recidivism, it would have to be considered to be excessive; no general need to obliterate all capital offenders could have been demonstrated, nor any specific need in individual cases.

D.

The three final purposes which may underlie utilization of a capital sanction—encouraging guilty pleas and confessions, eugenics, and reducing state expenditures—may be dealt with quickly. If the death penalty is used to encourage guilty pleas, and thus to deter suspects from exercising their rights under the Sixth Amendment to jury trials, it is unconstitutional. *United States v. Jackson*, 390 U.S. 570 (1968). Its elimination would do little to impair the State's bargaining position in criminal cases, since life imprisonment remains a severe sanction which can be used as leverage for bargaining for pleas or confessions in exchange either for charges of lesser offenses or recommendations of leniency.

Moreover, to the extent that capital punishment is used to encourage confessions and guilty pleas, it is not being used for punishment purposes. A State that justifies capital punishment on its utility as part of the conviction process could not profess to rely on capital punishment as a deterrent. Such a State's system would be structured with twin goals only: obtaining guilty pleas and confessions and imposing imprisonment as the maximum sanction. Since life imprisonment is sufficient for bargaining purposes, the death penalty is excessive if used for the same purposes.

In light of the previous discussion on deterrence, any suggestions concerning the eugenic benefits of capital punishment are obviously meritless. As I pointed out above, there is not even any attempt made to discover which capital offenders are likely to be recidivists, let alone which are positively incurable. No test or procedure presently exists by which incurables can be screened from those who would benefit from treatment. On the one hand, due process would seem to require that we have some procedure to demonstrate incurability before execution; and, on the other hand, equal protection would then seemingly require that all incurables be executed.... In addition, the "cruel and unusual" language would require that life imprisonment, treatment, and sterilization be inadequate for eugenic purposes. More importantly, this Nation has never formally professed eugenic goals, and the history of the world does not look kindly on them. If eugenics is one of our purposes, then the legislatures should say so forthrightly and design procedures to serve this goal. Until such time, I can only conclude, as has virtually everyone else who has looked at the problem,* that capital punishment cannot be defended on the basis of any eugenic purposes.

As for the argument that it is cheaper to execute a capital offender than to imprison him for life, even assuming that such an argument, if true, would support a capital sanction, it is simply incorrect. A disproportionate amount of money spent on prisons is attributable to death row. Condemned men are not productive members of the prison community, although they could be, and executions are expensive. Appeals are often automatic, and courts admittedly spend more time with death cases.

At trial, the selection of jurors is likely to become a costly, time-consuming problem in a capital case, and defense counsel will reasonably exhaust every possible means to save his client from execution, no matter how long the trial takes.

During the period between conviction and execution, there are an inordinate number of collateral attacks on the conviction and attempts to obtain executive clemency, all of which exhaust the time, money, and effort of the State. There are also continual assertions that the condemned prisoner has gone insane. Because there is a formally established policy of not executing insane persons, great sums of money may be spent on detecting and curing mental illness in order to perform the execution.† Since no one wants the responsibility for the execution, the condemned man is likely to be passed back and forth from doctors to custodial officials to courts like a ping-pong ball. The entire process is very costly.

When all is said and done, there can be no doubt that it costs more to execute a man than to keep him in prison for life.

E.

There is but one conclusion that can be drawn from all of this—i.e., the death penalty is an excessive and unnecessary punishment that violates the Eighth

---

*...We should not be surprised at the lack of merit in the eugenic arguments. There simply is no evidence that mentally ill persons who commit capital offenses constitute a psychiatric entity distinct from other mentally disordered patients, or that they do not respond as readily to treatment....

† To others, as well as to the author of this opinion, this practice seemed a strange way to spend money....

Amendment. The statistical evidence is not convincing beyond all doubt, but it is persuasive. It is not improper at this point to take judicial notice of the fact that, for more than 200 years, men have labored to demonstrate that capital punishment serves no purpose that life imprisonment could not serve equally well. And they have done so with great success. Little, if any, evidence has been adduced to prove the contrary. The point has now been reached at which deference to the legislatures is tantamount to abdication of our judicial roles as factfinders, judges, and ultimate arbiters of the Constitution. We know that, at some point, the presumption of constitutionality accorded legislative acts gives way to a realistic assessment of those acts. This point comes when there is sufficient evidence available so that judges can determine not whether the legislature acted wisely, but whether it had any rational basis whatsoever for acting. We have this evidence before us now. There is no rational basis for concluding that capital punishment is not excessive. It therefore violates the Eighth Amendment.*

VI

In addition, even if capital punishment is not excessive, it nonetheless violates the Eighth Amendment because it is morally unacceptable to the people of the United States at this time in their history.

---

*This analysis parallels in some ways the analysis used in striking down legislation on the ground that it violates Fourteenth Amendment concepts of substantive due process.... There is one difference, however. Capital punishment is unconstitutional because it is excessive and unnecessary punishment, not because it is irrational.

The concepts of cruel and unusual punishment and substantive due process become so close as to merge when the substantive due process argument is stated in the following manner: because capital punishment deprives an individual of a fundamental right (i.e., the right to life),... the State needs a compelling interest to justify it.... Thus stated, the substantive due process argument reiterates what is essentially the primary purpose of the Cruel and Unusual Punishments Clause of the Eighth Amendment—i.e., punishment may not be more severe than is necessary to serve the legitimate interests of the State.

The Chief Justice asserts that if we hold that capital punishment is unconstitutional because it is excessive, we will next have to determine whether a 10-year prison sentence rather than a five-year sentence, is also excessive, or whether a $5 fine would not do equally well as a $10 fine. He may be correct that such determinations will have to be made, but, as in these cases, those persons challenging the penalty will bear a heavy burden of demonstrating that it is excessive. These cases arise after 200 years of inquiry, 200 years of public debate and 200 years of marshaling evidence. The burden placed on those challenging capital punishment could not have been greater. I am convinced that they have met their burden. Whether a similar burden will prove too great in future cases is a question that we can resolve in time.

In judging whether or not a given penalty is morally acceptable, most courts have said that the punishment is valid unless "it shocks the conscience and sense of justice of the people."*

Judge Frank once noted the problems inherent in the use of such a measuring stick:

> [The court,] before it reduces a sentence as "cruel and unusual," must have reasonably good assurances that the sentence offends the "common conscience." And, in any context, such a standard—the community's attitude—is usually an unknowable. It resembles a slithery shadow, since one can seldom learn, at all accurately, what the community, or a majority, actually feels. Even a carefully taken "public opinion poll" would be inconclusive in a case like this.†

While a public opinion poll obviously is of some assistance in indicating public acceptance or rejection of a specific penalty, its utility cannot be very great. This is because whether or not a punishment is cruel and unusual depends not on whether its mere mention "shocks the conscience and sense of justice of the people," but on whether people who were fully informed as to the purposes of the penalty and its liabilities would find the penalty shocking, unjust, and unacceptable.‡

---

*... In *Repouille v. United States*, 165 F.2d 152 (CA2 1947), and *Schmidt v. United States*, 177 F.2d 450, 451 (CA2 1949), Judge Learned Hand wrote that the standard of "good moral character" in the Nationality Act was to be judged by "the generally accepted moral conventions current at the time."...Judge Frank, who was later to author the *Rosenberg* opinion [*United States v. Rosenberg*, 195 F.2d 583 (2d Cir. 1952)], in which a similar standard was adopted, dissented in *Repouille* and urged that the correct standard was the "attitude of our ethical leaders."... In light of *Rosenberg*, it is apparent that Judge Frank would require a much broader based moral approbation before striking down a punishment as cruel and unusual than he would for merely holding that conduct was evidence of bad moral character under a legislative act.

†*United States v. Rosenberg*, [195 F.2d 583 (2d Cir. 1952)] at 608.

‡ The fact that the constitutionality of capital punishment turns on the opinion of an informed citizenry undercuts the argument that, since the legislature is the voice of the people, its retention of capital punishment must represent the will of the people. So few people have been executed in the past decade that capital punishment is a subject only rarely brought to the attention of the average American. Lack of exposure to the problem is likely to lead to indifference, and indifference and ignorance result in preservation of the status quo, whether or not that is desirable, or desired.

It might be argued that, in choosing to remain indifferent and uninformed, *(cont'd)*

In other words, the question with which we must deal is not whether a substantial proportion of American citizens would today, if polled, opine that capital punishment is barbarously cruel, but whether they would find it to be so in the light of all information presently available.

This is not to suggest that, with respect to this test of unconstitutionality, people are required to act rationally; they are not. With respect to this judgment, a violation of the Eighth Amendment is totally dependent on the predictable subjective, emotional reactions of informed citizens.

It has often been noted that American citizens know almost nothing about capital punishment. Some of the conclusions arrived at in the preceding section and the supporting evidence would be critical to an informed judgment on the morality of the death penalty: e.g., that the death penalty is no more effective a deterrent than life imprisonment; that convicted murderers are rarely executed, but are usually sentenced to a term in prison; that convicted murderers usually are model prisoners, and that they almost always become law-abiding citizens upon their release from prison; that the costs of executing a capital offender exceed the costs of imprisoning him for life; that, while in prison, a convict under sentence of death performs none of the useful functions that life prisoners perform; that no attempt is made in the sentencing process to ferret out likely recidivists for execution; and that the death penalty may actually stimulate criminal activity.

This information would almost surely convince the average citizen that the death penalty was unwise, but a problem arises as to whether it would convince him that the penalty was morally reprehensible. This problem arises from the fact that the public's desire for retribution, even though this is a goal that the legislature cannot constitutionally pursue as is sole justification for capital punishment, might influence the citizenry's view of the morality of capital punishment. The solution to the problem lies in the fact that no one has ever seriously advanced retribution as a legitimate goal of our society. Defenses of capital punishment are always mounted on deterrent or other similar theories. This should not be surprising. It is the

citizens reflect their judgment that capital punishment is really a question of utility, not morality, and not one, therefore, of great concern. As attractive as this is on its face, it cannot be correct, because such an argument requires that the choice to remain ignorant or indifferent be a viable one. That, in turn, requires that it be a knowledgeable choice. It is therefore imperative for constitutional purposes to attempt to discern the probable opinion of an informed electorate.

people of this country who have urged in the past that prisons rehabilitate as well as isolate offenders, and it is the people who have injected a sense of purpose into our penology. I cannot believe that at this stage in our history, the American people would ever knowingly support purposeless vengeance. Thus, I believe that the great mass of citizens would conclude on the basis of the material already considered that the death penalty is immoral, and therefore unconstitutional.

But, if this information needs supplementing, I believe that the following facts would serve to convince even the most hesitant of citizens to condemn death as a sanction: capital punishment is imposed discriminatorily against certain identifiable classes of people; there is evidence that innocent people have been executed before their innocence can be proved; and the death penalty wreaks havoc with our entire criminal justice system. Each of these facts is considered briefly below.

Regarding discrimination, it has been said that "it is usually the poor, the illiterate, the underprivileged, the member of the minority group—the man who, because he is without means, and is defended by a court-appointed attorney—who becomes society's sacrificial lamb...."* Indeed, a look at the bare statistics regarding executions is enough to betray much of the discrimination. A total of 3,859 persons have been executed since 1930, of whom 1,751 were white and 2,066 were Negro.† Of the executions, 3,334 were for murder; 1,664 of the executed murderers were white and 1,630 were Negro; 455 persons, including 48 whites and 405 Negroes, were executed for rape. It is immediately apparent that Negroes were executed far more often than whites in proportion to their percentage of the population. Studies indicate that, while the higher rate of execution among Negroes is partially due to a higher rate of crime, there is evidence of racial discrimination.

Racial or other discriminations should not be surprising. In *McGautha v. California*, 402 U.S. at 402 U.S. 207, this Court held "that committing to the untrammeled discretion of the jury the power to pronounce life or death in capital cases is [not] offensive to anything in the Constitution."

*Hearings [on S. 1760 before the Subcommittee on Criminal Laws and Procedures of the Senate Committee on the Judiciary, 90th Cong., 2d Sess. (1968)] at 11 (statement of M. DiSalle).

†National Prisoner Statistics No. 45, *Capital Punishment 1930–1968*, p. 7 (Aug. 1969).

This was an open invitation to discrimination.

There is also overwhelming evidence that the death penalty is employed against men, and not women. Only 32 women have been executed since 1930, while 3,827 men have met a similar fate. It is difficult to understand why women have received such favored treatment, since the purposes allegedly served by capital punishment seemingly are equally applicable to both sexes.*

It also is evident that the burden of capital punishment falls upon the poor, the ignorant, and the underprivileged members of society. It is the poor, and the members of minority groups who are least able to voice their complaints against capital punishment. Their impotence leaves them victims of a sanction that the wealthier, better-represented, just-as-guilty person can escape. So long as the capital sanction is used only against the forlorn, easily forgotten members of society, legislators are content to maintain the status quo, because change would draw attention to the problem and concern might develop. Ignorance is perpetuated, and apathy soon becomes its mate, and we have today's situation.

Just as Americans know little about who is executed and why, they are unaware of the potential dangers of executing an innocent man. Our "beyond a reasonable doubt" burden of proof in criminal cases is intended to protect the innocent, but we know it is not foolproof. Various studies have shown that people whose innocence is later convincingly established are convicted and sentenced to death.†

Proving one's innocence after a jury finding of guilt is almost impossible. While reviewing courts are willing to entertain all kinds of collateral attacks where a sentence of death is involved, they very rarely dispute the jury's interpretation of the evidence. This is, perhaps, as it should be. But if an innocent man has been found guilty, he must then depend on the good faith of the prosecutor's office to help him establish his innocence. There is

---

*Men kill between four and five times more frequently than women.... Hence, it would not be irregular to see four or five times as many men executed as women. The statistics show a startlingly greater disparity, however....

†See, e.g., E. Borchard, *Convicting the Innocent* (1932); J. Frank & B. Frank, *Not Guilty* (1957); E. Gardner, *Court of Last Resort* (1952). These three books examine cases in which innocent persons were sentenced to die. None of the innocents was actually executed, however. Bedau has abstracted 74 cases occurring in the United States since 1893 in which a wrongful conviction for murder was alleged and usually proved "beyond doubt." In almost every case, the convictions were sustained on appeal. Bedau seriously contends that innocent persons were actually executed....

evidence, however, that prosecutors do not welcome the idea of having convictions, which they labored hard to secure, overturned, and that their cooperation is highly unlikely.

No matter how careful courts are, the possibility of perjured testimony, mistaken honest testimony, and human error remain all too real.* We have no way of judging how many innocent persons have been executed, but we can be certain that there were some. Whether there were many is an open question made difficult by the loss of those who were most knowledgeable about the crime for which they were convicted. Surely there will be more as long as capital punishment remains part of our penal law.

While it is difficult to ascertain with certainty the degree to which the death penalty is discriminatorily imposed or the number of innocent persons sentenced to die, there is one conclusion about the penalty that is universally accepted—i.e., it "tends to distort the course of the criminal law."†

As Mr. Justice Frankfurter said:

> I am strongly against capital punishment.... When life is at hazard in a trial, it sensationalizes the whole thing almost unwittingly; the

---

*Mr. Justice Douglas recognized this fact when he wrote:

> One who reviews the records of criminal trials need not look long to find an instance where the issue of guilt or innocence hangs in delicate balance. A judge who denies a stay of execution in a capital case often wonders if an innocent man is going to his death....
>
> Those doubts exist because our system of criminal justice does not work with the efficiency of a machine—errors are made and innocent as well as guilty people are sometimes punished....
>
> ...We believe that it is better for ten guilty people to be set free than for one innocent man to be unjustly imprisoned.
>
> Yet the sad truth is that a cog in the machine often slip: memories fail; mistaken identifications are made; those who wield the power of life and death itself—the police officer, the witness, the prosecutor, the juror, and even the judge—become overzealous in their concern that criminals be brought to justice. And at times there is a venal combination between the police and a witness. (Foreword, J. Frank & B. Frank, Not Guilty, 11–12 (1957)).

There has been an "incredible lag" between the development of modern scientific methods of investigation and their application to criminal cases. When modern methodology is available, prosecutors have the resources to utilize it, whereas defense counsel often may not.... This increases the chances of error.

†Ehrmann, The Death Penalty and the Administration of Justice, 284 Annals of the American Academy of Political and Social Science 73, 83 (1952).

effect on juries, the Bar, the public, the Judiciary, I regard as very bad. I think scientifically the claim of deterrence is not worth much. Whatever proof there may be, in my judgment, does not outweigh the social loss due to the inherent sensationalism of a trial for life.*

The deleterious effects of the death penalty are also felt otherwise than at trial. For example, its very existence "inevitably sabotages a social or institutional program of reformation."† In short "the presence of the death penalty as the keystone of our penal system bedevils the administration of criminal justice all the way down the line, and is the stumbling block in the path of general reform and of the treatment of crime and criminals."‡

Assuming knowledge of all the facts presently available regarding capital punishment, the average citizen would, in my opinion, find it shocking to his conscience and sense of justice.§ For this reason alone, capital punishment cannot stand.

VII

To arrive at the conclusion that the death penalty violates the Eighth Amendment, we have had to engage in a long and tedious journey. The amount of information that we have assembled and sorted is enormous.

* F. Frankfurter, *Of Law and Men* 81 (1956).

† B. Eshelman & F. Riley, *Death Row Chaplain* 222 (1962).

‡ McCafferty, Major Trends in the Use of Capital Punishment, 25 Fed.Prob., No. 3, pp. 15, 21 (Sept. 1961) (quoting Dr. S. Glueck of Harvard University).

§ Mr. Justice Powell suggests that this conclusion is speculative, and he is certainly correct. But the mere recognition of this truth does not undercut the validity of the conclusion. Mr. Justice Powell himself concedes that judges somehow know that certain punishments are no longer acceptable in our society; for example, he refers to branding and pillorying. Whence comes this knowledge? The answer is that it comes from our intuition as human beings that our fellow human beings no longer will tolerate such punishments.

I agree wholeheartedly with the implication in my Brother Powell's opinion that judges are not free to strike down penalties that they find personally offensive. But I disagree with his suggestion that it is improper for judges to ask themselves whether a specific punishment is morally acceptable to the American public. Contrary to some current thought, judges have not lived lives isolated from a broad range of human experience. They have come into contact with many people, many ways of life, and many philosophies. They have learned to share with their fellow human beings common views of morality. If, after drawing on this experience and considering the vast range of people and views that they have encountered, judges conclude that these people would not knowingly tolerate a specific penalty in light of its costs, then this conclusion is entitled to weight.... Judges can find assistance in determining whether they are being objective, rather than subjective, by referring to the attitudes of the persons whom most citizens consider our "ethical leaders." ... *(cont'd)*

Yet I firmly believe that we have not deviated in the slightest from the principles with which we began.

At a time in our history when the streets of the Nation's cities inspire fear and despair, rather than pride and hope, it is difficult to maintain objectivity and concern for our fellow citizens. But the measure of a country's greatness is its ability to retain compassion in time of crisis. No nation in the recorded history of man has a greater tradition of revering justice and fair treatment for all its citizens in times of turmoil, confusion, and tension than ours. This is a country which stands tallest in troubled times, a country that clings to fundamental principles, cherishes its constitutional heritage, and rejects simple solutions that compromise the values that lie at the roots of our democratic system.

In striking down capital punishment, this Court does not malign our system of government. On the contrary, it pays homage to it. Only in a free society could right triumph in difficult times, and could civilization record its magnificent advancement. In recognizing the humanity of our fellow beings, we pay ourselves the highest tribute. We achieve "a major milestone in the long road up from barbarism" and join the approximately 70 other jurisdictions in the world which celebrate their regard for civilization and humanity by shunning capital punishment. I concur in the judgments of the Court.
[*Appendixes omitted.*]

I must also admit that I am confused as to the point that my Brother Powell seeks to make regarding the underprivileged members of our society. If he is stating that this Court cannot solve all of their problems in the context of this case, or even many of them, I would agree with him. But if he is opining that it is only the poor, the ignorant, the racial minorities, and the hapless in our society who are executed; that they are executed for no real reason other than to satisfy some vague notion of society's cry for vengeance; and that, knowing these things, the people of this country would not care, then I most urgently disagree.

There is too much crime, too much killing, too much hatred in this country. If the legislatures could eradicate these elements from our lives by utilizing capital punishment, then there would be a valid purpose for the sanction, and the public would surely accept it. It would be constitutional. As the Chief Justice and Mr. Justice Powell point out, however, capital punishment has been with us a long time. What purpose has it served? The evidence is that it has served none. I cannot agree that the American people have been so hardened, so embittered, that they want to take the life of one who performs even the basest criminal act knowing that the execution is nothing more than bloodlust. This has not been my experience with my fellow citizens. Rather, I have found that they earnestly desire their system of punishments to make sense in order that it can be a morally justifiable system...

Gregg v. Georgia, 428 U.S. 153 (1976)

After the Supreme Court's decision in *Furman v. Georgia*, the Georgia legislature amended its death penalty statute to provide for bifurcated trials, with guilt or innocence decided separately from the sentence, and to require specified aggravating circumstances before the death penalty could be imposed.

The defendant in this case was charged with committing armed robbery and murder on evidence that he had killed and robbed two men. The defendant was convicted and sentenced to death under the amended death penalty statute, and the Georgia Supreme Court upheld the conviction and sentence on appeal.

The defendant made a final appeal to the U.S. Supreme Court on the ground that the death sentence was cruel and unusual punishment barred by the Eighth Amendment. A divided Court affirmed the death sentence. Seven justices agreed that the Eighth Amendment did not always bar capital punishment. Justice Marshall filed the dissent included here; Justice William J. Brennan, Jr., also dissented.

In the Supreme Court of the United States
Troy Leon Gregg, Petitioner, vs. State of Georgia

Decided July 2, 1976
Certiorari to the Supreme Court of Georgia

DISSENT
[Some citations and footnotes have been omitted for easier reading. Other omissions are noted in the text with ellipses or an ornament for longer omissions.]

MR. JUSTICE MARSHALL, dissenting.

In *Furman v. Georgia*, 408 U.S. 238, 408 U.S. 314 (1972) (concurring opinion), I set forth at some length my views on the basic issue presented to the Court in these cases. The death penalty, I concluded, is a cruel and unusual punishment prohibited by the Eighth and Fourteenth Amendments. That continues to be my view.

I have no intention of retracing the "long and tedious journey," that led to my conclusion in *Furman*. My sole purposes here are to consider the suggestion that my conclusion in *Furman* has been undercut by developments since then, and briefly to evaluate the basis for my Brethren's holding that the extinction of life is a permissible form of punishment under the Cruel and Unusual Punishments Clause.

In *Furman*, I concluded that the death penalty is constitutionally invalid for two reasons. First, the death penalty is excessive.... And second, the American people, fully informed as to the purposes of the death penalty and its liabilities, would, in my view, reject it as morally unacceptable....

Since the decision in *Furman*, the legislatures of 35 States have enacted new statutes authorizing the imposition of the death sentence for certain crimes, and Congress has enacted a law providing the death penalty for air piracy resulting in death.... I would be less than candid if I did not acknowledge that these developments have a significant bearing on a realistic assessment of the moral acceptability of the death penalty to the American people. But if the constitutionality of the death penalty turns, as I have urged, on the opinion of an informed citizenry, then even the enactment of new death statutes cannot be viewed as conclusive. In *Furman*, I observed that the American people are largely unaware of the information critical to a judgment on the morality of the death penalty, and concluded that, if they were better informed, they would consider it shocking, unjust, and unacceptable.... A recent study, conducted after the enactment of the post-*Furman* statutes, has confirmed that the American people know little about the death penalty, and that the opinions of an informed public would differ significantly from those of a public unaware of the consequences and effects of the death penalty.*

Even assuming, however, that the post-*Furman* enactment of statutes authorizing the death penalty renders the prediction of the views of an informed citizenry an uncertain basis for a constitutional decision, the enactment of those statutes has no bearing whatsoever on the conclusion that the death penalty is unconstitutional because it is excessive. An excessive penalty is invalid under the Cruel and Unusual Punishments Clause "even though popular sentiment may favor" it.... The inquiry here, then, is simply whether the death penalty is

*Sarat & Vidmar, Public Opinion, The Death Penalty, and the Eighth Amendment: Testing the Marshall Hypothesis, 1976 Wis.L.Rev. 171.

necessary to accomplish the legitimate legislative purposes in punishment, or whether a less severe penalty—life imprisonment—would do as well. . . .

The two purposes that sustain the death penalty as non-excessive in the Court's view are general deterrence and retribution. In *Furman*, I canvassed the relevant data on the deterrent effect of capital punishment.... The state of knowledge at that point, after literally centuries of debate, was summarized as follows by a United Nations Committee: "It is generally agreed between the retentionists and abolitionists, whatever their opinions about the validity of comparative studies of deterrence, that the data which now exist show no correlation between the existence of capital punishment and lower rates of capital crime."*

The available evidence, I concluded in *Furman*, was convincing that "capital punishment is not necessary as a deterrent to crime in our society." . . .

The Solicitor General, in his amicus brief in these cases, relies heavily on a study by Isaac Ehrlich,† reported a year after *Furman*, to support the contention that the death penalty does deter murder. Since the Ehrlich study was not available at the time of *Furman*, and since it is the first scientific study to suggest that the death penalty may have a deterrent effect, I will briefly consider its import.

The Ehrlich study focused on the relationship in the Nation as a whole between the homicide rate and "execution risk"—the fraction of persons convicted of murder who were actually executed. Comparing the differences in homicide rate and execution risk for the years 1933 to 1969, Ehrlich found that increases in execution risk were associated with increases in the homicide rate. But when he employed the statistical technique of multiple regression analysis to control for the influence of other variables posited to have an impact on the homicide rate,‡ Ehrlich found a negative correlation between changes in the homicide rate and changes in execution risk. His

*United Nations, Department of Economic and Social Affairs, *Capital Punishment*, pt. II, 159, p. 123 (1968).

† I. Ehrlich, The Deterrent Effect of Capital Punishment: A Question of Life and Death (Working Paper No. 18, National Bureau of Economic Research, Nov. 1973); Ehrlich, The Deterrent Effect of Capital Punishment: A Question of Life and Death, 65 Am.Econ. Rev. 397 (June 1975).

‡ The variables other than execution risk included probability of arrest, probability of conviction given arrest, national aggregate measures of the percentage of the population between age 14 and 24, the unemployment rate, the labor force participation rate, and estimated per capita income.

tentative conclusion was that, for the period from 1933 to 1967, each additional execution in the United States might have saved eight lives.

The methods and conclusions of the Ehrlich study have been severely criticized on a number of grounds.* It has been suggested, for example, that the study is defective because it compares execution and homicide rates on a nationwide, rather than a state-by-state, basis. The aggregation of data from all States—including those that have abolished the death penalty—obscures the relationship between murder and execution rates. Under Ehrlich's methodology, a decrease in the execution risk in one State combined with an increase in the murder rate in another State would, all other things being equal, suggest a deterrent effect that quite obviously would not exist. Indeed, a deterrent effect would be suggested if, once again all other things being equal, one State abolished the death penalty and experienced no change in the murder rate, while another State experienced an increase in the murder rate.

The most compelling criticism of the Ehrlich study is that its conclusions are extremely sensitive to the choice of the time period included in the regression analysis. Analysis of Ehrlich's data reveals that all empirical support for the deterrent effect of capital punishment disappears when the five most recent years are removed from his time series—that is to say, whether a decrease in the execution risk corresponds to an increase or a decrease in the murder rate depends on the ending point of the sample period. This finding has cast severe doubts on the reliability of Ehrlich's tentative conclusions. Indeed, a recent regression study, based on Ehrlich's theoretical model but using cross-section state data for the years 1950 and 1960, found no support for the conclusion that executions act as a deterrent.

The Ehrlich study, in short, is of little, if any, assistance in assessing the deterrent impact of the death penalty.... The evidence I reviewed in *Furman* remains convincing, in my view, that "capital punishment is not necessary as a deterrent to crime in our society." 408 U.S. at 353. The justification for the death penalty must be found elsewhere.

---

*... In addition to the items discussed in text, criticism has been directed at the quality of Ehrlich's data, his choice of explanatory variables, his failure to account for the interdependence of those variables, and his assumptions as to the mathematical form of the relationship between the homicide rate and the explanatory variables.

The other principal purpose said to be served by the death penalty is retribution.* The notion that retribution can serve as a moral justification for the sanction of death finds credence in the opinion of my Brothers Stewart, Powell, and Stevens, and that of my Brother White in *Roberts v. Louisiana*, ... 428 U.S. 337.... It is this notion that I find to be the most disturbing aspect of today's unfortunate decisions.

The concept of retribution is a multifaceted one, and any discussion of its role in the criminal law must be undertaken with caution. On one level, it can be said that the notion of retribution or reprobation is the basis of our insistence that only those who have broken the law be punished, and, in this sense, the notion is quite obviously central to a just system of criminal sanctions. But our recognition that retribution plays a crucial role in determining who may be punished by no means requires approval of retribution as a general justification for punishment. It is the question whether retribution can provide a moral justification for punishment—in particular, capital punishment—that we must consider.

My Brothers Stewart, Powell, and Stevens offer the following explanation of the retributive justification for capital punishment:

> The instinct for retribution is part of the nature of man, and channeling that instinct in the administration of criminal justice serves an important purpose in promoting the stability of a society governed by law. When people begin to believe that organized society is unwilling or unable to impose upon criminal offenders the punishment they "deserve," then there are sown the seeds of anarchy—of self-help, vigilante justice, and lynch law.

... This statement is wholly inadequate to justify the death penalty. As my Brother Brennan stated in *Furman*, "there is no evidence whatever that utilization of imprisonment, rather than death, encourages private blood feuds and other disorders." 408 U.S. at 303 (concurring opinion). It simply defies belief to suggest that the death penalty is necessary to prevent the American people from taking the law into their own hands.

---

*In *Furman*, I considered several additional purposes arguably served by the death penalty.... The only additional purpose mentioned in the opinions in these case is specific deterrence—preventing the murderer from committing another crime. Surely life imprisonment and, if necessary, solitary confinement would fully accomplish this purpose....

In a related vein, it may be suggested that the expression of moral outrage through the imposition of the death penalty serves to reinforce basic moral values—that it marks some crimes as particularly offensive, and therefore to be avoided. The argument is akin to a deterrence argument, but differs in that it contemplates the individual's shrinking from antisocial conduct not because he fears punishment, but because he has been told in the strongest possible way that the conduct is wrong. This contention, like the previous one, provides no support for the death penalty. It is inconceivable that any individual concerned about conforming his conduct to what society says is "right" would fail to realize that murder is "wrong" if the penalty were simply life imprisonment.

The foregoing contentions—that society's expression of moral outrage through the imposition of the death penalty preempts the citizenry from taking the law into its own hands and reinforces moral values—are not retributive in the purest sense. They are essentially utilitarian, in that they portray the death penalty as valuable because of its beneficial results. These justifications for the death penalty are inadequate because the penalty is, quite clearly I think, not necessary to the accomplishment of those results.

There remains for consideration, however, what might be termed the purely retributive justification for the death penalty—that the death penalty is appropriate not because of its beneficial effect on society, but because the taking of the murderer's life is itself morally good. Some of the language of the opinion of my Brothers Stewart, Powell, and Stevens...appears positively to embrace this notion of retribution for its own sake as a justification for capital punishment. They state: "The decision that capital punishment may be the appropriate sanction in extreme cases is an expression of the community's belief that certain crimes are themselves so grievous an affront to humanity that the only adequate response may be the penalty of death."

They then quote with approval from Lord Justice Denning's remarks before the British Royal Commission on Capital Punishment: "'The truth is that some crimes are so outrageous that society insists on adequate punishment because the wrongdoer deserves it, irrespective of whether it is a deterrent or not.'"

Of course, it may be that these statements are intended as no more than observations as to the popular demands that it is thought must be responded to in order to prevent anarchy. But the implication of the statements appears to me to be quite different—namely, that society's judgment that the murderer "deserves" death must be respected not simply because the preservation of order requires it, but because it is appropriate that society make the judgment and carry it out. It is this latter notion, in particular, that I consider to be fundamentally at odds with the Eighth Amendment. The mere fact that the community demands the murderer's life in return for the evil he has done cannot sustain the death penalty, for as Justices Stewart, Powell, and Stevens remind us, "the Eighth Amendment demands more than that a challenged punishment be acceptable to contemporary society." To be sustained under the Eighth Amendment, the death penalty must "comport with the basic concept of human dignity at the core of the Amendment"; the objective in imposing it must be "[consistent] with our respect for the dignity of [other] men."...Under these standards, the taking of life "because the wrongdoer deserves it" surely must fall, for such a punishment has as its very basis the total denial of the wrongdoer's dignity and worth.

The death penalty, unnecessary to promote the goal of deterrence or to further any legitimate notion of retribution, is an excessive penalty forbidden by the Eighth and Fourteenth Amendments. I respectfully dissent from the Court's judgment upholding the sentences of death imposed upon the petitioners in these cases.

———

5. "A Living Document": 1977–1991

Justice Thurgood Marshall, passing Chief Justice Warren Burger in the hallways of the Supreme Court Building, would greet him: "What's shakin', Chief baby?" But Marshall's customary bonhomie disguised his disappointment as the Court grew more conservative during the 1970s and 1980s.

During Justice Marshall's first decade on the Court, he had frequently voted with the majority, in cases including *Roe v. Wade* (1973), protecting a woman's right to choose abortion. As justices were replaced over the years, however, Marshall found himself frequently in the minority and often authored or joined dissents from the majority's rulings. One such dissent was in *Regents of the University of California v. Bakke*, included here, in which Marshall provided a history of racial discrimination in the United States for those who needed reminding.

During Marshall's 1967 Supreme Court confirmation hearings, segregationist senator Sam Ervin of North Carolina had asked Marshall whether judges should stick to "what was written in the Constitution." He replied, "Yes, Senator, with the understanding that the Constitution is meant to be a living document."[1] On the bicentennial of the Constitution, Marshall reiterated this long-held view in one of the numerous speeches he gave during these years.

Marshall's remark that gave this book its title—that he believed in doing what he thought was right and letting the law catch up—reflected his lived understanding of the Constitution as a work in progress. It began its life as a very defective document; after all, it countenanced and facilitated the trade in kidnapped and enslaved human beings and ratified and enforced their continued captivity. But the Constitution, like the Union, has become "more perfect" through struggle, suffering, sacrifice, amendment, argument, and interpretation. Some have given all to this effort; Marshall gave much. He retired in 1991 after a long period of declining health.

President George H. W. Bush nominated Clarence Thomas to replace Justice Marshall. The Senate hearings on Thomas's nomination became a sensation when a former employee, Anita Hill, testified that Thomas had made crude sexual remarks to her. Thomas was nevertheless confirmed in a close vote. Marshall was reportedly deeply hurt by the selection of his replacement, which felt like a slap in the face: Thomas supported the death penalty, opposed abortion rights, opposed affirmative action, and had even criticized *Brown v. Board of Education* as based on sociology rather than law.[2]

Regents of Univ. of California v. Bakke, 438 U.S. 265 (1978)

Allan Bakke applied to the medical school at the University of California, Davis, but was rejected twice, even though the score assigned to him by the admissions committee was higher than the scores of several other applicants, classified as disadvantaged, who were admitted to the medical school. Bakke sued in state court to challenge the constitutionality of the medical school's affirmative action program. The California Supreme Court struck down the program as unconstitutional and ordered Bakke to be admitted. The university appealed to the U.S. Supreme Court.

A divided Court agreed that the program violated the rights of white applicants and that Bakke had to be admitted to the medical school. The justices disagreed on their reasoning, and the majority joined only parts of Justice Lewis Powell's opinion announcing the ruling. That opinion stated that affirmative action in general was allowed but also held that the medical school's affirmative action program went too far. Four justices dissented from that holding; Marshall's dissent is included here.

Justice Marshall wrote, "At every point from birth to death, the impact of the past is reflected in the still disfavored position of the Negro. In light of the sorry history of discrimination and its devastating impact on the lives of Negroes, bringing the Negro into the mainstream of American life should be a state interest of the highest order. To fail to do so is to ensure that America will forever remain a divided society."

The decision did not have as much impact on affirmative action programs as was feared when it was announced. The fractured votes on the Court in favor of the ruling left some in doubt about whether the ruling would apply to other affirmative action programs. This question was not settled until 2003, when the Supreme Court decided *Grutter v. Bollinger*, 539 U.S. 306, ruling that admissions procedures that favored underrepresented minority groups were constitutionally acceptable as long as other factors were also evaluated individually for each student.

In the Supreme Court of the United States
Regents of the University of California, Petitioner, vs. Allan Bakke

Decided June 28, 1978
Certiorari to the Supreme Court of California

DISSENT ANNOUNCEMENT

THURGOOD MARSHALL: Some of what I have to say will be repetitious but I feel obliged to say it.

I agree with the judgment of the Court, this Court only insofar as it permits a university to consider the race of an applicant in making admissions decisions.

I do not agree that petitioner's admissions program violates the Constitution.

For it must be remembered that, during most of the past 200 years, the Constitution, as interpreted by this Court, did not prohibit the most ingenious and pervasive forms of discrimination against the Negro.

Now, when a State acts to remedy the effects of that legacy of discrimination, I cannot believe that this same Constitution stands as a barrier.

Three hundred and fifty years ago, the Negro was dragged to this country in chains to be sold into slavery and the system of slavery brutalized and dehumanized both master and slave.

An implicit protection of slavery was embodied in the Declaration of Independence and was made explicit in the Constitution.

The individual States likewise established the machinery to protect the system of slavery through the promulgation of the Slave Codes, which were designed primarily to defend the property interest of the owner and his slave.

The position of the Negro slave as mere property was then confirmed by this Court in *Dred Scott against Sandford.*

The status of the Negro as property was officially erased by his emancipation at the end of the Civil War.

But the long-awaited emancipation, while freeing the Negro from slavery, did not bring him citizenship or equality in any meaningful way.

Despite the passage of the Thirteenth, Fourteenth, and Fifteenth Amendments, the Negro was systematically denied the rights that those Amendments were supposed to secure.

The combined actions and inactions of the State and Federal Governments maintained Negroes in a position of legal inferiority for another century after the Civil War.

The Southern States took the first steps and immediately following the end of the Civil War, many of the provisional legislatures passed Black Codes, similar to the Slave Codes, which, among other things, limited the rights of a Negro to own or rent property and permitted imprisonment for breach of employment contracts.

Congress responded to these legal disabilities by enacting the Reconstruction Acts and the Civil Rights Acts.

Thus for a time back there, it seemed as if the Negro might be protected from the continued denial of his civil rights and might be relieved of the disability that prevented him from taking his rightful place as a free and equal citizen.

That time, however, was short-lived. Reconstruction came to a close, and, with the assistance of this Court, the Negro was rapidly stripped of his new civil rights.

The Court began by interpreting the Civil War Amendments in a manner that sharply curtailed their substantive protections.

Then in the notorious *Civil Rights Cases*, the Court strangled Congress' efforts to use its power to promote racial equality.

The Court's ultimate blow to the Civil War Amendments and to the equality of Negroes was of course, *Plessy against Ferguson*.

In upholding that Louisiana law, they said that, "equal but separate" accommodations for whites and Negroes.

The Court held that the Fourteenth Amendment was not intended "to abolish distinctions upon color, or to enforce social, as distinguished from political equality, or a commingling of the two races upon terms unsatisfactory to either."

Ignoring totally the realities of the positions of the two races, Mr. Justice Harlan's dissenting opinion recognized the bankruptcy of the Court's reasoning.

He expressed his fear that if like laws were enacted in other States, "the effect would be in the highest degree mischievous."

The fears of Mr. Justice Harlan were soon to be realized.

In the wake of *Plessy*, many States began expand their Jim Crow laws, which had up until that time been limited primarily to passenger trains and schools.

The segregation of the races was extended to residential areas, parks, hospitals, theaters, waiting rooms, and bathrooms, you name it. The enforced segregation of the races continued into the middle of the 20th century.

In both World Wars, Negroes were for the most part confined to separate military units.

It was not until 1948 that an end to segregation in the military was ordered by President Truman and the history of the exclusion of Negro children from white public schools is too well known and recent to require repeating here.

That Negroes were deliberately excluded from public graduate and professional schools and thereby denied the opportunity to become doctors, lawyers, engineers, and the like is too well established.

The position of the Negro today in America is a tragic, but inevitable consequence of centuries of unequal treatment measured by any benchmark of comfort or achievement, meaningful equality remains a distant dream for the Negro.

A Negro child today has a life expectancy which is shorter by more than five years than of a white child, that's today.

The median income of the Negro family is only 60% of the median of a white family, and the percentage of Negroes who live in families with incomes below the poverty line is nearly four times greater than that of whites.

Today, when the Negro child reaches working age, he finds that America offers him significantly less than it offers his white counterpart.

For Negro adults, the unemployment rate is twice that of whites, at least whites and the unemployment rate for Negro teenagers is three to four times that of white teenagers, I am talking about today.

The relationship between those figures and the history of unequal treatment afforded to the Negro cannot be denied and I haven't heard it denied.

At every point from birth to death, the impact of the past is reelected to the still disfavored position of the Negro.

In light of the sorry history of discrimination and the devastating impact on the lives of Negroes, bringing the Negro into the mainstream of American life should be a state interest of the highest order.

To fail to do so is to ensure that America will remain a divided society.

I do not believe that the Fourteenth Amendment requires us to accept that fate.

Neither its history nor our past cases lend support to the conclusion that a university may not remedy the cumulative effects of society's discrimination by giving consideration to race in an effort to increase the number and percentage of Negro doctors in this country.

The experience of Negroes in America has been different in kind, not just in degree, from that of other ethnic groups.

It's not merely the history of slavery alone, but also that a whole people were marked as inferior by the law and that mark has endured.

The dream of America as great melting pot has not been realized for the Negro: because of his skin color, he never even made it into the pot.

These differences in the experience of the Negro make it difficult for me to accept that Negroes cannot be afforded greater protection under the Fourteenth Amendment where it is necessary to remedy the effects of past discrimination.

In the *Civil Rights Cases*, this Court wrote that the Negro, emerging from slavery must cease "to be the special favorite of the laws."

We cannot in light of the history of the last century yield to that view.

Had this Court been willing in 1896, in *Plessy and Ferguson* to hold that the Equal Protection Clause forbids difference in treatment based on race, we would not be faced with this dilemma in 1978.

We must remember, however, that the principle that the "Constitution is color-blind" appeared only in the dissenting opinion.

The majority of the Court rejected the principle of color blindness, and for the next 60 years, from *Plessy* to *Board of Education*, ours was a Nation where, by law, an individual could be given "special" treatment based on the color of his skin.

It is because of a legacy of unequal treatment that we now must permit the institutions of this society to give consideration to race to making decisions about who will hold the positions of influence, prestige and influence in America.

Far too long, the doors to those positions have been shut to Negroes.

If we are ever to become a fully integrated society, one in which the color of a person's skin will not determine the opportunities available to him, we must be willing to take steps to open those doors.

I do not believe that anyone can truly look into America's past and still find that a remedy for the effects of that past is impermissible.

It has been said that this case involves only the individual, Bakke and nobody else and on the other hand it says it only involves Davis University.

I doubt, however, that there is a computer capable of determining the number of persons and institutions that may be affected by the decision in this case today.

For example, we are told by the Attorney General of the United States that at least 27 federal agencies have adopted regulations, requiring recipients of federal funds to take "affirmative action to overcome the effects of conditions which resulted in limiting participation by persons of a particular race, color, or national origin."

I cannot even guess the number of state and local governments that have set up similar affirmative-action programs, which may be affected by today's decision.

I for one, fear that we have come full circle.

After the Civil War our Government started several "affirmative action" programs.

This Court in the *Civil Rights Cases* and *Plessy against Ferguson* destroyed the movement toward complete equality through affirmative actions and then for almost a century, no action was taken and this non-action was with the tacit approval of the courts.

Then we had *Brown versus [Board of] Education* and the Congressional Civil Rights Act followed by numerous affirmative-action programs.

But now today, we have this Court again stepping in this time to stop affirmative-action program of the type used by the University of California in doing so; I cannot go along.

DISSENT

[*Some citations and footnotes have been omitted for easier reading. Other omissions are noted in the text with ellipses or an ornament for longer omissions.*]

MR. JUSTICE MARSHALL, dissenting:

I agree with the judgment of the Court only insofar as it permits a university to consider the race of an applicant in making admissions decisions. I do not agree that petitioner's admissions program violates the Constitution. For it must be remembered that, during most of the past 200 years, the Constitution, as interpreted by this Court, did not prohibit the most ingenious and pervasive forms of discrimination against the Negro. Now, when a State acts to remedy the effects of that legacy of discrimination, I cannot believe that this same Constitution stands as a barrier.

I.

A.

Three hundred and fifty years ago, the Negro was dragged to this country in chains to be sold into slavery. Uprooted from his homeland and thrust into bondage for forced labor, the slave was deprived of all legal rights. It was unlawful to teach him to read; he could be sold away from his family and friends at the whim of his master; and killing or maiming him was not a crime. The system of slavery brutalized and dehumanized both master and slave.*

The denial of human rights was etched into the American Colonies' first attempts at establishing self-government. When the colonists determined to seek their independence from England, they drafted a unique document cataloguing their grievances against the King and proclaiming as "self-evident" that "all men are created equal" and are endowed "with certain unalienable Rights," including those to "Life, Liberty and the pursuit of Happiness." The self-evident truths and the unalienable rights were intended, however, to apply only to white men. An earlier draft of the Declaration of Independence, submitted by Thomas Jefferson to the Continental Congress, had included among the charges against the King that "he has waged cruel war against human nature itself, violating its most sacred rights of life and liberty in the persons of a distant people who never offended him, captivating and carrying them into slavery in another hemisphere, or to incur miserable death in their transportation thither." Franklin 88. The Southern delegation insisted that the charge be deleted; the colonists themselves were implicated in the slave trade, and inclusion of this claim might have made it more difficult to justify the continuation of slavery once the ties to England were severed. Thus, even as the colonists embarked on a course to secure their own freedom and equality, they ensured perpetuation of the system that deprived a whole race of those rights.

The implicit protection of slavery embodied in the Declaration of

*The history recounted here is perhaps too well known to require documentation. But I must acknowledge the authorities on which I rely in retelling it. J. Franklin, *From Slavery to Freedom* (4th ed., 1974) (hereinafter Franklin); R. Kluger, *Simple Justice* (1975) (hereinafter Kluger); C. Woodward, *The Strange Career of Jim Crow* (3d ed., 1974) (hereinafter Woodward).

Independence was made explicit in the Constitution, which treated a slave as being equivalent to three-fifths of a person for purposes of apportioning representatives and taxes among the States. Art. I, § 2. The Constitution also contained a clause ensuring that the "Migration or Importation" of slaves into the existing States would be legal until at least 1808, Art. I, § 9, and a fugitive slave clause requiring that, when a slave escaped to another State, he must be returned on the claim of the master, Art. IV, § 2. In their declaration of the principles that were to provide the cornerstone of the new Nation, therefore, the Framers made it plain that "we the people," for whose protection the Constitution was designed, did not include those whose skins were the wrong color. As Professor John Hope Franklin has observed, Americans "proudly accepted the challenge and responsibility of their new political freedom by establishing the machinery and safeguards that insured the continued enslavement of blacks." Franklin 100.

The individual States likewise established the machinery to protect the system of slavery through the promulgation of the Slave Codes, which were designed primarily to defend the property interest of the owner in his slave. The position of the Negro slave as mere property was confirmed by this Court in *Dred Scott v. Sandford*, 19 How. 393 (1857), holding that the Missouri Compromise—which prohibited slavery in the portion of the Louisiana Purchase Territory north of Missouri—was unconstitutional because it deprived slave owners of their property without due process. The Court declared that, under the Constitution, a slave was property, and "the right to traffic in it, like an ordinary article of merchandise and property, was guaranteed to the citizens of the United States...." 60 U.S. 451. The Court further concluded that Negroes were not intended to be included as citizens under the Constitution, but were "regarded as beings of an inferior order...altogether unfit to associate with the white race, either in social or political relations; and so far inferior that they had no rights which the white man was bound to respect...." 60 U.S. 407.

B.

The status of the Negro as property was officially erased by his emancipation at the end of the Civil War. But the long-awaited emancipation, while freeing the Negro from slavery, did not bring him citizenship or equality in any meaningful way. Slavery was replaced by a system of "laws which imposed upon the colored race onerous disabilities and burdens, and curtailed their rights in the pursuit of life, liberty, and property to such an extent that their freedom was of little value." *Slaughter-House Cases*, 16 Wall. 36, 83 U.S. 70 (1873). Despite the passage of the Thirteenth, Fourteenth, and Fifteenth Amendments, the Negro was systematically denied the rights those Amendments were supposed to secure. The combined actions and inactions of the State and Federal Governments maintained Negroes in a position of legal inferiority for another century after the Civil War.

The Southern States took the first steps to re-enslave the Negroes. Immediately following the end of the Civil War, many of the provisional legislatures passed Black Codes, similar to the Slave Codes, which, among other things, limited the rights of Negroes to own or rent property and permitted imprisonment for breach of employment contracts. Over the next several decades, the South managed to disenfranchise the Negroes in spite of the Fifteenth Amendment by various techniques, including poll taxes, deliberately complicated balloting processes, property and literacy qualifications, and, finally, the white primary.

Congress responded to the legal disabilities being imposed in the Southern States by passing the Reconstruction Acts and the Civil Rights Acts. Congress also responded to the needs of the Negroes at the end of the Civil War by establishing the Bureau of Refugees, Freedmen, and Abandoned Lands, better known as the Freedmen's Bureau, to supply food, hospitals, land, and education to the newly freed slaves. Thus, for a time, it seemed as if the Negro might be protected from the continued denial of his civil rights, and might be relieved of the disabilities that prevented him from taking his place as a free and equal citizen.

That time, however, was short-lived. Reconstruction came to a close, and, with the assistance of this Court, the Negro was rapidly stripped of his new civil rights. In the words of C. Vann Woodward: "By narrow and ingenious interpretation [the Supreme Court's] decisions over a period of years had whittled away a great part of the authority presumably given the government for protection of civil rights." Woodward 139.

The Court began by interpreting the Civil War Amendments in a manner that sharply curtailed their substantive protections. See, e.g., *Slaughter-House Cases*; *United States v. Reese*, 92 U.S. 214 (1876); *United States v. Cruikshank*, 92 U.S. 542 (1876). Then, in the notorious *Civil Rights Cases*, 109 U.S. 3 (1883), the Court strangled Congress' efforts to use its power to promote racial equality. In those cases, the Court invalidated sections of the Civil Rights Act of 1875 that made it a crime to deny equal access to "inns, public conveyances, theatres and other places of public amusement." ...According to the Court, the Fourteenth Amendment gave Congress the power to proscribe only discriminatory action by the State. The Court ruled that the Negroes who were excluded from public places suffered only an invasion of their social rights at the hands of private individuals, and Congress had no power to remedy that....

"When a man has emerged from slavery, and, by the aid of beneficent legislation, has shaken off the inseparable concomitants of that state," the Court concluded, "there must be some stage in the progress of his elevation when he takes the rank of a mere citizen, and ceases to be the special favorite of the laws...."

...As Mr. Justice Harlan noted in dissent, however, the Civil War Amendments and Civil Rights Acts did not make the Negroes the "special favorite" of the laws, but instead "sought to accomplish in reference to that race ...—what had already been done in every State of the Union for the white race—to secure and protect rights belonging to them as freemen and citizens; nothing more."

—

The Court's ultimate blow to the Civil War Amendments and to the equality of Negroes came in *Plessy v. Ferguson*, 163 U.S. 537 (1896). In upholding a Louisiana law that required railway companies to provide "equal but separate" accommodations for whites and Negroes, the Court held that the Fourteenth Amendment was not intended "to abolish distinctions based upon color, or to enforce social, as distinguished from political, equality, or a commingling of the two races upon terms unsatisfactory to either."

... Ignoring totally the realities of the positions of the two races, the Court remarked: "We consider the underlying fallacy of the plaintiff's argument to consist in the assumption that the enforced separation of the two races stamps the colored race with a badge of inferiority. If this be so, it is not by reason of anything found in the act, but solely because the colored race chooses to put that construction upon it."

—

Mr. Justice Harlan's dissenting opinion recognized the bankruptcy of the Court's reasoning. He noted that the "real meaning" of the legislation was "that colored citizens are so inferior and degraded that they cannot be allowed to sit in public coaches occupied by white citizens." 163 U.S. 560. He expressed his fear that, if like laws were enacted in other States, "the effect would be in the highest degree mischievous." ...Although slavery would have disappeared, the States would retain the power "to interfere with the full enjoyment of the blessings of freedom; to regulate civil rights, common to all citizens, upon the basis of race; and to place in a condition of legal inferiority a large body of American citizens...."

———

The fears of Mr. Justice Harlan were soon to be realized. In the wake of *Plessy*, many States expanded their Jim Crow laws, which had, up until that time, been limited primarily to passenger trains and schools. The segregation of the races was extended to residential areas, parks, hospitals, theaters, waiting rooms, and bathrooms. There were even statutes and ordinances which authorized separate phone booths for Negroes and whites, which required that textbooks used by children of one race be kept separate from those used by the other, and which required that Negro and white prostitutes be kept in separate districts. In 1898, after *Plessy*, the *Charlestown News and Courier* printed a parody of Jim Crow laws:

> If there must be Jim Crow cars on the railroads, there should be Jim Crow cars on the street railways. Also on all passenger boats.... If there are to be Jim Crow cars, moreover, there should be Jim Crow waiting saloons at all stations, and Jim Crow eating houses.... There should be Jim Crow sections of the jury box, and a separate Jim Crow dock and witness stand in every court—and a Jim Crow Bible for colored witnesses to kiss. (Woodward 68)

The irony is that, before many years had passed, with the exception of the Jim Crow witness stand, "all the improbable applications of the principle suggested by the editor in derision had been put into practice—down to and including the Jim Crow Bible."

———

Nor were the laws restricting the rights of Negroes limited solely to the Southern States. In many of the Northern States, the Negro was denied the right to vote, prevented from serving on juries, and excluded from theaters, restaurants, hotels, and inns. Under President Wilson, the Federal Government began to require segregation in Government buildings; desks of Negro employees were curtained off; separate bathrooms and separate tables in the cafeterias were provided; and even the galleries of the Congress were segregated. When his segregationist policies were attacked, President Wilson responded that segregation was "not humiliating, but a benefit,'" and that he was "'rendering [the Negroes] more safe in their possession of office, and less likely to be discriminated against.'" Kluger 91.

The enforced segregation of the races continued into the middle of the 20th century. In both World Wars, Negroes were, for the most part, confined to separate military units; it was not until 1948 that an end to segregation in the military was ordered by President Truman. And the history of the exclusion of Negro children from white public schools is too well known and recent to require repeating here. That Negroes were deliberately excluded from public graduate and professional schools—and thereby denied the opportunity to become doctors, lawyers, engineers, and the like is also well established. It is, of course, true that some of the Jim Crow laws (which the decisions of this Court had helped to foster) were struck down by this Court in a series of decisions leading up to *Brown v. Board of Education*, 347 U.S. 483 (1954). See, e.g., *Morgan v. Virginia*, 328 U.S. 373 (1946); *Sweatt v. Painter*, 339 U.S. 629 (1950); *McLaurin v. Oklahoma State Regents*, 339 U.S. 637 (1950). Those decisions, however, did not automatically end segregation, nor did they move Negroes from a position of legal inferiority to one of equality. The legacy of years of slavery and of years of second-class citizenship in the wake of emancipation could not be so easily eliminated.

II.

The position of the Negro today in America is the tragic but inevitable consequence of centuries of unequal treatment. Measured by any benchmark of comfort or achievement, meaningful equality remains a distant dream for the Negro.

A Negro child today has a life expectancy which is shorter by more than five years than that of a white child.* The Negro child's mother is over three times more likely to die of complications in childbirth, and the infant mortality rate for Negroes is nearly twice that for whites. The median income of the

---

*U.S. Dept. of Commerce, Bureau of the Census, *Statistical Abstract of the United States* 65 (1977) (Table 94).

Negro family is only 60% that of the median of a white family,* and the percentage of Negroes who live in families with incomes below the poverty line is nearly four times greater than that of whites.

When the Negro child reaches working age, he finds that America offers him significantly less than it offers his white counterpart. For Negro adults, the unemployment rate is twice that of whites,† and the unemployment rate for Negro teenagers is nearly three times that of white teenagers. A Negro male who completes four years of college can expect a median annual income of merely $110 more than a white male who has only a high school diploma.‡ Although Negroes represent 11.5% of the population,§ they are only 1.2% of the lawyers and judges, 2% of the physicians, 2.3% of the dentists, 1.1% of the engineers and 2.6% of the college and university professors.

The relationship between those figures and the history of unequal treatment afforded to the Negro cannot be denied. At every point from birth to death, the impact of the past is reflected in the still disfavored position of the Negro.

In light of the sorry history of discrimination and its devastating impact on the lives of Negroes, bringing the Negro into the mainstream of American life should be a state interest of the highest order. To fail to do so is to ensure that America will forever remain a divided society.

III.

I do not believe that the Fourteenth Amendment requires us to accept that fate. Neither its history nor our past cases lend any support to the conclusion that a university may not remedy the cumulative effects of society's discrimination by giving consideration to race in an effort to increase the number and percentage of Negro doctors.

---

*U.S. Dept. of Commerce, Bureau of the Census, Current Population Reports, Series P-60, No. 107, p. 7 (1977) (Table 1).

† U.S. Dept. of Labor, Bureau of Labor Statistics, *Employment and Earnings*, January, 1978, p. 170 (Table 44).

‡ U.S. Dept. of Commerce, Bureau of the Census, *Current Population Reports*, Series P-60, No. 105, p. 198 (1977) (Table 47).

§ U.S. Dept. of Commerce, Bureau of the Census, *Statistical Abstract*, 25 (Table 24).

A.

This Court long ago remarked that "in any fair and just construction of any section or phrase of these [Civil War] amendments, it is necessary to look to the purpose which we have said was the pervading spirit of them all, the evil which they were designed to remedy...." *Slaughter-House Cases*, 16 Wall. at 83 U.S. 72. It is plain that the Fourteenth Amendment was not intended to prohibit measures designed to remedy the effects of the Nation's past treatment of Negroes. The Congress that passed the Fourteenth Amendment is the same Congress that passed the 1866 Freedmen's Bureau Act, an Act that provided many of its benefits only to Negroes.... Although the Freedmen's Bureau legislation provided aid for refugees, thereby including white persons within some of the relief measures,... the bill was regarded, to the dismay of many Congressmen, as "solely and entirely for the freedmen, and to the exclusion of all other persons...." Cong. Globe, 39th Cong., 1st Sess., 544 (1866) (remarks of Rep. Taylor).... Indeed, the bill was bitterly opposed on the ground that it "undertakes to make the Negro in some respects...superior..., and gives them favors that the poor white boy in the North cannot get." Cong. Globe, 39th Cong., 1st Sess., 401 (remarks of Sen. McDougall).... The bill's supporters defended it not by rebutting the claim of special treatment, but by pointing to the need for such treatment:

> The very discrimination it makes between "destitute and suffering" Negroes and destitute and suffering white paupers proceeds upon the distinction that, in the omitted case, civil rights and immunities are already sufficiently protected by the possession of political power, the absence of which in the case provided for necessitates governmental protection. Cong. Globe, 39th Cong., 1st Sess., at App. 75 (remarks of Rep. Phelps).

Despite the objection to the special treatment the bill would provide for Negroes, it was passed by Congress. President Johnson vetoed this bill, and also a subsequent bill that contained some modifications; one of his principal objections to both bills was that they gave special benefits to Negroes. Rejecting the concerns of the President and the bill's opponents, Congress overrode the President's second veto.

Since the Congress that considered and rejected the objections to the 1866

Freedmen's Bureau Act concerning special relief to Negroes also proposed the Fourteenth Amendment, it is inconceivable that the Fourteenth Amendment was intended to prohibit all race-conscious relief measures. It "would be a distortion of the policy manifested in that amendment, which was adopted to prevent state legislation designed to perpetuate discrimination on the basis of race or color," *Railway Mail Assn. v. Corsi*, 326 U.S. 88, 94 (1945), to hold that it barred state action to remedy the effects of that discrimination. Such a result would pervert the intent of the Framers by substituting abstract equality for the genuine equality the Amendment was intended to achieve.

B.

As has been demonstrated in our joint opinion, this Court's past cases establish the constitutionality of race-conscious remedial measures. Beginning with the school desegregation cases, we recognized that, even absent a judicial or legislative finding of constitutional violation, a school board constitutionally could consider the race of students in making school assignment decisions. We noted, moreover, that a

> flat prohibition against assignment of students for the purpose of creating a racial balance must inevitably conflict with the duty of school authorities to disestablish dual school systems. As we have held in *Swann*, the Constitution does not compel any particular degree of racial balance or mixing, but when past and continuing constitutional violations are found, some ratios are likely to be useful as starting points in shaping a remedy. An absolute prohibition against use of such a device—even as a starting point—contravenes the implicit command of *Green v. County School Board*, 391 U.S. 430 (1968), that all reasonable methods be available to formulate an effective remedy. *Board of Education v. Swann*, 402 U.S. 43, 46 (1971).

As we have observed, "any other approach would freeze the status quo that is the very target of all desegregation processes." *McDaniel v. Barresi*, at 402 U.S. 41.

Only last Term, in *United Jewish Organizations v. Carey*, 430 U.S. 144 (1977) [*UJO*], we upheld a New York reapportionment plan that was deliberately drawn on the basis of race to enhance the electoral power of Negroes and

Puerto Ricans; the plan had the effect of diluting the electoral strength of the Hasidic Jewish community. We were willing in *UJO* to sanction the remedial use of a racial classification even though it disadvantaged otherwise "innocent" individuals. In another case last Term, *Califano v. Webster*, 430 U.S. 313 (1977), the Court upheld a provision in the Social Security laws that discriminated against men because its purpose was "the permissible one of redressing our society's long-standing disparate treatment of women."...We thus recognized the permissibility of remedying past societal discrimination through the use of otherwise disfavored classifications.

Nothing in those cases suggests that a university cannot similarly act to remedy past discrimination.* It is true that, in both *UJO* and *Webster*, the use of the disfavored classification was predicated on legislative or administrative action, but in neither case had those bodies made findings that there had been constitutional violations or that the specific individuals to be benefited had actually been the victims of discrimination. Rather, the classification in each of those cases was based on a determination that the group was in need of the remedy because of some type of past discrimination. There is thus ample support for the conclusion that a university can employ race-conscious measures to remedy past societal discrimination without the need for a finding that those benefited were actually victims of that discrimination.

IV.

While I applaud the judgment of the Court that a university may consider race in its admissions process, it is more than a little ironic that, after several hundred years of class-based discrimination against Negroes, the Court is unwilling to hold that a class-based remedy for that discrimination is permissible. In declining to so hold, today's judgment ignores the fact that, for several hundred years, Negroes have been discriminated against not as individuals, but rather solely because of the color of their skins. It is unnecessary in 20th-century America to have individual Negroes demonstrate that they have been victims of racial discrimination; the racism of our society has

---

*Indeed, the action of the University finds support in the regulations promulgated under Title VI by the Department of Health, Education, and Welfare and approved by the President, which authorize a federally funded institution to take affirmative steps to overcome past discrimination against groups even where the institution was not guilty of prior discrimination. 45 CFR § 80.3(b)(6)(ii) (1977).

been so pervasive that none, regardless of wealth or position, has managed to escape its impact. The experience of Negroes in America has been different in kind, not just in degree, from that of other ethnic groups. It is not merely the history of slavery alone, but also that a whole people were marked as inferior by the law. And that mark has endured. The dream of America as the great melting pot has not been realized for the Negro; because of his skin color, he never even made it into the pot.

These differences in the experience of the Negro make it difficult for me to accept that Negroes cannot be afforded greater protection under the Fourteenth Amendment where it is necessary to remedy the effects of past discrimination. In the *Civil Rights Cases*, the Court wrote that the Negro emerging from slavery must cease "to be the special favorite of the laws." ...We cannot, in light of the history of the last century, yield to that view. Had the Court, in that decision and others, been willing to "do for human liberty and the fundamental rights of American citizenship what it did...for the protection of slavery and the rights of the masters of fugitive slaves," 109 U.S. at 53 (Harlan, J., dissenting), we would not need now to permit the recognition of any "special wards."

Most importantly, had the Court been willing in 1896, in *Plessy v. Ferguson*, to hold that the Equal Protection Clause forbids differences in treatment based on race, we would not be faced with this dilemma in 1978. We must remember, however, that the principle that the "Constitution is colorblind" appeared only in the opinion of the lone dissenter. 163 U.S. at 559. The majority of the Court rejected the principle of color blindness, and for the next 60 years, from *Plessy* to *Brown v. Board of Education*, ours was a Nation where, by law, an individual could be given "special" treatment based on the color of his skin.

It is because of a legacy of unequal treatment that we now must permit the institutions of this society to give consideration to race in making decisions about who will hold the positions of influence, affluence, and prestige in America. For far too long, the doors to those positions have been shut to Negroes. If we are ever to become a fully integrated society, one in which the color of a person's skin will not determine the opportunities available to him or her, we must be willing to take steps to open those doors. I do not believe that anyone can truly look into America's past and still find that a remedy for the effects of that past is impermissible.

It has been said that this case involves only the individual, Bakke, and this University. I doubt, however, that there is a computer capable of determining the number of persons and institutions that may be affected by the decision in this case. For example, we are told by the Attorney General of the United States that at least 27 federal agencies have adopted regulations requiring recipients of federal funds to take *"affirmative action* to overcome the effects of conditions which resulted in limiting participation... by persons of a particular race, color, or national origin." Supplemental Brief for United States as Amicus Curiae 16 (emphasis added). I cannot even guess the number of state and local governments that have set up affirmative action programs, which may be affected by today's decision.

I fear that we have come full circle. After the Civil War, our Government started several "affirmative action" programs. This Court, in the *Civil Rights Cases* and *Plessy v. Ferguson*, destroyed the movement toward complete equality. For almost a century, no action was taken, and this nonaction was with the tacit approval of the courts. Then we had *Brown v. Board of Education* and the Civil Rights Acts of Congress, followed by numerous affirmative action programs. Now, we have this Court again stepping in, this time to stop affirmative action programs of the type used by the University of California.

Equality Speech (1978)

Marshall gave this informal speech when Wiley Branton, an old friend, became the dean of Marshall's alma mater, Howard Law School. The two had worked together on the integration of Central High School in Little Rock during the late 1950s (see chapter 2). Marshall warned his audience, quoting his old mentor at Howard, Charles Hamilton Houston:

> There are people that tell us today, and there are movements that tell us, tell Negroes, "Take it easy man. You made it. No more to worry about. Everything is easy." Again, I remind you about what Charlie Houston said, "You have got to be better, boy. You better move better." ...Don't listen to this myth that...it has already been solved. Take it from me, it has not been solved.

SPEECH

Installation of Wiley Branton as dean of Howard Law School, Washington, D.C., November 18, 1978

Mr. Chief Justice, Mr. President, my friends...It is a great day. We are all here because it is a great day. I am particularly happy that people like the Chief Justice of the United States is here; and other Chief Judges. [*Applause.*] I want to confess, I begged him not to come; because I know how much work he has to do. By statute, he has jurisdiction over I don't know how many different outfits in this country, which he has to go to. And then he has to preside over some five hundred Federal Judges, each of whom is an individual prima donna. [*Laughter.*] And with all of that, he shouldn't find time to come something like this. But, he insisted. To him, it was that important; and to me that truly demonstrates how important it is.

I would like to start off by having a couple of true stories on the record. I do not have a written speech. I have gotten away from written speeches since I heard about that legislator who had a speech committee in his office...and they would write up these speeches for him. He wouldn't even look at them before he delivered them. He just read them off. And this day he said, "Look! Next Monday night I am speaking for Senator Johnson; and I want a speech, twenty minutes [long]; and I want it on energy." And they said, "What are...?" And he said, "That's it. Just go do it." And they did. And on Monday they gave him the speech and he went out, got in his car, got in the place, got there, got in another car, went there. When he was called on to speak, he opened up his speech, and on the first page he went on telling stories like this... [*Laughter from the audience.*] Except mine is true. [*Laughter.*] Then he went on talking in general about the energy problem. And then he said, he has "an airtight program for taking care of the entire energy program. It was very elaborate; and it was set up in five different phases, all five of which, I shall set forth before you tonight." And he turned over the page and to his utter surprise, he saw "Now, you sucker, you are on your own." [*Laughter and applause.*] I have given up that idea... [*Laughter.*]

...When I decided to come. [*Laughter.*] ...I am not too much in the line of notes. But the one that really is what I am going to talk about today is a Las Vegas story.

This guy went out from California to Las Vegas and did what all others do. He lost his money. [*Laughter.*] All of it including his fare home. And he was commiserating with himself; and as sometimes happens, he had to go. And when he got to the toilet room... [*Laughter*], he found out, that they had not nickel or dime: they had quarter ones. [*Laughter.*] And he didn't have a nickel. So he was in pretty bad shape. [*Laughter.*] And just then a gentleman came by and he told the gentleman his problem... The guy said, "I will give you a quarter." And the guy said, "Well look, you don't know me... I don't care if you give it back to me or not. You are no problem. Here's a quarter." He took the quarter and went in the room there, and just as he was about to put the quarter in the slot to open the door, the door had been left open for somebody. So he put the quarter in his pocket. He went on in; and when he finished, he went upstairs. A quarter wasn't going to get him back to Los Angeles. A quarter wasn't even going to feed him. So, he put the quarter in the slot machine. And it wouldn't be any story if he didn't hit the jackpot. [*Laughter.*] Then he hit the bigger jackpot... and he went to the crap table; he went to the roulette table. He ended up with about ten or fifteen thousand dollars' worth.

He went back to Los Angeles, invested in the right stock. He got the right business together. And in pretty short order, about fifteen years, he became the second wealthiest man in the world. And on television, they asked him about it; and he said he would like to tell his story. And he told the story. And he said, "I am so indebted to that benefactor of mine. That man who made all of this possible. And if he comes forth and proves it; that he was the man, I will give him half of my wealth in cash. [*Laughter.*] So a man came forth... They had all the elaborate... private detective investigation; and sure enough, "That was the man."... The guy said, "Well look. Are you sure you are the one I am looking for?" He said, "Why certainly." He said, "Who are you?" He said, "I am the man that gave you that quarter." He said, "Heck, I'm not looking for him. I am looking for the man who left the door opened. [*Applause and laughter.*] Because you see, if he hadn't left the door open, I would have had to put the quarter in the slot." [*Laughter.*]

I figure at a stage like this in our development of our law school, we have to be sure we know just what we are after.

Why do we have occasions like this? Well, I will tell you why. Everything in any question of education depends on the reputation of the school. And a part of the reputation of the school, is the reputation of the dean. And being so old as I am, you almost scared me to death, Wiley, talking about the oldest graduate was here. [*Laughter.*]

... In order to find out just where we stand, and to be in a room like this, and on a campus I like this, I had to go back... But you know it's an awful long way from 25th Street [*a former location for Howard Law School*]; which incidentally, I went by not too long ago. These of you that hadn't been by, it's gone. They have torn it down. It was a marvelous place when it was there.

But today, you know, we have reached the place where people say, "We've come a long way." But so [have] other people come a long way. And so have other schools come a long way. Has the gap been getting smaller? It's getting bigger. Everybody's been doing better.

And so, as you took at the law school today, and that's what you have to look at. You look back, and people say we are better off today. Better than what?

You know, I used to be amazed at people who would say that, "The poorest Negro kid in the South was better off than the kid in South Africa." So what! We are not in South Africa. [*Applause.*] We are here. [*Applause.*] "You ought to go around the country and show yourself to Negroes; and give them inspiration." "For what? These Negro kids are not fools. They know to tell them there is a possibility that someday you'll have a chance to be the o-n-l-y Negro on the Supreme Court, those odds aren't too good." [*Applause.*]

When I do get around the country like recently, I have been to places like...unfortunately for funerals; like New Orleans, Houston, Dallas, etc. When I get out and talk with the people in the street, I still get the same problems. "You know, like years ago, you told us things were going to get better. But they are not a darn bit better for me. I am still having trouble getting to work. I have trouble eating." And guess what I am getting now? "... You not only told me that; you told my father that. And he's no better off; and neither am I. And can you tell me my children will be better off." Well, all I am trying to tell you...there's a lot more to be done. Now, think of those good old days. We started at Howard with Charlie Houston as dean [*Charles H. Houston, Dean of Howard University Law School, 1930–1935*]...The school had several things that they did not have would be more important. They did not have a reputation, and they did not have any accreditation; and they did not have anything, it looked to me.

Charlie Houston took over and in two or three years got full accreditation: American Bar Association, Association of American Law Schools, etc. He did it the hard way.

And for any students that might be interested, for these of you who came to this school later, and had complaints, you should have been there when I was there.

We named Charlie the only repeatable names I could give him as "Iron Shoes and Cement Pants." [*Laughter.*] We had a lot of others but... [*Laughter.*]

He even installed the cutback system that would keep you on the books all the time. And that was that, a professor could take five points off your mark for no reason at all. So the only way you could really make it is to get around 95 ...

He gave an examination in Evidence in our second year that started at nine o'clock in the morning and ended at five in the afternoon. One subject.

In our first year he told us, "Look at the man on your right, took at the man on your left, and at this time next year, two of you won't be here." [*Laughter.*] ...

I know my class started, as I remember, it was around thirty; and it ended up with six...He brought in people not on the faculty, but who were coming by Washington. And because of his reputation and background he could get them.

And the people I would list. Every time they came to Washington, they would come by; and we would close up the school and listen to them, in our moot courtroom, which held about fifteen.

For example, a man by the name of Roscoe Pound who just happened to be Dean of Harvard Law School, would talk and lecture to us on the Common Law.

And it just so happened that at that time he was the greatest authority in the world... Then we had Bill Lewis, a Negro lawyer from Boston, Massachusetts, who had the distinction of being Assistant Attorney General, a little while back, under Theodore Roosevelt. He would tell us about how to try a lawsuit; and how to argue with the Judges; because he was a master of it. And we would run to the Supreme Court and hear him argue.

Then Garfield Hayes would drop by from the American Civil Liberties Union. The first time, I was very impressed with the fact, he was en route from Birmingham, Alabama, where he had defended a poor Negro. He was then en route to Boston, Massachusetts, to defend the Ku Klux Klan... He explained to me about the Constitution being color-blind.

Then you had people like Clarence Darrow who told us the importance of sociology and other studies rather than law—which he considered to be unimportant. As witness one time, he was trying a case in North Carolina. A Negro beating up a white man. And his whole argument... to the jury was (he had never touched the facts of the case),... that this was a waste of time for him to stand up there and argue to this all white Southern prejudiced jury; that no way in the world they could give this Negro a chance. They just couldn't do it because they were too prejudiced. And he argued that for two and a half hours; and the jury went out and came back and proved to him that they weren't prejudiced. [*Laughter.*] And they turned the man loose. [*Laughter.*]

We had Vaughn S. Cooke, a great expert on Conflict Law. People like that because the emphasis was not theory. The emphasis in this school was on practice. How to get it done.

Harvard was training people to join big Wall Street firms. Howard was teaching lawyers to go out and go in court. Charlie's phrase was Social Engineer. To be a part of the community. And have the lawyer to take over the leadership in the community.

And we used to hold fort in our little library down there, after school, at night. And start out on research problems sometimes sponsored by him and sometimes on our own.

Indeed, I remember one time, one night. One guy, I believe it was Oliver Hill... He got to work on something, we all joined in. And we found out that in codifying the Code of the District of Columbia, they had just left out the Civil Rights Statute. So, since it didn't apply to anybody but us, they left it out. We eventually got through in court and got that straightened out. And we got to work on segregation. What are we going to do about that?

I for one was very interested in it because I couldn't go to the University of Maryland. I had to ride the train everyday, twice a day. Back and forth. I didn't like that ...

Well, it ended up Bill Hastie [*William H. Hastie, Dean of Howard University Law School, 1939–1946*] went down to North Carolina and filed our first University case which we lost on a technicality. But Hastie laid the groundwork for the future.

Then we had a criminal case dealing with a man named Crawford. We did more litigating, I guess, than any school I ever did.

But I emphasize that it was aimed at working in the community. The other thing that Charlie beat in our heads... I think that is very important. He says, "You know when a doctor makes a mistake, he buries his mistake. When a lawyer makes a mistake, he makes it in front of God and everybody else." [*Laughter.*]

When you get in the courtroom you can't say, "Please, Mr. Court, have mercy on me because I am a Negro." You are in competition with a well-trained white lawyer and you better be at least as good as he, and if you expect to win, you better be better. [*Applause.*] If I give you five cases to read overnight, you read eight. And when I say eight, you read ten. You go that step further; and you might make it. And then you had all these other people, Charles H. Houston, William H. Hastie, George E. C. Hayes, Leon A. Ransom, Edward P. Lovett, James Nabrit, Spottswood W. Robinson III.

Then later you had Robert L. Carter, Constance Baker Motley, A. T. Walden in Atlanta, Arthur Shores in Birmingham, A. P. Tureaud, Sr., in New Orleans.

Then on the other side you had a very good group of professors from other schools. Charles Black... and others.

Then we had a certain wild guy over there in Arkansas. [*Laughter.*] I would just like to mention it at this point, because it is very important, I think, to realize that in those days, "it was rough." And I think Wiley is an example of one part of it. I got the credit mostly. But I would go to those places, and

I would get out on the fastest damn thing that moved. [*Laughter.*] I couldn't wait for the plane. And then I couldn't wait for the jet. [*Laughter.*] I am talking about... He stayed there. He didn't go. He stayed right there. He had not once, but crosses were burned on his lawn. He had everything they could try. He laughed at them. He stayed there, and made them take it and like it. I mentioned that because it seems to me, that while we had this whole movement going along, we were beginning to touch it.

Then we had those Damon [*Damon J. Keith, Judge, U.S. Court of Appeals for the Sixth Circuit*] was talking about. Those dry runs. We would have both of the Lawyers who were going to argue tomorrow's case before the Supreme Court, to come before a panel of judges in our old moot courtroom, when we were in the library down there on the campus. This went on all during the 1940's. The faculty members who set as members of the Court were deliberately urged to be rougher and excuse me, "nastier" than the judges would be. And you know, it worked well; because once you got through with that slugging match with them, you didn't worry about anything the next day. It was like going to an ice cream party...because the members of the court were so polite and nice to you. Well, I keep reminding you that this was done at Howard; all of it. How much it was necessary to the success of those cases, is left to anybody. And finally on that point, I want you to know, that starting with that research in the library of finding the Civil Rights Statute, through all these cases in the Supreme Court, clean up to the present time, in the *Bakke* case, I will tell anybody, and I will dispute anybody who does not agree, that the brief filed by Herb Reid [*Herbert O. Reid Sr., Charles Hamilton Houston Distinguished Professor of Law at Howard University*] was one of the best briefs. [*Standing ovation.*] He didn't pay me a nickel for it. [*Laughter.*]

Now, you know, Wiley integrated the University of Arkansas. He went back down in there; and cases that were mentioned, I know several other criminal cases that were just unbelievable. He went from there to Atlanta; and up here to Washington. I hate to get down into the gutter; but "Wiley" stands for, "brains and guts." I know both of them; I have seen him in action. It seems to me, that what are we going to do now, other than, all of us to give our blessings to what I consider a perfect marriage: Branton and the Howard Law School. [*Applause.*]

That's not enough because we have got to look to the future. They are still laying traps for us.

I have just requested a book which I heard about. Believe it or not, somebody found out the Klan [*Ku Klux Klan*] is still around. I could have told them that. [*Laughter.*] The Klan never died. They just stopped wearing the sheets, because the sheets cost too much. [*Laughter.*] When I say "they," I think we all know who "they" would include. We have them in every phase of American life. And as we dedicate this courtroom, as we launch Wiley on his road, we just have to continue that basic theory of practice; and not just theory. With these clinics that have been set up, you note we can give the poor people in the ghettoes for peanuts better legal protection than the millionaires get. If we could just get them to bring their legal problems to the lawyer, before they sign them. That's how to stay out of trouble. And that can be done with clinics. And I think this law school has to insist on that. And here I have a note which says all of this has to be done and it has to be done together.

There are people that tell us today, and there are movements that tell us, tell Negroes, "Take it easy man. You made it. No more to worry about. Everything is easy." Again, I remind you about what Charlie Houston said, "You have got to be better, boy. You better move better."

Be careful of these people who say, "You have made it. Take it easy; you don't need any more help."...I would like to read...for these people who tell you, "to take it easy. Don't worry, etc."

"The great enemy of truth very often is not the lie—deliberate, contrived and dishonest—but the myth—persistent, persuasive, and unrealistic."—John F. Kennedy

Be aware of that myth, that everything is going to be all right. Don't give in. I add that, because it seems to me, that what we need to do today is to refocus. Back in the 1930s and 40s, we could go no place but to court. We knew then, the court was not the final solution. Many of us knew the final solution would have to be politics, if for no other reason, politics is cheaper than lawsuits. So now we have both. We have our legal arm, and we have our political arm. Let's use them both. And don't listen to this myth that it can be solved by either or that it has already been solved. Take it from me, it has not been solved.

I will conclude if I may with a conclusion from another great American, the late Chief Justice Warren in his one book. And this is the conclusion of his book. And more important and as we move more in what I consider to be his new phase. He says, "Those who won our independence believed that the greatest menace to freedom is an inert people. That public discussion is a political duty. That this should be a fundamental principle of the American government. They eschewed silence coerced by law."

And then again, Chief Justice Warren:

> No, the democratic way of life is not easy. It conveys great privileges with constant vigilance needed to preserve them. This vigilance must be maintained by those responsible for the government. And in our country those responsible are we the people, no one else. Responsible citizenship is therefore the... anchor of our republic. With it we can withstand the storm. Without it, we are helplessly at sea.

It is beyond question... Benjamin Franklin had it in mind when he said: "A republic, if you can keep it."

To me, that means much. It's not "a republic, if we keep it." With me, "It's a democracy, if we can keep it. And in order to keep it, you can't stand still. You must move, and if you don't move, they will run over you."

This law school has been in the front. It's been the bellwether. It's been the fulcrum of pressure.

In driving on, I am just as certain as I have ever been in my life, that under the leadership of Wiley Branton, it will not only continue: it will broaden, increase and continue to be the bulwark that we all can be proud of.

This is a great day. We are entering a great era. And let's do as many of us did back home. You know some people have been going home with the *Roots* [*a popular 1970s television miniseries tracing the history of a fictional Black American family*] business and all that. [*Laughter.*] I have been going over these since the late 1950s. When Kenya got its independence in 1963, and to see all those hundreds of thousands of people, when freedom was declared,... in unison yelled, "Harambee": [*meaning*] "Pull Together."

We could, and with Wiley and this school, we will continue to do it. Anything I can do to help, I will do—that is, except raise money. Because there are a couple of committees of the Judiciary that say, "No." [*Standing ovation.*]

The Sword and the Robe (1981)

After Ronald Reagan's election to the White House in 1980, the United States and the Supreme Court both became increasingly conservative. Chief Justice Warren Burger, who had been appointed by President Richard Nixon, spoke before the American Bar Association (ABA) in February 1981, blaming the judicial system for providing "massive safeguards for accused persons" while failing to provide "elementary protection for its decent, law-abiding citizens."[3] Many saw the speech that follows, which Marshall gave at the Second Circuit Judicial Conference three months later, as a direct rejoinder to the chief justice's address to the ABA.

SPEECH
Second Circuit Judicial Conference, May 8, 1981

The task of interpretation is the cornerstone of the judicial process. As we undertake it, we must strive for neutrality. None of us is perfect, and I recognize that neutrality is more ideal than real. Each of us brings along to the judicial role certain preconceived biases. It is, I suppose, impossible to make a decision totally uninfluenced by them. But we as judges must try to do so to the extent we possibly can.

This ideal of neutrality is particularly hard to maintain in times such as these, when our society faces major unsolved problems. Indeed, we judges are frequently criticized these days for our neutrality. For example, it is argued by some members of our society that the judiciary has not taken an active enough role in combating crime. It is urged that we as judges, should take sides, that we should stand shoulder to shoulder with the police and prosecutors. Convictions should be easier, appellate review more rapid and resort to habeas corpus—what the founders of this republic called the Great Writ—drastically curtailed. All of this frightens me, because when I was in law school, I was taught not that judges were there to see the defendant convicted and punished in every case but that they were there to see justice done in every case. Of course the state had to carry a heavy burden to obtain a conviction. Of course appellate judges would weigh each case carefully. Of course an individual, once convicted, could attack his sentence later. This, so I was taught, was not to coddle the guilty but to protect the innocent. I was raised in the days when the prevailing maxim was: "It is better that a thousand guilty people go free than that one innocent person suffer unjustly."

Well, that's just what I was taught, and maybe I was taught wrong. But the suggestion that we as judges take sides frightens me for another, more fundamental reason as well. As I have said, judges are required in our system to be as neutral as they possibly can, to stand above the political questions in which the other branches of government are necessarily entangled. The Constitution established a legislative branch to make the laws and an executive branch to enforce them. Both branches are elected and are designed to respond to ever-changing public concern, and problems. Indeed, as we were reminded just last November, the failure of either branch to respond to the will of the majority can quickly be remedied at the polls.

But the framers of the Constitution recognized that responsiveness to the will of the majority may, if unchecked, become a tyranny of the majority. They therefore created a third branch—the judiciary—to check the actions of the legislature and the executive. In order to fulfill this function, the judiciary was intentionally isolated from the political process and purposely spared the task of dealing with changing public concerns and problems. Article III judges are guaranteed life tenure. Similarly, their compensation cannot be decreased during their term in office—a provision, as we have recently seen, that certainly has its tangible benefits. Finally, the constitutional task we are assigned as judges is a very narrow one. We cannot make the laws, and it is not our duty to see that they are enforced. We merely interpret them through the painstaking process of adjudicating actual "cases or controversies" that come before us.

We have seen what happens when the courts have permitted themselves to be moved by prevailing political pressures and have deferred to the mob rather than interpret the Constitution. *Dred Scott* [*the 1857 case holding that the U.S. Constitution did not extend American citizenship to people of African descent, whether enslaved or not*], *Plessy* [*the 1896 case sustaining the legality of racial segregation*], *Korematsu* [*the 1944 case upholding the compulsory exclusion of Japanese Americans from the West Coast during wartime*], and the trial proceedings in *Moore v. Dempsey* [*a 1923 case in which the judge in the capital murder trial of twelve Black Arkansas farmers, for allegedly killing whites during a riot, permitted the proceedings to be dominated by a lynch mob*], come readily to mind as unfortunate examples. They are decisions of which the entire judicial community, even after all these years, should be ashamed. There have also been times when the courts have stood proudly as a bulwark against what was politically expedient but also unconstitutional. One need only recall the school desegregation cases to understand why this ability to stand above the fray is so important.

Our central function is to act as neutral arbiters of disputes that arise under the law. To this end, we bind ourselves through our own code of ethics to avoid even the appearance of impropriety or partiality. We must handle the cases that come before us without regard for what result might meet with public approval. We must decide each case in accordance with the law. We must not reach for a result that we, in our arrogance, believe will further some goal not related to the concrete case before us. And we must treat the litigants in every case in an evenhanded manner. It would be as wrong to favor the prosecution in every criminal case as it would be to favor the plaintiff in every tort suit.

We must never forget that the only real source of power that we as judges can tap is the respect of the people. We will command that respect only as long as we strive for neutrality. If we are perceived as campaigning for particular policies, as joining with other branches of government in resolving questions not committed to us by the Constitution, we may gain some public acclaim in the short run. In the long run, however, we will cease to be perceived as neutral arbiters, and we will lose that public respect so vital to our function.

I do not suggest that we as judges should not be concerned about the problem of crime. Every thinking American is worried about it. And just about all of us have lurking somewhere in the back of our minds what we consider the ideal solution.

But when we accepted the judicial mantle, we yielded our right to advocate publicly our favored solutions for society's problems. The tools for solving these problems are in the hands of the other branches of government because that is where the Constitution has placed them. That is also where we should leave them. I therefore urge that you politely disregard any suggestion that you give up the robe for the sword.

The Constitution's Bicentennial (1987)

Marshall used the occasion of the two-hundredth anniversary of the writing of the U.S. Constitution to give listeners a history lesson. He noted that though the Founders carefully avoided using the word "slave" in the document, they reached a clear understanding that the trade in kidnapped and enslaved human beings that was enriching both New England and the Southern states at the time of the Constitutional Convention of 1787 would continue under the new Constitution. It took a Civil War, constitutional amendments, and continued "suffering, struggle, and sacrifice" for Americans to triumph over "much of what was wrong with the original document." Marshall found the Constitution worth celebrating only as a work in progress, "a living document, including the Bill of Rights and the other amendments protecting individual freedoms and human rights."

SPEECH

Annual Seminar of the San Francisco Patent and Trademark Law Association, Maui, Hawaii, May 6, 1987

1987 marks the 200th anniversary of the United States Constitution. A Commission has been established to coordinate the celebration. The official meetings, essay contests, and festivities have begun.

The planned commemoration will span three years, and I am told 1987 is "dedicated to the memory of the Founders and the document they drafted in Philadelphia."* We are to "recall the achievements of our Founders and the knowledge and experience that inspired them, the nature of the government they established, its origins, its character, and its ends, and the rights and privileges of citizenship, as well as its attendant responsibilities."†

* Commission on the Bicentennial of the United States Constitution, *First Full Year's Report*, at 7 (Sept. 1986).

† Commission on the Bicentennial of the United States Constitution, *First Report*, at 6 (Sept. 17, 1985).

Like many anniversary celebrations, the plan for 1987 takes particular events and holds them up as the source of all the very best that has followed. Patriotic feelings will surely swell, prompting proud proclamations of the wisdom, foresight, and sense of justice shared by the Framers and reflected in a written document now yellowed with age. This is unfortunate—not the patriotism itself, but the tendency for the celebration to oversimplify, and overlook the many other events that have been instrumental to our achievements as a nation. The focus of this celebration invites a complacent belief that the vision of those who debated and compromised in Philadelphia yielded the "more perfect Union" it is said we now enjoy.

I cannot accept this invitation, for I do not believe that the meaning of the Constitution was forever "fixed" at the Philadelphia Convention. Nor do I find the wisdom, foresight, and sense of justice exhibited by the Framers particularly profound. To the contrary, the government they devised was defective from the start, requiring several amendments, a civil war, and momentous social transformation to attain the system of constitutional government, and its respect for the individual freedoms and human rights, we hold as fundamental today. When contemporary Americans cite "The Constitution," they invoke a concept that is vastly different from what the Framers barely began to construct two centuries ago.

For a sense of the evolving nature of the Constitution we need look no further than the first three words of the document's preamble: "We the People." When the Founding Fathers used this phrase in 1787, they did not have in mind the majority of America's citizens. "We the People" included, in the words of the Framers, "the whole Number of free Persons."* On a matter so basic as the right to vote, for example, Negro slaves were excluded, although they were counted for representational purposes at three-fifths each. Women did not gain the right to vote for over a hundred and thirty years.†

These omissions were intentional. The record of the Framers' debates on the slave question is especially clear: The Southern States acceded to the demands of the New England States for giving Congress broad power to regulate commerce, in exchange for the right to continue the slave trade. The economic

---

* U.S. Const. art. 1, § 2 (Sept. 17, 1787).

†. U.S. Const. amend. XIX (ratified 1920).

interests of the regions coalesced: New Englanders engaged in the "carrying trade" would profit from transporting slaves from Africa as well as goods produced in America by slave labor. The perpetuation of slavery ensured the primary source of wealth in the Southern States.

Despite this clear understanding of the role slavery would play in the new republic, use of the words "slaves" and "slavery" was carefully avoided in the original document. Political representation in the lower House of Congress was to be based on the population of "free Persons" in each State, plus three-fifths of all "other Persons."* Moral principles against slavery, for those who had them, were compromised, with no explanation of the conflicting principles for which the American Revolutionary War had ostensibly been fought: the self-evident truths "that all men are created equal, that they are endowed by their Creator with certain unalienable Rights, that among these are Life, Liberty and the pursuit of Happiness."†

It was not the first such compromise. Even these ringing phrases from the Declaration of Independence are filled with irony, for an early draft of what became that Declaration assailed the King of England for suppressing legislative attempts to end the slave trade and for encouraging slave rebellions.‡ The final draft adopted in 1776 did not contain this criticism. And so again at the Constitutional Convention eloquent objections to the institution of slavery went unheeded, and its opponents eventually consented to a document which laid a foundation for the tragic events that were to follow.

Pennsylvania's Gouverneur Morris provides an example. He opposed slavery and the counting of slaves in determining the basis for representation in Congress. At the Convention he objected that

> the inhabitant of Georgia [or] South Carolina who goes to the coast of Africa, and in defiance of the most sacred laws of humanity tears away his fellow creatures from their dearest connections and damns them to the most cruel bondages, shall have more votes in a Government instituted for protection of the rights of mankind, than the

* U.S. Const. art. 1, § 2 (Sept. 17, 1787).

† Declaration of Independence (July 4, 1776).

‡ See C. Becker, *The Declaration of Independence: A Study in the History of Political Ideas* 147 (1942).

Citizen of Pennsylvania or New Jersey who views with a laudable horror, so nefarious a practice.*

And yet Gouverneur Morris eventually accepted the three-fifths accommodation. In fact, he wrote the final draft of the Constitution, the very document the Bicentennial will commemorate.

As a result of compromise, the right of the Southern States to continue importing slaves was extended, officially, at least until 1808. We know that it actually lasted a good deal longer, as the Framers possessed no monopoly on the ability to trade moral principles for self-interest. But they nevertheless set an unfortunate example. Slaves could be imported, if the commercial interests of the North were protected. To make the compromise even more palatable, customs duties would be imposed at up to ten dollars per slave as a means of raising public revenues.†

No doubt it will be said, when the unpleasant truth of the history of slavery in America is mentioned during this Bicentennial year, that the Constitution was a product of its times, and embodied a compromise which, under other circumstances, would not have been made. But the effects of the Framers' compromise have remained for generations. They arose from the contradiction between guaranteeing liberty and justice to all, and denying both to Negroes.

The original intent of the phrase, "We the People," was far too clear for any ameliorating construction. Writing for the Supreme Court in 1857, Chief Justice Taney penned the following passage in the *Dred Scott* case,‡ on the issue whether, in the eyes of the Framers, slaves were "constituent members of the sovereignty," and were to be included among "We the People":

> We think they are not, and that they are not included, and were not intended to be included. . . .

> They had for more than a century before been regarded as beings of an inferior order; and altogether unfit to associate with the white race . . . ; and so far inferior, that they had no rights which the white

---

* 2 *The Records of the Federal Convention of 1787*, at 222 (M. Farrand, ed., 1911).

† U.S. Const. art. 1, § 9 (Sept. 17, 1787).

‡ *Scott v. Sandford*, 60 U.S. (19 How.) 393, 405, 407–408 (1857).

Let the Law Catch Up / 244

man was bound to respect; and that the Negro might justly and lawfully be reduced to slavery for his benefit.

Accordingly, a Negro of the African race was regarded...as an article of property, and held, and bought and sold as such.... No one seems to have doubted the correctness of the prevailing opinion of the time.*

And so, nearly seven decades after the Constitutional Convention, the Supreme Court reaffirmed the prevailing opinion of the Framers regarding the rights of Negroes in America. It took a bloody civil war before the Thirteenth Amendment could be adopted to abolish slavery, though not the consequences slavery would have for future Americans.

While the Union survived the Civil War, the Constitution did not. In its place arose a new, more promising basis for justice and equality, the Fourteenth Amendment, ensuring protection of the life, liberty, and property of all persons against deprivations without due process, and guaranteeing equal protection of the laws. And yet almost another century would pass before any significant recognition was obtained of the rights of Black Americans to share equally even in such basic opportunities as education, housing, and employment, and to have their votes counted, and counted equally. In the meantime, Blacks joined America's military to fight its wars and invested untold hours working in its factories and on its farms, contributing to the development of this country's magnificent wealth and waiting to share in its prosperity.

What is striking is the role legal principles have played throughout America's history in determining the condition of Negroes. They were enslaved by law, emancipated by law, disenfranchised and segregated by law; and, finally, they have begun to win equality by law. Along the way, new constitutional principles have emerged to meet the challenges of a changing society. The progress has been dramatic, and it will continue.

The men who gathered in Philadelphia in 1787 could not have envisioned these changes. They could not have imagined, nor would they have accepted, that the document they were drafting would one day be construed by a Supreme Court to which had been appointed a woman and the descendant of an

---

* Scott v. Sandford, 60 U.S. 407–408.

African slave. "We the People" no longer enslave, but the credit does not belong to the Framers. It belongs to those who refused to acquiesce in outdated notions of "liberty," "justice," and "equality," and who strived to better them.

And so we must be careful, when focusing on the events which took place in Philadelphia two centuries ago, that we not overlook the momentous events which followed, and thereby lose our proper sense of perspective. Otherwise, the odds are that for many Americans the Bicentennial celebration will be little more than a blind pilgrimage to the shrine of the original document now stored in a vault in the National Archives. If we seek, instead, a sensitive understanding of the Constitution's inherent defects, and its promising evolution through 200 years of history, the celebration of the "Miracle at Philadelphia"* will, in my view, be a far more meaningful and humbling experience. We will see that the true miracle was not the birth of the Constitution, but its life, a life nurtured through two turbulent centuries of our own making, and a life embodying much good fortune that was not.

Thus, in this Bicentennial year, we may not all participate in the festivities with flag-waving fervor. Some may more quietly commemorate the suffering, struggle, and sacrifice that has triumphed over much of what was wrong with the original document, and observe the anniversary with hopes not realized and promises not fulfilled. I plan to celebrate the Bicentennial of the Constitution as a living document, including the Bill of Rights and the other amendments protecting individual freedoms and human rights.

---

* C. Bowen, *Miracle at Philadelphia: The Story of the Constitutional Convention, May to September, 1787* (1966).

Afterword

After his retirement, Marshall was honored with the Liberty Medal on July 4, 1992. In his acceptance speech, he passionately offered an agenda for change and a call for optimism and unity in the face of differences:

We cannot play ostrich. Democracy just cannot flourish amid fear. Liberty cannot bloom amid hate. Justice cannot take root amid rage. America must get to work. In the chill climate in which we live, we must go against the prevailing wind. We must dissent from the indifference. We must dissent from the apathy. We must dissent from the fear, the hatred and the mistrust. We must dissent from a nation that has buried its head in the sand, waiting in vain for the needs of its poor, its elderly, and its sick to disappear and just blow away. We must dissent from a government that has left its young without jobs, education or hope. We must dissent from the poverty of vision and the absence of moral leadership. We must dissent because America can do better, because America has no choice but to do better.

The legal system can force open doors and sometimes even knock down walls. But it cannot build bridges. That job belongs to you and me. Afro and White, rich and poor, educated and illiterate, our fates are bound together. We can run from each other but we cannot escape each other. We will only attain freedom if we learn to appreciate what is different and muster the courage to discover what is fundamentally the same. America's diversity offers so much richness and opportunity. Take a chance, won't you? Knock down the fences that divide. Tear apart the walls that imprison. Reach out, freedom lies just on the other side. We should have liberty for all.[1]

Thurgood Marshall died on January 24, 1993. He lay in repose in the United States Supreme Court Building's Great Hall and was buried in Arlington National Cemetery.

Marshall has inspired many over the years. The late Supreme Court justice Ruth Bader Ginsburg credited him for her strategy in attacking gender discrimination as an attorney with the American Civil Liberties Union in the 1970s:

> He was my model as a lawyer...I took a step-by-step, incremental approach; well, that's what Marshall did. He didn't come to the Court on day one and say, "End apartheid in America." He started with law schools and universities, and until he had those building blocks, he didn't ask the Court to end separate-but-equal. Of course, there was a huge difference between the litigation for gender equality in the '70s and the civil rights struggles in the '50s and '60s. The difference between Thurgood Marshall and me, most notably, is that my life was never in danger. His was. He would go to a Southern town to defend people and he literally didn't know whether he would be alive at the end of the day.[2]

The U.S. Congress passed a resolution, included here, honoring Marshall on the hundredth anniversary of his birth, July 2, 2008—in the same year as the United States elected its first Black president.

In May 2010, President Barack Obama appointed Elena Kagan, who had served as Marshall's clerk, to the Supreme Court to replace Justice John Paul Stevens. In announcing the nomination, Obama noted that Kagan "often referred to Supreme Court Justice Thurgood Marshall, for whom she clerked, as her hero....She credits him with reminding her that, as she put it, 'behind law there are stories—stories of people's lives as shaped by the law, stories of people's lives as might be changed by the law.'"[3] Kagan herself unequivocally called Marshall the "greatest lawyer of the twentieth century. No one did more to advance justice."[4]

Vice President Kamala Harris used Thurgood Marshall's Bible when she was sworn into the office of the vice presidency in Washington, D.C., on January 20, 2021. Harris earlier described Marshall as "one of the heroes and inspirations of my youth." "Thurgood was a fighter. He was a boxer in the courtroom," Harris wrote. "Our nation is made better because of his work and presence. His legacy calls us to continue to be a voice for justice and truth."[5]

Honoring Thurgood Marshall on the 100th Anniversary of His Birth

House Congressional Resolution 381, July 16, 2008 (from the Congressional Record [bound edition], vol. 154 (2008), part 11.)

Whereas Thurgood Marshall was born in Baltimore, Maryland, on July 2, 1908, the grandson of a slave;

Whereas Thurgood Marshall developed an interest in the Constitution and the rule of law in his youth;

Whereas Thurgood Marshall graduated from Lincoln University in Pennsylvania with honors in 1930, but was denied acceptance at the all-white University of Maryland Law School because he was African-American;

Whereas Thurgood Marshall attended law school at Howard University, the country's most prominent Black university, and graduated first in his class in 1933;

Whereas Thurgood Marshall served as the legal director of the National Association for the Advancement of Colored People (NAACP) from 1940 to 1961;

Whereas Thurgood Marshall argued 32 cases before the Supreme Court of the United States, beginning with the case of Chambers v. Florida in 1940, and won 29 of them, earning more victories in the Supreme Court than any other individual;

Whereas, as Chief Counsel of the NAACP, Thurgood Marshall fought to abolish segregation in schools and challenged laws that discriminated against African-Americans;

Whereas Thurgood Marshall argued *Brown v. Board of Education* before the Supreme Court in 1954, which resulted in the famous decision declaring racial segregation in public schools unconstitutional, overturning the 1896 decision in *Plessy v. Ferguson*;

Whereas Thurgood Marshall was nominated to the United States Court of Appeals for the Second Circuit by President John F. Kennedy in 1961, and was confirmed by the United States Senate in spite of heavy opposition from many Southern Senators;

Whereas Thurgood Marshall served on the United States Court of Appeals for the Second Circuit from 1961 to 1965, during which time he wrote 112 opinions, none of which were overturned on appeal;

Whereas Thurgood Marshall was nominated as Solicitor General of the United States by President Lyndon Johnson, and served as the first African-American Solicitor General from 1965 to 1967;

Whereas Thurgood Marshall was nominated as an Associate Justice of the Supreme Court by President Johnson in 1967, and served as the first African-American member of the Supreme Court;

Whereas Thurgood Marshall sought to protect the rights of all Americans during his 24 years as a justice on the Supreme Court;

Whereas Thurgood Marshall was honored with the Liberty Medal in 1992, in recognition of his long history of protecting the rights of women, children, prisoners, and the homeless; and

Whereas Thurgood Marshall died on January 24, 1993, at the age of 84: Now, therefore, be it

Resolved by the House of Representatives (the Senate concurring), that Congress—

(1) honors the dedication and achievements of Thurgood Marshall;

(2) recognizes the contributions of Thurgood Marshall to the struggle for equal rights and justice in the United States; and

(3) celebrates the lifetime achievements of Thurgood Marshall on the 100th anniversary of his birth.

Notes

Introduction

1. Deborah L. Rhode, "Letting the Law Catch Up," in "A Tribute to Justice Thurgood Marshall," *Stanford Law Review* 44 (Summer 1992): 1259–1265.
2. Thurgood Marshall, speech at Dillard University, reproduced in "A Supreme Court Justice's Warning to Fellow Negroes," *U.S. News and World Report*, May 19, 1969.
3. NAACP, "Civil Rights Leaders: Thurgood Marshall," n.d., https://naacp.org/find-resources/history-explained/civil-rights-leaders/thurgood-marshall.
4. Miles Parks, "Confederate Statues Were Built to Further a 'White Supremacist Future,'" NPR, August 20, 2017, https://www.npr.org/2017/08/20/544266880/confederate-statues-were-built-to-further-a-white-supremacist-future; "Whose Heritage? Public Symbols of the Confederacy," Southern Poverty Law Center, n.d., https://www.splcenter.org/whose-heritage#findings.
5. Larry S. Gibson, *Young Thurgood: The Making of a Supreme Court Justice* (New York: Prometheus Books, 2012), 24.
6. Gibson, *Young Thurgood*, 24–25; Patricia Sullivan, *Lift Every Voice: The NAACP and the Making of the Civil Rights Movement* (New York: New Press, 2009), 101.
7. Gibson, *Young Thurgood*, 20, 54–55.
8. Gibson, *Young Thurgood*, chaps. 2, 3; Carl T. Rowan, *Dream Makers, Dream Breakers: The World of Justice Thurgood Marshall* (New York: Welcome Rain, 2002), chap. 3.
9. Rowan, *Dream Makers, Dream Breakers*, chaps. 3, 5; Gibson, *Young Thurgood*, chap. 4.
10. Rowan, *Dream Makers, Dream Breakers*, 46.
11. Juan Williams, *Thurgood Marshall: American Revolutionary* (New York: Random House, 1998), 57–58.
12. Gibson, *Young Thurgood*, 107.
13. Mark V. Tushnet, ed., *Thurgood Marshall: His Speeches, Writings, Arguments, Opinions, and Reminiscences* (Chicago: Lawrence Hill Books, 2001), 91.
14. Gibson, *Young Thurgood*, chap. 1.
15. Gibson, *Young Thurgood*, chap. 7.
16. Gibson, *Young Thurgood*, chaps. 9, 10.

Chapter 1. Mr. Civil Rights: 1934—1950

1. Juan Williams, *Thurgood Marshall: American Revolutionary* (New York: Random House, 1998), 84–85; Carl T. Rowan, *Dream Makers, Dream Breakers: The World of Justice Thurgood Marshall* (New York: Welcome Rain, 2002), 48.
2. Larry S. Gibson, *Young Thurgood: The Making of a Supreme Court Justice* (New York: Prometheus Books, 2012), chaps. 10, 11.
3. Gibson, *Young Thurgood*, chap. 16.
4. Gibson, *Young Thurgood*, chap. 16.
5. Gilbert King, *Devil in the Grove: Thurgood Marshall, the Groveland Boys, and the Dawn of a New America* (New York: HarperCollins, 2012), 5.
6. Patricia Sullivan, *Lift Every Voice: The NAACP and the Making of the Civil Rights Movement* (New York: New Press, 2009), 311–314; Williams, *Thurgood Marshall*, chap. 10.
7. Rowan, *Dream Makers, Dream Breakers*, chap. 8.
8. Williams, *Thurgood Marshall*, 126, 136–137.
9. Sullivan, *Lift Every Voice*, chap. 9.

10. James Poling, "Thurgood Marshall and the 14th Amendment," *Collier's Magazine*, February 23, 1952, quoted in Rowan, *Dream Makers, Dream Breakers*, 186.

11. Rowan, *Dream Makers, Dream Breakers*, 237, quoting Marshall's interview in *TIME* magazine, September 1955.

12. Thurgood Marshall, "The Legal Attack to Secure Civil Rights," speech given at the NAACP Wartime Conference, Chicago, Illinois, July 13, 1944, in Mark V. Tushnet, ed., *Thurgood Marshall: His Speeches, Writings, Arguments, Opinions, and Reminiscences* (Chicago: Lawrence Hill Books, 2001)

13. "Constitutional Amendments and Major Civil Rights Acts of Congress Referenced in *Black Americans in Congress* [exhibit]," History, Art & Archives, U.S. House of Representatives, https://history.house.gov/Exhibitions-and-Publications/BAIC/Historical-Data/Constitutional-Amendments-and-Legislation/.

Chapter 2. "That Is Not What Our Constitution Stands For": 1950–1960

1. Carl T. Rowan, *Dream Makers, Dream Breakers: The World of Justice Thurgood Marshall* (New York: Welcome Rain, 2002), 158.

2. Rowan, *Dream Makers, Dream Breakers*, chap. 12; Juan Williams, *Thurgood Marshall: American Revolutionary* (New York: Random House, 1998), 169–172.

3. Rowan, *Dream Makers, Dream Breakers*, chap. 14; Williams, *Thurgood Marshall*, chap. 21.

4. Rowan, *Dream Makers, Dream Breakers*, chap. 14; Williams, *Thurgood Marshall*, chap. 21.

5. Rowan, *Dream Makers, Dream Breakers*, chap. 15; Williams, *Thurgood Marshall*, chap. 22.

6. Williams, *Thurgood Marshall*, 229.

7. Williams, *Thurgood Marshall*, chap. 25.

8. Thurgood Marshall, "The Meaning of Liberty," speech, Independence Hall, Philadelphia, Pennsylvania, July 4, 1992, quoted in "Thurgood Marshall's Stirring Acceptance Speech After Receiving the Prestigious Liberty Award on July 4, 1992," NAACP Legal Defense and Educational Fund, July 1, 2015, https://www.naacpldf.org/press-release/thurgood-marshalls-stirring-acceptance-speech-after-receiving-the-prestigious-liberty-award-on-july-4-1992/.

9. "A Revealing Experiment: *Brown v. Board* and 'The Doll Test,'" NAACP Legal Defense and Educational Fund, n.d., https://www.naacpldf.org/ldf-celebrates-60th-anniversary-brown-v-board-education/significance-doll-test/.

10. "Dissenting Opinion, *Briggs v. Elliott*," June 21, 1951, "Documented Rights" exhibit, https://www.archives.gov/exhibits/documented-rights/exhibit/section5/detail/briggs-dissent-transcript.html.

11. Cecil Williams, the then thirteen-year-old photographer who captured the image on the cover of this book—of Marshall arriving in South Carolina to work on the *Briggs* case—says the reason *Briggs* was not treated as the lead case on appeal was that former South Carolina governor James F. Byrnes, who had served as a Supreme Court justice for just over a year in the early 1940s before resigning, asked his former colleagues not to embarrass South Carolina by connecting the state so prominently to the problem of school segregation. Photographer Williams now is responsible for a civil rights museum in Orangeburg, South Carolina, and, with the Briggs family, is involved in an effort to rename the consolidated appeal: "It's never too late to do the right thing." Interview with Cecil Williams, November 5, 2021; see Peter Keating, "Take a Virtual Tour of South Carolina's Only Civil Rights Museum," with photographs by Cecil Williams, September 16, 2020, *National Geographic*, https://www.nationalgeographic.com/travel/article/visit-historic-cecil-williams-civil-rights-museum.

12. Rowan, *Dream Makers, Dream Breakers*, chap. 15; Williams, *Thurgood Marshall*, chap. 25.

13. Alex McBride, "Supreme Court History: Landmark Cases—*Cooper v. Aaron* (1958)," WNET, n.d., https://www.thirteen.org/wnet/supremecourt/democracy/landmark⊠ cooper.html.

Chapter 3: The Right Time, the Right Man: 1960–1971

1. Juan Williams, *Thurgood Marshall: American Revolutionary* (New York: Random House, 1998), 285.
2. Williams, *Thurgood Marshall*, chap. 28.
3. Seth P. Waxman, "'Presenting the Case of the United States as It Should Be': The Solicitor General in Historical Context," address to the Supreme Court Historical Society, June 1, 1998.
4. Carl T. Rowan, *Dream Makers, Dream Breakers: The World of Justice Thurgood Marshall* (New York: Welcome Rain, 2002), 297.
5. Williams, *Thurgood Marshall*, chap. 30.
6. Walter Rugaber, "Mississippi Jury Convicts 7 of 18 in Rights Killings," *New York Times*, October 21, 1967.
7. Federal Bureau of Investigation, "Famous Cases & Criminals: Mississippi Burning," n.d., https://www.fbi.gov/history/famous-cases/mississippi-burning.
8. Mark V. Tushnet, ed., *Thurgood Marshall: His Speeches, Writings, Arguments, Opinions, and Reminiscences* (Chicago: Lawrence Hill Books, 2001), 91.
9. Peniel E. Joseph, "From Ronald Reagan in Philadelphia, Miss., to Donald Trump in Tulsa, a Pattern of Racially Divisive Politics," *Washington Post*, June 19, 2020.
10. Niraj Chokshi, "Behind the Race to Publish the Top-Secret Pentagon Papers," *New York Times*, December 20, 2017; John T. Correll, "The Pentagon Papers," *Air Force Magazine*, February 1, 2007; Stephen Robertson, "*New York Times Co. v. United States* (1971)," *The First Amendment Encyclopedia*, https://www.mtsu.edu/first-amendment/ article/505/new-york-times-co-v-united-states.

Chapter 4. "The Humanity of Our Fellow Beings": 1971–1977

1. "Death Row," Death Penalty Information Center, Capital Punishment Project of the NAACP Legal Defense and Educational Fund, n.d., https://deathpenaltyinfo. org/death-row/overview.
2. Larry S. Gibson, *Young Thurgood: The Making of a Supreme Court Justice* (New York: Prometheus Books, 2012), 207–209.
3. Juan Williams, *Thurgood Marshall: American Revolutionary* (New York: Random House, 1998), 66.
4. Carl T. Rowan, *Dream Makers, Dream Breakers: The World of Justice Thurgood Marshall* (New York: Welcome Rain, 2002), 386.
5. Williams, *Thurgood Marshall*, 360–361.

Chapter 5. "A Living Document": 1977–1991

1. Juan Williams, *Thurgood Marshall: American Revolutionary* (New York: Random House, 1998), 335.
2. Williams, *Thurgood Marshall*, 393–395.
3. "Burger Urges Drive to Fight Crime and End 'Reign of Terror' in Cities: Excerpts from Address," *New York Times*, February 9, 1981.

Afterword

1. Thurgood Marshall, "Liberty Medal Acceptance Speech," Independence Hall, Philadelphia, July 4, 1992, https://constitutioncenter.org/liberty-medal/recipients/thurgood-marshall.

2. Robert Cohen and Laura J. Dull, "Teaching About the Feminist Rights Revolution: Ruth Bader Ginsburg as 'The Thurgood Marshall of Women's Rights,'" *American Historian*, November 2017, https://www.oah.org/tah/issues/2017/november/teaching-about-the-feminist-rights-revolution-ruth-bader-ginsburg-as-the-thurgood-marshall-of-womens-rights/.

3. "Remarks by the President and Solicitor General Elena Kagan at the Nomination of Solicitor General Elena Kagan to the Supreme Court," press release, White House Office of the Press Secretary, May 10, 2010, https://obamawhitehouse.archives.gov/the-press-office/remarks-president-and-solicitor-general-elena-kagan-nomination-solicitor-general-el.

4. Andrew Hamm, "Kagan on Marshall: 'Greatest Lawyer of the 20th Century,'" *SCOTUSblog*, October 17, 2017, https://www.scotusblog.com/2017/10/kagan-marshall-greatest-lawyer-20th-century/.

5. Kamala Harris, Facebook post and video, August 30, 2019.